Oasis of Dreams

Oasis of Dreams
Teaching and Learning Peace
in a Jewish-Palestinian Village in Israel

Grace Feuerverger

RoutledgeFalmer
New York   London

Published in 2001 by
RoutledgeFalmer
29 West 35th Street
New York, NY 10001

Published in Great Britain by
RoutledgeFalmer
11 New Fetter Lane
London EC4P 4EE

RoutledgeFalmer is an imprint of the Taylor & Francis Group.

Printed in the United States of America on acid-free paper.

Design and typography: Clarinda Publication Services

A CIP catalogue record for this book is available at the Library of Congress.

10 9 8 7 6 5 4 3 2 1

ISBN 0-4159-2938-5 (hb)
ISBN 0-4159-2939-3 (pbk)

To the memory of Bruno Hussar, who had a dream

To accomplish great things
We must not only act, but also dream;
Not only plan, but also believe.
—Anatole France

Contents

Acknowledgments

There are so many people to thank. I wish to express my sincere and heart-felt appreciation to the people of Neve Shalom/Wahat Al-Salam and to those from the neighboring villages who so generously shared their personal and professional stories with me. To my mind, educational innovation always involves risk taking. The inhabitants of Neve Shalom/Wahat Al-Salam search for a new meaning to life, and a better future for their children. I will always stand in awe of their hope and their courage in spite of all the obstacles that are in the way.

My genuine gratitude goes to Coral Aron, the "elder" of the village, who fed me body and soul. During our many dinners at her home, we talked about everything under the sun. I especially appreciated the stories about her late husband, Wellesley Aron, who was a very positive force in the village and who, in fact, had brought Coral to live in Neve Shalom/Wahat Al-Salam with him. During every one of my sojourns, Coral fussed over me like a mother hen and I will always love her for that.

I also admire and warmly thank Anne LeMeignen, who dreamed the dream along with Father Bruno and who was also among the early pioneers. I regret that we only had brief periods of time together; she was often abroad, usually fund-raising for the village, during most of my stays there. Anne is also founder and editor of the French version of the village newsletter entitled *La Lettre de la Colline.*

My heartfelt thanks go to Bob Mark, who teaches in the elementary school, and to his wife, Michal Zak, who is a facilitator at the "School for Peace," for their wonderful hospitality and for the many great conversations that we had together. Right from the start, they made me feel at home. In fact, it was Bob to whom I first spoke (long distance) about my research proposal back in 1991. He was head of the village educational committee at the time, and I thank him from the bottom of my heart for taking a chance and giving me the "go-ahead" to come to the village and start this research.

A sincere "thank you" to Leila Hassoun and to her whole family from Abu Ghosh, an Arab village near Neve Shalom/Wahat Al-Salam. Leila is a dedicated teacher at the school and a strong human being in her very special, quiet way. I will never forget the meaningful discussions (not to mention the splendid meals) I had with her and her family in their home. We talked not only about pain and suffering but also about reconciliation and goodwill. I will also always remember that wonderful trip with them to the West Bank to visit their relatives. It was a very emotional experience.

I am indebted to Anwar Daoud, Ety Edlund, Boaz Kitain, Diana Shalufi-Rizek, and Nava Sonnenschein, among others, who gave me carte blanche to carry out my research in the elementary school and in the "School for Peace." I deeply appreciate their openness and generosity of spirit. Many thanks to Raida and Ibrahim Hatib, who live and teach in the village, for the great conversations about language and identity.

Thanks also to Howard Shippin, who was always just an e-mail away when I needed a question answered, and also to his wife, Dorrit, who made my stays in the village guest house very pleasant. Howard and Coral Aron are in charge of editing the English and Hebrew versions of the village newsletter. I appreciate Abed Najjar's work on the Arabic version of the newsletter and on community relations.

I owe an inexpressible debt of gratitude to Rayek Rizek, whose quiet passion and gentle diplomacy are nothing short of extraordinary. My discussions with him have changed me forever.

Un très grand merci à Père Paul Sauma, Abbot of the Latrun Monastery, who told me not to worry about who would publish my manuscript because "la main de Dieu" was behind it. I have kept the promise that he asked of me to include in my book a photo of the beautiful *PAX* mosaic which stands on the grounds in front of the monastery and symbolizes the Benedictine commitment to working for "peace on earth."

My very special thanks go to all the children attending the elementary school and the students participating in the "School for Peace" at Neve Shalom/Wahat Al-Salam. They will forever be a source of inspiration for me.

I thank Karita Dos Santos, former Education Editor at Routledge in New York, for her enthusiasm about this book from our very first telephone conversation and for the many interesting discussions that we shared. Many thanks also to Seema Shah, Jonathan Herder, and Amy Matthusen at Routledge, for pulling it all together and keeping me on top of things. I appreciate Jennifer Crisp's great work on the cover design, which shows two flags shaking hands, based on artwork created in class by children in the village elementary school. Also, I appreciate the very generous attitude of Tom Wang who allowed me to include more photos than had originally been planned. His organizational skills were very reassuring during the production process. I am very grateful to Mary Verrill of Clarinda Publication Services for her meticulous work in coordinating the production of the manuscript.

I was very fortunate to have met Richard Rodriguez at just the right moment. He encouraged me as a first-time author and put me in contact with Bill Goodman, the editor and literary agent who helped him when he was a first-time author. I sent off my final manuscript by FedEx to Routledge from Berkeley on a sunny day in August and then took the Bay Area Rapid Transit (BART) to San Francisco to have lunch with Richard. We spoke for hours about the writing process. It was a perfect moment of closure for the manuscript.

I am thankful for the professional generosity and insight of Bill Goodman, who took me under his wing and guided me through the maze of the prepublication process. He is truly a "prince of the old school."

A special "thank you" goes to Michael Connelly, head of the Center for Teacher Development at the Ontario Institute for Studies in Education of the University of Toronto. He opened the door to new professional worlds, and gave me "permission" to embark on qualitative inquiry by telling me that "doing narrative is not a crime."

Other special mentions and thanks go to Sandra Acker, Mary Beattie, Kathy Bickmore, Jim Cummins, David Corson, Marcel Danesi, Monica Heller, Normand Labrie, and Howard Russell at OISE/University of Toronto, who put up with listening to me and freely offered their suggestions at various stages during the research process.

I thank Michael Gayner, Gary Pyper, Lisa Richards, Frances Tolnai, and Gina Valle for their meticulous help in transcribing the interview data. I also thank the Social Sciences and Humanities Research Council of Canada (SSHRC) and the Ontario Institute of Studies in Education (OISE) of the University of Toronto for funding various parts of this project.

I spent much of the time writing this book while on study leave at the Department of Language and Literacy in the School of Education at the University of California, Berkeley. I warmly thank Eugene Garcia, Dean of the School of Education, for the encouraging discussions we had about the progress of the manuscript during that time. I also acknowledge here the great "vibes" at Caffe Strada, Musical Offering, Brewed Awakening, and especially at the Berkeley City Club, the magnificent architectural gem designed by Julia Morgan, where I did much of my writing using my trusty MAC laptop.

I am very grateful to Arlene and Wolf Homburger for the valuable times that we shared. I admire their deep personal commitment to Neve Shalom/Wahat Al-Salam.

Many thanks to Jesse Perry, a dedicated, long-time educator, for being so enthusiastic about this book. When I first told him about it, he had just returned from a pilgrimage to the Holy Land, and was disappointed that he hadn't known about the village then. "I'll read the book and then go back to Israel," he told me.

Many others also contributed to this book both directly and indirectly in ways that they themselves may not fully realize: Salim Abu-Rabia, Gila Bar-David, Dan Bar-On, Pierre Bourdieu, Lorie and David Brillinger, Sharon Burde, Mahmoud Darwich, Sheryllyn Doherty, Shoshi Fogelman, Ilan Frisch, Joan Fujimura, Michael Fullan, Clifford Geertz, Sigrun Gudmundsdottir, Maxine Greene, Angela Hildyard, Blythe Hinitz, Wsevolod Isajiw, Shoshana

Keiny, Joe Kincheloe, Boaz and Daniella Kitain, Julia Kristeva, Merle Lefkoff, Cardinal Jean-Marie Lustiger, Mariana Masterson, André Elias Mazawi, Anne Melis, Carol Mullen, Abdelssalam (Abed) and Aishe Najjar, Peter Nelde, Roseann Runte, Edward Said, Anton Shammas, Elana Shohamy, Roger Simon, Sally and Terry Speed, Bernard Spolsky, Shirley Steinberg, Bernard and Phyllis Shapiro, Shlomo Swirski, Monica Taylor, Hesh Troper, and Witold Tulasiewicz.

I will never, ever, be able to repay the kindness and wisdom of Benjamin Geneen, who loved me like a parent and taught me to have faith in myself. Without him, this book would never have been written.

And greatest thanks of all go to my life partner, Andrey, whose constant love, unwavering support, and clarity of thought are utterly beyond measure. He is my Rock of Gibraltar, my "knight in shining armor," my soul mate.

Grace Feuerverger

Introduction

I would have wanted
(but I am only telling this to you privately)
to be a child in another country.
In a country where there would be no news
about the dead and wounded and wars.
In a country which wouldn't need an army or soldiers;
and where one would not be afraid or worried all the time.
In a country where there would always be peace;
and one could walk anywhere and travel anywhere;
In a country where, except for the cars on the highway,
there would be nothing dangerous.
I would have wanted to be in another country,
but this is my country [Israel],
my home with its sunshine, the sea, and the anemones;
with my Mommy and Daddy and aunts and uncles.
It is my State and I am devoted to it.
I just wish it would have been a different country.

—Translated from *La Lettre de la Colline*, December 1994

This poem, which reveals the landscape of Jewish-Arab conflict and violence that confronts all students in Israel, was written by a twelve-year-old child living in a village called Neve Shalom/Wahat Al-Salam. The village is situated on a rocky hill some 30 kilometers west of Jerusalem. This book is about the people of this village, both Palestinians and Jews, who decided to try to live in peace. This cooperative community was founded in 1972 as an intercultural experiment, and the first families took up residence there in 1978. Today it is a small but thriving village with a growing sheepfold and a large olive orchard planted on its hilly slopes. Its purpose is to create a social, cultural, and political framework of equality and mutual respect for the residents while maintaining the cultural heritage, language, and identity of each individual. The aim of this book is to provide an interpretive/ethnographic inquiry into the relationship between the Jews and Palestinians who live in this small village and into its two schools, which are devoted to the principle of peaceful coexistence.

Neve Shalom/Wahat Al-Salam, which is Hebrew and Arabic for "Oasis of Peace," is no ordinary place, and neither are its educational institutions. It is a social-psychological experiment—a place where people with a strong personal conviction and a deep level of moral commitment have come together to enact a collective vision of justice and caring. The villagers are in general well educated, liberal minded, and interested in giving their children a chance for a peaceful future. Their philosophy of a Jewish-Arab village in Israel, living and teaching peace and equality, is rooted in the democratic ideals of dialogue, negotiation, and cooperative problem solving. But things in everyday life are never as simple and utopian as that. The village is a "flesh-and-blood" place within a difficult arena of intergroup conflict, and the ensuing moral problems and dilemmas are constantly being played out and negotiated. It is not an island unto itself by any means. Many of the villagers work in nearby Jerusalem, Ramle, or Tel Aviv, and they are subject to the social and political turmoil that envelops all of Israel. Since the Neve Shalom/Wahat Al-Salam school is open not only to the village children but also now serves children from various neighboring Jewish and Arab villages, it therefore finds itself within the wider atmosphere of mutual fear, distrust, prejudice, and stereotype. The peacemaking efforts of these villagers are thus embedded within a psychological terrain of vulnerability and risk taking. The residents are involved in an emotionally intense endeavor taking place on the cutting edge of conflict resolution and education for peace.

This book, therefore, is an exploration into the desolate psychological landscape that Jews and Palestinians must navigate, and into their emotional journey toward breaking down the barriers of fear and mistrust that have saturated their daily existence. I explore the social and psychological dimensions of this educational odyssey toward peaceful coexistence, and discuss the sites of struggle, ambiguities, and negotiation in the "border dialogues" that the villagers have gradually created for themselves in their search to give equal expression to their national identities. I look at these two national groups which are cultivating new cultural spaces, new realms of discourse, and new modes of thought in spite of the profound difficulties that envelop them on a daily basis. I study the epistemologically complex implications of understanding conflict resolution as a dialogical relation (Buber, 1959), the ultimate purpose of which is to create a geography of inclusion within the context of an Israeli community setting. Through the observation of pedagogical experiences as well as sharing personal and professional stories, I focus on meaning-making as grounded in personal life history—that is, on the social, linguistic, and cultural texts of my participants (and myself), in an attempt at a more nuanced view of peacemaking in education. This book focuses on the multidimensional relationship between autobiographical narrative, educational discourse, and the intercultural quest for peaceful coexistence in the Neve Shalom/Wahat Al-Salam village school programs. Indeed, through the exploration of the social, linguistic, and psychological complexities inherent in Neve Shalom/Wahat Al-Salam's pedagogical experiment toward peace, this book provides a portrait of the lived experiences of these Jewish and Palestinian students, teachers, and parents.

In recent years there have been several grassroots educational innovations in Israel that attempt to turn around the destructive patterns of intergroup conflict and war resulting from the ongoing struggle between Jews and Arabs in Israel and in the Middle East. Formal and informal social and linguistic projects encourage Jewish-Arab coexistence in a growing number of Palestinian and Jewish schools in some parts of the country (see for example, Maroshek-Klarman, 1993; Shohat, 1993; Shohamy & Spolsky, 2000). I have invested much energy and time over the last nine years in documenting these cooperative efforts toward peacemaking at Neve Shalom/Wahat Al-Salam. This village presents an ideal of a small society in its attempt to respect differences and to inspire a moral vision of dialogue and equality in the midst of a geopolitical framework of conflict. Furthermore, there also is a moral imperative for the villagers to maintain their respective Jewish and Palestinian identities as separate entities. The tension between these two goals becomes evident in the various moral dilemmas that constantly confront the villagers in their efforts for peaceful coexistence, and also affects their schools' objectives—both the elementary school and the peace education program called the "School for Peace"—which are the central foci of this ethnographic study.

Both of these educational institutions in the village, the elementary school and the "School for Peace," exemplify a genuine attempt at partnership between two peoples whose cultures are in geopolitical and sociohistorical conflict. They are innovative in their attempts to deconstruct the traditional school discourses in Israel, which generally perpetuate the dominant/subordinate status of Hebrew and Arabic, respectively, within the curriculum. The elementary school opened its doors in 1984; the preschool and kindergarten three years earlier. What is unique about this Neve Shalom/Wahat Al-Salam village school is that it provides the possibility for Jewish and Arab children to learn *together* on a daily basis in a full Hebrew-Arabic bilingual, bicultural, binational setting. It is coordinated by a teaching team of Jewish and Arab educators, some of whom are residents of the village and others who commute from nearby towns and villages. The use of both languages has become a symbol for inclusiveness and mutual understanding in formal and informal school activities.

When the elementary school opened in 1984 there were 12 children from the village in attendance. In September 2000, 250 children were enrolled in the elementary school which has become a regional institution with 80% of its population from 20 different villages. The kindergarten has 28 children; the pre-kindergarten has 12 children, and the nursery has 5 children. For the first nine years of its existence, the school received no government help. Official recognition came in 1993. In spite of very limited financial support, it set a strong precedent by giving legitimacy to Hebrew-Arabic bilingual education and paved the way for further attempts in other parts of the country. In June 1997 the school won even more government recognition by being registered as an "experimental school." It was only one of two elementary schools which received this status out of hundreds of schools that applied. There are approximately 30 teachers in the school and their salaries are paid by the village.

The "School for Peace" conflict resolution program is geared toward bringing Jewish and Palestinian adolescents from all over Israel and the West Bank together for workshops conducted by well-trained facilitators in the village; it has been operating since 1979. The underlying message of the elementary school and the "School for Peace" workshops is the overriding importance of maintaining personal, social, and national identity for both Jews and Arabs within an egalitarian perspective. This framework assures the legitimacy of every participant's position.

By 2000, more than 20,000 Palestinian and Jewish adolescent have had the opportunity to attend the "School for Peace" workshops. In addition, the School for Peace has a growing outreach program that includes not only encounter workshops for adolescents but also teachers' workshops (which have been approved and accredited as in-service training by the Ministry of Education); encounter opportunities between professionals from the West Bank, Gaza, and Israel; postgraduate courses in collaboration with a number of Israeli universities; and work with groups and individuals from other parts of the world where conflict and racial tension is prevalent (e.g., groups from Northern Ireland, ex-Yugoslavia, and the United States, to date).

This kind of thoughtful teaching and learning is a dynamic process which appreciates the complexities of bilingual, bicultural, and binational education within a backdrop of conflict and war. Indeed, it embodies the late Brazilian educator and social philosopher Paulo Freire's (1970) revolutionary perspective of social liberation. The innovative initiatives at Neve Shalom/Wahat Al-Salam have opened a space for reshaping the pedagogical processes in classrooms and in school policies. These initiatives are also in concert with American educational researcher Henry Giroux's (1988) theoretical notion of "border pedagogy." They have made it possible for the villagers to become free to be "border crossers" and thus to challenge and redefine the limitations created by hegemonic domination. Such an atmosphere allows teachers and students to rethink the space where dominant and subordinate groups are situated, and thus to transform their own relationships. Neve Shalom/Wahat Al-Salam can thus be envisioned as a new "borderland," to use Gloria Anzaldua's (1987) eloquent metaphor, where emancipatory discourses of national, cultural, and linguistic equality are being created.

The theoretical and methodological approach adopted here is exploratory and flexible rather than definitive and static; I search for the words that will adequately describe the potent ideas and works of these villagers. This book is a story about peacemaking and conflict resolution between two peoples who have been apart for centuries in enmity (Benvenisti, 1995; Shipler, 1986). This quest for peace in the midst of conflict is a meta-theme which has resided in the collective consciousness of both peoples for a very long time; it will undoubtedly continue to unfold. I can only capture it here as a snapshot of this particular moment in history—this desire for peace between these Jews and Arabs in this village in the land of Israel. I try to weave together memories, daydreams, reflections, imaginations, retrospections, anticipations, hopes, terrors, desires, delusions—in short, to put, as Samuel Beckett (1961, p. 23) suggested, "the chaos of experience" into a narrative. He said that the goal of the artist is "to find a form that accommodates the mess." So too is it the task of the researcher/writer to heed Beckett's words again: "It is the shape that matters."

Through in-depth interviewing, participant observation, and journal writing techniques, I explore the interaction between the students and their teachers in the everyday classroom activities of the bilingual/bicultural/binational elementary school, as well as in the "School for Peace" education program. These are symbolically intertwined and emerge out of the same desire for Jewish-Arab coexistence. It is probably safe to assert that most individuals from fundamentalist Islamic or ultra-Orthodox Jewish backgrounds are opposed to this village. Indeed, the impression I gained from informal discussions with people in other parts of Israel, both Arab and Jewish, was that this village is looked on by some with uncertainty and skepticism; by others, with admiration and even curiosity. Almost all see it as experimental ("out on a limb") and based on a self-selected group of committed people dedicated to an integrated Jewish-Palestinian school system. This is perhaps so. Nevertheless, it does not negate the fact that if peace can happen in this village, there is the possibility it can happen in other areas of Israel and, indeed, elsewhere in conflict zones around the world. It is important, however, to stress at the outset that this is a real place like any other, and therefore subject to all the vicissitudes of human society—the interpersonal problems, misunderstandings, and tensions that regularly occur among neighbors regardless of culture, race, religion, or nationality anywhere on Earth. These people are not saints; nor is this village a utopia. In spite of how much we might yearn in our hearts for the fantasy of a perfect peace, we must recognize the reality of the dilemmas and difficulties challenging these villagers every day. It would be easy to put them up on a pedestal and expect them to perform miracles. What is much more difficult to do is to respect the nobility of their attempt at peaceful coexistence in spite of the very human frailties and flaws of their everyday lives.

One of the underlying themes of this book is that if we are to develop valued models of peace education, we must first listen closely to the voices in conflict. This process of sensitive listening is essential to all forms of professional development, both for the learner and for the teacher. One of the major objectives of this research was to recontextualize the emotional upheaval and dilemmas within the narratives of the participants and place them in a social, cultural, and educational perspective. I examined the stories collected from my participants in order to highlight the multiplicity of tensions, failed hopes, dreams, and traumas that are pivotal within the configuration of their personal and professional lives. Finally, this book attempts to capture the dynamics and subtlety of the acts of resistance by the villagers against the hegemonic social and linguistic framework of the wider Israeli society. Their endurance, courage, and cautious optimism give their enterprise of conflict resolution and peaceful coexistence its strength. I have attempted to bring forth the voices of these villagers (both children and adults) in order to critically negotiate the relationship between the two national identities and the intricacies of teaching and learning intercultural understanding within the midst of conflict. In the transcultural movement of the late twentieth century and the beginning of the twenty-first century our identities are constantly in flux. What is identity if not fluid and unstable and flexible? It means being at the crossroads of history: what we have inherited as identity is therefore open to interrogation, to retelling and to renaming. But we cannot simply rub it out; it is there as our baggage, both precious and heavy, and cannot be abandoned or denied. Its force may never be truly understood or resolved, but it offers us the keys to new possibilities, to new pedagogies and to new stories that we construct in the no-man's-land where we can recognize ourselves for the first time in the narratives of the "other" (Kristeva, 1999). Neve Shalom/Wahat Al-Salam embodies for me the frontier—where creating interconnections between people in conflict happens in spite of all the imperfections and is sustained as much by imagination and fantasy as by physical reality. It is the magnificent potential that lies within all of us.

All the chapters of this book consider the powerful notion of interconnections within a variety of contexts. Chapter 1 introduces the village and the elementary school. It offers my initial glimpses of Neve Shalom/Wahat Al-Salam and describes how my personal and professional life has been deeply influenced by the experiences I have shared with these people who have found a way to peace in spite of the deadly conflict all around them. Chapter 2 is concerned with the village and its elementary school as a community of moral education in Israel. It is devoted to the complexity and aesthetic of the moral development that has been taking place in this village and to the evolving relationships among myself as researcher and the villagers as participants. Stories of moral dilemmas and accomplishments are detailed. Chapter 3 focuses on peacemaking through emancipatory discourse in the elementary school in order to reflect on the complex relationship among language awareness, educational discourse, and the quest for Jewish-Palestinian coexistence in the village. Chapter 4 discusses the theoretical and conceptual framework underpinning the issues around the pedagogy of hope in the "School for Peace" workshops. It provides a reflexive narrative of my participant observation during a three-day encounter between Jewish and Palestinian teenagers and also focuses on the interviews I carried out with the two facilitators and some of the participants. Chapter 5 details my in-depth interview with Father Bruno Hussar, the Jewish-born Dominican priest whose dream created the village. I was humbled by this man who belongs to a "subversive" group of people in our world: those who recognize no boundaries. By believing in the possibility of peace and reconciliation, he defied the political rhetoric that unfortunately controls so many places on this globe, a rhetoric that separates, excludes, and destroys.

The second part of Chapter 5 is devoted to the interview I conducted with Rayek Rizek, who was mayor of the village at the time. He is a Palestinian from Nazareth. In the interview, we discuss the complex and multifaceted image of national identity. This section is called "Longing to Belong: A Tale of Two Identities" because we were both astonished to realize how similar our minority group "lenses" were, in spite of the fact that he is Palestinian and I am Jewish. The last section of this chapter discusses my interview with Abbé Père Paul Sauma of the Latrun Monastery, which has figured so large in the creation of the village. Chapter 6 highlights my conversations with a number of educators at the elementary school and the "School for Peace," who shared with me their pedagogical insights and showed me how teaching offers the power of love, art, and imagination. I also reflect on my personal reasons for going into education in the first place. Chapter 7 provides the concluding remarks of this book and pays homage to all researchers and participants working together in their quest to create a world more articulate, more beautiful, more creative, more intelligent, more loving, and more joyful than it is now. The implications of Hillary Rodham Clinton's visit to the village on December 13, 1998 when she was First Lady of the United States, is also discussed. This chapter also offers a reflective overview of my place in this village as researcher, witness, listener, teller, and fellow dreamer of peace.

This ethnographic study has been an all-encompassing endeavour since I first entered the village of Neve Shalom/Wahat Al-Salam in 1991. The people in this village motivated me to observe the spiritual as well as intellectual complexity of their cooperative Jewish-Palestinian enterprise and to reflect on the power of self-affirmation through a morally valuable educational pursuit. I became immersed in a journey of consciousness raising from my perspective of educational ethnographer. Neve Shalom/Wahat Al-Salam came to feel like "home"—a place which enables and promotes negotiation where we can discover new ways of seeing reality, new ways of confronting difference, and new ways of understanding ourselves and others.

Narrating the experiences of my participants, remembering my sojourns, reflecting on my actions and reactions in the village (at conferences, in academic articles, in graduate courses that I teach), has provided me the intellectual grounding, validation, and justification that I required in order to continue my professional journey to other places and with other peoples. I have been enriched and forever changed by the process of listening to and writing about my observations and interviews in this village.

Indeed, who can tell where the truth lies? Who can tell what is important in this life? We may be educated by others' words or comforted by them or angered by them, but we will be redeemed by our own words and we will find justice there. We will be reborn in our own voices, for nobody knows our stories the way we do, and it is our birthright to tell them. The building and sharing of peaceful coexistence in Neve Shalom/Wahat Al-Salam is the means of coming one step closer to repairing the broken shards of humanity. It is one step closer to returning to the wholeness of being. This is what true human spirit and caring is all about. This is what real education is about—opening our naked, scarred, vulnerable, precious souls to each other. How fortunate I am that these villagers shared their stories with me. This is why I decided to write this book, in order to describe the transformative power of the social and educational enterprise carried out by those who live in this extraordinary place of peace—this oasis of dreams.

Chapter One

An Oasis of Peace:
The Village of
Neve Shalom/Wahat Al-Salam

Peace is every step.

—Thich Nhat Hahn

True to its name, the village of Neve Shalom/Wahat Al-Salam is a small "oasis of peace" within a deeply polarized country. Nestled on a rocky hilltop, it is surrounded by green fields full of dazzling wildflowers and olive groves (in winter) and by other collective rural settlements such as kibbutzim and moshavim.[1] At the bottom of the hill several kilometers away is the Latrun Monastery and its vineyards, run by French Trappist monks who originally leased this land (a part of their holdings) to the village at the beginning of its existence in 1972.[2]

There are two means of access to the village: an old, picturesque dirt road, very bumpy and muddy in bad weather, and a newer asphalt road which meanders around fields and orchards. In the fields not far from this road, hidden by small trees, are the tents and sheep of a Bedouin family who has lived there since well before the village's existence. As one enters the village, the first buildings encountered are the youth hostel, the guest house with separate free-standing rooms, and the dining hall. The view of the rolling and tranquil Ayalon Valley below is breathtaking. Looking westward on a very clear day at sunset, one can sometimes catch a glimpse of the Mediterranean Sea in the far distance. I cannot count the times I stood in silence marveling at that sublime sight. A small main road runs through the middle of the village with white houses and red roofs of different shapes and sizes on both sides. The houses reflect the diversity of the population. Some have a traditional Arabic style; others are a mixture of European and Middle Eastern design. Each home has an interesting garden filled with all sorts of spices, vegetables, fruit, and flowers. Many plants grow in abundance all over the village. The lushness of the vegetation and the colors and scents of the flowers (made possible through irrigation) are a magnificent

Figure 1–1   A view of the village of Neve Shalom/Wahat Al-Salam with the Doumia/Sakina at left. (Courtesy of NS/WAS. Used with permission.)

sight, especially to one who was born and raised in North America north of the 49th parallel! In a lovely secluded corner of the hillside beneath the village houses and sheltered by an orchard is the "House of Silence" or Doumia/Sakina. It is a place of meditation, reflection and prayer. This white domeshaped building is a common sanctuary for all. (See Figures 1–1 and 1–2.)

   Approximately forty families and a number of single members comprise the population of the village. There is a waiting list of almost three hundred families who have applied to live in the village. The community is administered by a steering committee, the secretariat, which meets regularly once a week as well as whenever necessary. All matters requiring a decision of principle are considered by the plenum. The plenum consists of all residents, but only full members are entitled to vote. The plenum may return matters to the secretariat with the authority to make a final decision. The secretariat may decide to put matters to a vote in the plenum for a final decision. Once made, a final decision must be adhered to by the community. The community is governed by a constitution, which is reviewed from time to time. Several internal committees supervise various activities in the life of the community. All members of the secretariat and the committees are elected democratically each year. It is interesting to note that a balanced ratio of Jews and Arabs is observed throughout the community. The secretariat is always served by two Arabs and

Figure 1–2   The Bedouin family's tent and sheep in the Ayalon Valley below the village. (Courtesy of the author.)

two Jewish members, plus the secretary. The secretary, who basically takes on the role of mayor of the village, is elected on merit and availability, but not strictly in rotation.

The elementary school is at the northeast side of the village; the entrance to the village is at the southwest border, about half a kilometer away. When I first arrived in 1991, the school consisted of three small buildings: a kindergarten, the multigrade elementary schoolhouse with a kitchen/staff room in the middle, and a bomb shelter[3] which doubled as another classroom. In 1997 a new building was erected to accommodate the growing school population—an open plan design with large windows and much space, allowing a lot of freedom of movement. It is a closely knit environment; most of the students have at least one sibling attending along with them. Some of the teachers have their own children in the school. There are almost 300 children from kindergarten to grade six, with two kindergarten teachers and almost 30 elementary teachers. Each class has one Jewish and one Arab teacher; they work in a team-teaching mode. There is also a nursery and pre-kindergarten with about twenty toddlers. Many children are from the village, but a very large percentage of the children are bused into the school from nearby Jewish and

Palestinian villages. One can sense that they feel very comfortable in the school. It is definitely their school (See Figure 1–3). I was immediately struck by their sense of ownership and the sense of empowerment which derives from it. Several village dogs are always sniffing around the entrance to the school and in the yard, waiting for the children to come out and play with them at recess, lunch, and at the end of the day. It is a noisy, gregarious, happy place.

This school is unique in its commitment to educating its students in a full Arabic-Hebrew bilingual, bicultural setting. The following box on page 5 is a brief statement of the school's main educational goals.

During that first sojourn in 1991, Bob Mark, who is the school's English teacher, was my host. He first took me to the preschool where the children were scampering about amid toys in the company of two very cheerful caregivers. Bob explained that one of the caregivers was Arab and the other one was Jewish; this was in fact the paradigm for all levels of schooling. In this way the children always have the opportunity to speak the language with which they are most familiar, and to identify with "their" teachers. Bob and I then walked up a stony pathway to the kindergarten. Inside, a very busy scene greeted us. The children, about fifteen of them, were involved in making decorations for a Christmas tree—a pine tree standing bare at the back of the room. Scissors and colored paper and tinsel sparkled in the air. Naomi, Bob's daughter, approached us excitedly and showed me the little reindeer decorations and candy cane pictures that she was going to place on the tree. She whispered to me about how she was looking forward to the Christmas Eve party and how she had enjoyed the

Figure 1–3   Four children on the school playground. (Courtesy of the author.)

Educational Goals of the Neve Shalom/Wahat Al-Salam Primary School

Introduction

Consistent with its definition as a binational school* the NS/WAS Primary School strives to realize the principle of egalitarian co-existence between the two nations. There can be co-existence between members of the two peoples if, first of all, each child's own identity is nurtured, and commensurate space is given for his/her language, culture and customs, so that the child feels on an equal footing with classmates of the other national group.

The fact that differences are accepted and seen as natural provides the basis for an educational system which emphasizes the uniqueness, and respects the freedom of choice, of every child.

The curriculum is designed to allow the primary school's graduates to integrate into any high school in Israel, and therefore provides methodical study of all subjects learned in other schools: mathematics, English, nature, language, geography and others.

Both Jewish and Arab teachers teach in the school, with the guiding principle that each teacher instructs in his/her own language.

Goals

1. To create an environment where the meeting between children of the two cultures is as natural as possible.
2. To develop the child's openness, sensitivity and tolerance towards his/her Jewish and Arab friends.
3. To nurture, strengthen and foster each child's identity.
4. To deepen the child's acquaintance with, and knowledge of, the cultural values of the group to which he/she belongs.
5. To introduce the child to the literature, traditions and customs of the child from the other nation.
6. To inculcate a knowledge of both Hebrew and Arabic as primary languages.
7. To develop in the child an awareness of what is happening in Israel and throughout the world, while cultivating an understanding that events can be seen in more than one way.
8. To develop independent learning by letting the child choose subjects for study.
9. To allow the child to place particular emphasis on, and to deepen knowledge of, subjects which are dear to him/her.
10. To impart knowledge and develop proficiency in primary subjects such as mathematics, nature, etc.
11. To encourage the child's impulse to creativity.
12. To transform study into an enjoyable and positive experience.

The Management

*We use *nation* in reference to Jews and Palestinian Arabs, each of which see themselves as a distinct people with their own national culture, traditions and language.

Hannukah celebration a week earlier. She asked me if I was going to attend. One of the teachers said, "I'm sure Grace will come to the party; it's a very special event." I was, of course, ecstatic at the prospect.

Some of the children came up to me, curious to know who I was. In a small village, a stranger does not get lost. I spoke with the two teachers: one was a Moslem Arab; the other was Jewish. The person in charge of the decorating lesson was a teacher's aide who was a Christian Arab. It should be noted that both Moslem and Christian Arabs, as well as Jews, live in Neve Shalom/Wahat Al-Salam. One part of the curriculum is devoted to the teaching of Jewish and Arab identity. Each child is taught to understand what his or her culture is all about and also learns about the other children's cultures. The underlying principle is coexistence and tolerance and friendship, but not assimilation. Maintaining personal, social, and national identity is considered of utmost importance. Religion is taught separately, but there are joint discussions as well. The children learn about all the holidays of these three great religions during class time. They had just finished learning about Hannukah, the Jewish Festival of Lights, and prior to that about Milad-Un-Nabi, the birthday of the Islamic prophet Mohammed. And now it was time to prepare for Christmas. The children explained to me that it is important to respect each person's religion. What I sensed was that in this school environment the holidays were enjoyed and treated equally, but that their religious meaning was taught separately. All the children were sharing their decorations and helping each other with the cutting and pasting tasks.

Then Bob and I left the kindergarten and walked to the elementary school not far away. It was a little stone building. A few dogs were ambling about. I walked in and was swept away in the flurry of classroom activities. My first impression was how cheerful and busy the atmosphere was—easygoing yet hardworking at the same time. I noticed a picture on the wall of Santa Claus that had been painted by one of the students. It was an unusual portrait that embodied, I think, the message of this village. There were gold Jewish stars on top of the Baba Noel and Arabic words on the bottom. The three religions were living peacefully together in this picture just as they were in the village. There was also a mural on the wall, created by the children, composed of drawings of Jerusalem from varying religious and cultural perspectives. For example, there was the Al-Aqsa Mosque along with the Arabic text describing it; the Western Wall with a text in Hebrew explaining its significance; and the Church of the Holy Sepulchre, with an Arabic explanation. It was a sacred moment for me. (See Figure 1–4.)

During that first sojourn, I also had the opportunity to visit the monks at the Latrun Monastery not far from the village. I sat in the lovely chapel meditating in the stillness of their vows of silence. I also had the occasion to taste (and purchase) their brandy, wine, and marmalade in the little shop that they run for tourists and local residents. In fact, I was lucky enough to accompany some of the villagers to the monastery for midnight mass on Christmas Eve. The church bells rang loudly in the pouring rain. Inside, the ceremony was conducted in Latin, French, Arabic, and Hebrew. After the

Figure 1–4   A teacher with her students in class. (Courtesy of the author.)

mass, all the visitors were invited to partake in refreshments of hot mulled wine and cakes. During Christmas, the monks are allowed to speak, and the discussion between those who live in the monastery and the villagers was lively. What impressed me most was the deep respect each group had for one another's religions: Jewish, Roman Catholic, Greek Orthodox, and Moslem. This experience spoke powerfully to me, I a child of Holocaust survivors.

Reflexive Ethnography on the Border of Hope

When freedom is the question, it is always time to begin.

—Maxine Greene (1988)

My personal and professional life has been greatly informed by the revolutionary landscape of Neve Shalom/Wahat Al-Salam. Indeed, the fieldwork experience has affected me in myriad ways and has allowed me to reflect more deeply on my life story. It is highly significant that I, the researcher in this study, was situated in the dual role of outsider/insider; as "outsider," because I do not live in the village, but also as "insider" due to my being Jewish. Being an insider/outsider presupposes that there is a border—on one side you belong; on the other side you do not. Indeed, this book is all about borders: both imaginary and real, both positive and negative. My excursion into the landscape of Jewish-Palestinian coexistence and conflict resolution focuses on narratives of longing for and belonging to a homeland—the Jewish homeland of Israel that now exists and the Palestinian homeland that longs to be created. Both sides understand the troubling dimension of cultural displacement within their collective psyches. I adopted an ethnographic gaze on the life stories of my participants fueled by the desire arising from my own personal history to focus on this painful polarity of longing and belonging; the tension between personal and national aspirations of Jew and Palestinian in Israel. I wanted my "psychic signature" to be evident and for my interpretations to be understood through the embodiment of my own life story.

In contrast to the classical ethnographic approach, where the researcher is expunged from the text, the method of inquiry I offer here is more in concert with postmodern ethnographers who, in spite of having their qualms about the "authorial voice," make themselves visible and sometimes even central to their research enterprise as a means of better understanding and interpreting the interaction of their past life experiences with the life experiences of their participants during their fieldwork, during their data analysis, and in the discussion of their findings (Behar, 1996; Britzman, 1998; Grimshaw, 1992; Marcus, 1998; Oakley, 1992; Rosaldo, 1993). My sense of "entitlement" to this reflexive approach comes from the research of James Banks, Ruth Behar, Michael Connelly, Elliot Eisner, Robert Coles, Jonathon Kozol, George Marcus, Clifford Geertz, Charlotte Davies, Norman Denzin, Maxine Greene, Yvonna Lincoln, and Renato Rosaldo to name only a few, who show that inquiring into another organizational life through embodied experiences does not compromise intellectual credibility. On the contrary, they emphasize that it strengthens the ways in which researchers construct their ethnographic text as well as the ways in which they read those of others. These scholars explain that reflexivity is inherent in social research at all stages and in all forms. For example, Charlotte Davies (1999) explains that this interest in *reflexivity* (the use of autobiography in ethnography) is a positive feature of ethnographic research, and indeed, a legitimate methodological approach. The central way in which ethnographers have established the validity of their written ethnographies— which Geertz (1988, p. 4–5) sees "as essentially the same as establishing their own authority, is through a variety of literary or rhetorical forms that demonstrate their having actually penetrated or been penetrated by another form of life, of having one way or another truly 'been there.'" Embedded within these notions of reflexivity in ethnographic research lies the possibility of resolving the "signature dilemma," which is a fundamental issue in terms of how the author is to be positioned in the text.

Reflexivity, however, is not the end purpose of my research; it is the means through which knowledge of a social reality outside ourselves (such as this cooperative Jewish-Palestinian village) can be approached and can be explored and presented in various formats. Among these formats are the research practices of "engaging in open and critical dialogue with our research subjects— dialogues that may be acted out as well as spoken—and in seeking out varying perspectives" (Davies, 1999, p. 222). In fact, reflexivity, dialogic forms, and polyvocality are essential elements of postmodern writing, and to a great extent, of postmodern ethnography as well. Feminist researchers, for example, have focused on reflexivity in terms of personal experience, but also "in the recognition of the situatedness of the observer and its effect on social interactions and theoretical perceptions" (Mascia-Lees, Sharpe & Cohen, 1989; Strathern, 1987, Wolf, 1992). I draw from Sandra Harding's work on feminist methodology (1987, 1991), which gives permission to the researcher to "openly locate her history, values, and assumptions in the text so that she, like those researched, is open to critical scrutiny by her readers. Such openness places the researcher on the same critical plane as the researched" (Bloom, 1998, p. 148).

The perspective of this book then suggests that an informed reflexivity, as Davies (1999, p. 178–9) claims, is "compatible with a commitment to social scientific knowledge in the sense of knowledge that is based in, and can inform us about, a real social world and that it is public and open to critical analysis." It is simply recognized that ethnographic knowledge is in part a product of the social situation of ethnographers and that this must be acknowledged and its significance addressed during analysis (Rosaldo, 1993). Another use of autobiography in ethnography is the "consideration of the effects upon the ethnographer of the experience of fieldwork, using others to learn more about and reflect upon oneself" (Briggs, 1970; Church, 1994; Gilligan, 1987; Okley, 1992). In keeping with this line of inquiry, this book offers glimpses into my own personal and professional narrative: as a child of Holocaust survivors growing up in Montreal, as a former elementary school teacher, and as a university professor and educational researcher of minority language issues, in order to articulate my reasons for embarking on this journey to Neve Shalom/Wahat Al-Salam—perceived both as a geographical space and also a psychospiritual border zone.

Autobiographical Ruminations: Introducing the Author

The significance of the border zone is perhaps in its power to give voice not only locally but also to those around the globe who dwell in between borders and in between identities. I am one of those "border dwellers," and I have always longed to articulate my psychic state of "inbetweenness" which is in fact shared by many individuals in this postmodern and postcolonial world riddled with diasporas emerging out of global migrancy and movement. The historical spaces of the twentieth century have been inhabited, in unprecedented numbers, by those fleeing war, poverty, and famine. Their sense of rootlessness, as well as their struggle to find voice, meaning, and balance in their new lives, can be regarded as a metaphor for the postmodern urban condition. This immigrant/refugee experience has created complex transformations in all metropolitan centers around the world, but especially in those Western countries which encourage immigration and offer a sense of possibility and hope for the displaced. Immigrant students and their parents arrive in large urban centers in our global society, often overwhelmed by forces of oppression and violence in their home countries, and are immediately faced with economic struggle and language barriers in their new places of residence. At the dawn of this new millennium we are faced with a sense of urgency engendered by this societal reality. More than ever before, it is essential to critically examine international educational initiatives that promote peacemaking and conflict resolution in order to provide a window to investigate the broader issues of war, violence, social justice, and human rights and their implications for the culturally diverse classroom. Neve Shalom/Wahat Al-Salam may well be an excellent role model for this purpose.

My life has always represented a curious residence on a psychological border—always on the margins, never in the center; always looking in through the window of loss and alienation, never quite belonging. I identify with E. Morin's (1989, p. 17) interpretation: "One foot is here and the other always elsewhere; straddling both sides of the border." I must elaborate on this notion, as it is significantly linked to my professional involvement with Neve Shalom/Wahat Al-Salam. As a member of the Jewish people, I identify strongly with the state of Israel and a Jewish-Israeli identity. As a child of Holocaust survivors, my life has been engulfed in the dark shadow of the genocide of the Jews in Europe by the Nazis from 1933 to 1945—a horror which forced the desperate need to recreate a Jewish homeland. In this respect I am at one with my Jewish Israeli sisters and brothers and consider myself very much an insider. I was not socialized in Israel, however, and as such, I am an outsider.

My parents immigrated in 1948 to Canada, and not to Israel, because my father's oldest sister had moved to Montreal from Poland in 1929. My aunt was the only other member of his nuclear and extended family left alive after the war. The rest were murdered in the ghettos and the concentration camps of Poland. As for my mother's family, she is the lone survivor. My brother arrived at the end of the war, the only Jewish child to be born in the convent of the Black Madonna Shrine, Matka Boszka, at Jasna Gora Monastery in the city of Czestochowa, my parents' hometown, a famous Polish Catholic pilgrimage destination. My parents and brother (who was one year old at the time) decided to leave Poland under very risky and illegal circumstances because of the startling news that Jews had just been murdered in a postwar pogrom in Kielce, a small town in southeastern Poland. I remember my mother telling me years later in Montreal when I was old enough to hear these stories that she was terribly shocked by this pogrom, which took place in July 1946, more than a year after the war in Europe ended. I will always remember her sad words: "The Nazi annihilation of Jews was horrible enough and I thought naively that after the war there would never again be such a plague as anti-Semitic pogroms. But when this pogrom in Kielce took place, we knew that we could never live in Poland again."

My parents and my brother languished for nearly three years in a displaced persons (DP) camp in the American zone in postwar Germany. It was not until 1948 that my parents were permitted to emigrate to Canada. This delay (in spite of the sponsorship of a blood relative) was due to the now well-documented anti-Semitic policies of Frederic Charles Blair, the director of the Immigration Branch of the Department of Mines and Resources,[4] who ensured that restriction on Jewish immigration was upheld (Abella & Troper, 1983, p. 7). In fact, my parents and brother were among the first Jewish refugees to enter Canada after the war. I was born in Montreal a few years later. Some of my parents' friends, however, who were also survivors, went to Israel (known as Palestine under the British Mandate) either out of Zionist motivation or, in many cases, because they simply were not welcome anywhere else—they had no other place to go. Their children were born in the newly created state of Israel of 1948 and became "sabras"—the term for "born Israelis," referring metaphorically to an indigenous cactus fruit of the same name—tough on the outside (because they must build and fight for and defend their homeland) but sweet on the inside. I am not a sabra, although I think psychologically it would have been better for me to have been one. Growing up as child of survivors would have been difficult anywhere, but perhaps in Israel I would not have felt quite so alone or "deviant" in society. (I firmly believed this as a child, but now I am not so certain about that belief.) Suffice to say that I am heavily invested emotionally and spiritually in the enterprise of the state of Israel.

I continually envied my Jewish Israeli peers as I was growing up. From a distance half a world away, I watched them thrive in a majority culture and coveted the strength and pride that were part and parcel of existence in that magical space. How I longed for such a fairy tale life; but of course it was not at all the idyll that I imagined it to be, as the grim Middle East conflicts vividly demonstrate. Nevertheless, it certainly represented a psychological improvement over my childhood, which was relentlessly assaulted by the nightmares of my emotionally wounded parents. And there was no real societal (mainstream) support to help our plight—nobody spoke about the Holocaust in those days. Some were indifferent to it and looked away; for others the magnitude of the trauma was just too shocking, and they felt guilty. Therefore, the awakening of the new identity and national culture in Israel seemed like a magnificent gift for Jews trying to reconstruct their homeland. It was, however, an unattainable dream for someone like me, who had no choice but to wander in the desert of exile. In fact, it was much more than exile: I felt a devastating sense of personal loss and mourning—indeed, of near annihilation. My parents suffered their sorrow in deafening silence or sudden bursts of hysteria. We, their children, knew that it was forbidden to enter that unspeakable, untouchable, unthinkable territory. (For more information on this plight of the children of Holocaust survivors, see Bar-On, 1989, 1996; Epstein, 1979.) In my childhood, the demon Hitler was always around the corner, ready to pounce—especially if I was not alert at every moment. It took all the emotional resources I could muster to simply hang on to the delicate thread of life. (I discuss this issue in greater detail in Chapter 5.)

I finally did get to Israel during the summer of my nineteenth year when I was awarded a scholarship to study Italian language and literature at the Università per Stranieri in Perugia, Italy. Before arriving in Italy, I decided to take a month-long holiday in Israel and finally see this mythic homeland of my dreams. This visit unleashed a wellspring of emotions. For the first time in my life I felt that being Jewish did not solely entail suffering and marginality. Israel seduced me with the dazzling possibility of normalcy for my cultural identity. Its geopolitical reality offered me the romantic sense of belonging and being "at home." I imagined that my nomadic existence, my wandering about without a fixed identity, could end. I had planned to enter a master's degree program in comparative literature at the Hebrew University in Jerusalem after I graduated from McGill, but life had its own agenda. By a twist of fate, I ended up in Berkeley, California, took a graduate course in bilingual educational research, and decided to pursue a career in sociolinguistics and education. I also found my life partner in Berkeley and did not return to Israel until more than a decade later, when we spent a university sabbatical year in Jerusalem. It was on our return to North America that I heard about the village of Neve Shalom/Wahat Al-Salam in a casual conversation at a social gathering. I was very disappointed that I hadn't known about this place while I was in Israel.

I did, however, have the opportunity to return to Israel and to visit the village a number of years later. In fact, it was at the beginning of the first year of my faculty position at the Ontario Institute for Studies in Education (OISE) in the University of Toronto that I wrote a research proposal to the Social Sciences and Humanities Research Council of Canada (SSHRC) in order to explore issues of language, culture, and identity within the intergroup setting of Jewish-Palestinian coexistence (to which this book is devoted). This project was funded, in part, by a grant from the SSHRC. I flew to Israel in December of 1991, and stayed for a number of weeks into January 1992, to begin the ethnographic journey in Neve Shalom/Wahat Al-Salam, which I have tried to distill in the pages of this book. I would return five more times in the nine years that followed. Most of this book was written during my stay as visiting scholar in the Department of Language and Literacy, School of Education, University of California at Berkeley. The next section contains the first few pages of the journal entry I wrote on my return from that first research sojourn in Neve Shalom/Wahat Al-Salam in the winter of 1992.

"In the Beginning": A First Glimpse of Peace

From my journal of February 1992:

> *In the beginning there were words staring up at me with silent hope. Neve Shalom/Wahat Al-Salam. Words with an exotic flavor. "Oasis of Peace." An adventure of faith and goodwill. An adventure in which I wanted to participate. I could only see the village in my imagination. It actually began in October 1984, when I had returned from a year as visiting graduate scholar at the Hebrew University in Jerusalem. My mind and heart were still filled with the power of my experiences in Israel. That year changed my emotional life forever. I learned to accept my personal destiny as a child of Holocaust survivors and I finally tasted the sweet fruit of belonging to a "majority culture." I, who can still hear the screams of the children at Auschwitz over and over again like an endless satanic tape in my head, was being offered a new role model. Instead of*

bleakness and despair, I saw energy and color and hope. It was a revelation for me. I sensed that if I had grown up in Israel with my fellow Jews that I might not have been so imprisoned in my suffering. I don't know; but it's possible. There were many Holocaust survivors in Israel and their suffering had meaning in this land of Jewish resurrection. All during the year I could feel a stirring in my soul, a yearning for "home," a need to finally be with my people in my land—in spite of all the social and political turmoil. The sheer power of Israel was intoxicating. It awakened in me a sense of belonging that had been buried so deep that I had given up trying to retrieve it. I became familiar with that magnificent spiritual presence that is Jerusalem. I was in exile no longer. This presence has nourished me since that year and has offered me a more whole and balanced outlook on my life. . . .

Upon return from my year in Jerusalem, I attended a social gathering in Toronto and someone, on hearing of my year's sojourn, asked me whether I had visited this special village where Jews and Arabs were living together peacefully. I could not believe that I had heard nothing of this place during my year in Israel. I called the appropriate authority to find out about this place and tucked away the information in a file folder which I named "For the Future." The years that followed were full of personal and professional growth. The charisma of "Eretz Israel" unleashed an energy within me to find meaning and voice in my life. I raced through the writing of my doctoral thesis, "Jewish-Canadian Non-native Language Learning and Ethnic Identity," at the University of Toronto with the speed of someone who had just been let out of prison. I also spent a couple of years doing postdoctoral work which focused on perceptions of university students from a variety of ethnocultural backgrounds toward issues of linguistic and cultural diversity in Canada.

Every so often, in my search through my filing system for some paper or other, I would pass the folder with the big letters "For the Future" and take a few minutes out to daydream. I had a feeling that I would get there someday. Certainly, at that particular moment my plate was full and there was much to do. I believed that if it was meant to be, then it would happen. Then the time finally came for me to realize my research interest in this tiny village halfway around the world from where I lived. I received a faculty position in the Centre for Teacher Development at the Ontario Institute for Studies in Education in the University of Toronto and the first research proposal I wrote as an assistant professor was to study the bilingual/bicultural school in Neve Shalom/Wahat Al-Salam. I was very busy as a first-year professor and wondered at the soundness of my judgment to fly to Israel during the Christmas holidays instead of staying at home. I felt, however, that I owed it to myself and those villagers, whose social and educational efforts had heretofore been unrecognized in the academic world. Nobody knew about them! It seemed appropriate for this to be my first professional step forward . . .

So this is a story about a small group of people, Arabs and Jews, who decided on their own and for their own, to try to live in peace. A little village in a little country called Israel. This tiny spot on the map is precious to me not only because I am Jewish but because of my yearning to find myself in this vast, broken world of ours. I owe the sense of direction in my life to this little country which has the power of healing me forever in its wild earth. My spirit is always wandering back to this land in my dreams and in my waking hours. I shall never be free of its overwhelming grip on my destiny. . . .

The village is located on a barren hill thirty miles west of Jerusalem. When the first people came to live there in the early 1970s there were so many obstacles. This hill had neither been inhabited nor cultivated since the Byzantine era, many centuries earlier. [The people] arrived to see only rocks, thistles, and thorns. There wasn't a single tree . . . . Certain individuals and organizations helped along the way. It was a terribly difficult time and some said that they were foolish and would never make it. But the dream of peace buoyed them up and protected them. This village was the vision of a very special man, a Jewish Israeli Dominican priest named Father Bruno. . . .

I arrived in the village on a clear, cool early December evening. Bob and Anwar, two of the villagers, picked me up from the place where I was staying in Jerusalem at the Hebrew University. I was thirsting for adventure. We drove through East Jerusalem and Anwar, who is an Arab, went into a bakery to get delicious Arab bread spiced with za'atar[5] (colloquially called sumsum). I huddled inside my down jacket feeling oddly very safe and very warm. The confusion of the postmodern, urban world dissolved. Here reality was more palpable. There was a traditional conflict happening here, full of unresolved pain but full of concrete meaning. We ate the freshly baked bread with the spices and talked about ourselves as we drove in the quiet of the night. The lights of Jerusalem shone behind us as we headed westward. . . .

Concluding Remarks

The journal entry above is a small introductory piece to a larger narrative that I shared with my participants during subsequent interviews and during the many extraordinary conversations that emerged over the course of this research study in Neve Shalom/Wahat Al-Salam. It turned out that I as researcher, and they as participants, found it possible to identify with one another in the safe place of our respective cultural/national group vulnerabilities and dilemmas. Mary Catherine Bateson (1987, p. 29) says, "Composing a life involves a continual reimagining of the future and reinterpretation of the past to give meaning to the present." I must admit that I have always found safety and solace in my professional life. When I began this research work, I hoped that I was ready to confront my multiple cultural identities, my sense of being on the margins, my psychic "orphanhood" as a child of Holocaust survivors. My desire was to resurrect the lost texts of my past through the present by locating my professional work in this village, where people have dedicated their lives to peaceful coexistence in the midst of a deadly conflict—and thus are transforming their world. Neve Shalom/Wahat Al-Salam beckoned as a kind of border zone and as a way in which that border becomes the site for educational explorations, for creating traditions with futures, for offering niches where identity discourses get reinvented and authenticated. For me that border suggested a whole new set of pedagogical vistas, and became a destination both theoretically as well as practically, to a site of resistance, and adventure, as well as of ambiguity and tension. The desire to know "What happens there?" overwhelmed me. I knew that I needed to contextualize what lies behind the efforts of these villagers, to create and negotiate a new epistemological space that is right at the edge of possibility— right on the border of hope.

Endnotes

1. A kibbutz is a communal, rural farm where residents collectively share their property. A moshav is physically very similar, but property is privately owned.
2. In January 2000, the land was given as a gift to the villagers. For more details, see the interview with the Abbot of the Monastery in Chapter 5.
3. Every building in Israel is obliged to have a designated bomb shelter in the event of war.
4. This took place under the auspices of the Canadian Liberal Party, whose Prime Minister at the time was William Lyon MacKenzie King.
5. *Za'atar* is a Middle Eastern lemony herb mixture which combines sumac and sesame seeds with thyme, oregano, or marjoram.

Chapter Two

A Community of Moral Education

There is no way to Peace; Peace is the way.

—A. J. Muste

The ongoing struggle between Palestinians and Jews in Israel has created hatred and fear between the two peoples, aggravated by misunderstanding, mistrust, and misconceptions. It was in this atmosphere that Neve Shalom/Wahat Al-Salam was born. The members have joined forces, with a determination to harness their fears together in order to lead them onto a positive path. Their struggles will then not be directed against each other but will merge into a common quest to find a way to live and to work together side by side in a spirit of cooperation. Their joint commitment provides a better life for all of them, especially for their children, [and] a model for others to observe and adopt.

—Written by a former school codirector and village member

Moral Responsibility: A Theoretical Framework

Neve Shalom/Wahat Al-Salam can be considered a fragile space where the desire for peace is a state of being and a place called home. It represents a frontier in that it transcends the current hegemony through personal invention—something that its villagers have truly built by repairing a broken space. This chapter studies this transformative space as a "moral edifice."[1] It also explores those interactions among the students and teachers, emanating from their sense of shared purpose, which reflect their assumptions about the nature of education in their village and about the type of society they wish to promote through education. Within the theoretical framework of this study, the specific educational initiative of this village as a moral community provides a window through which the issues of schools' relationships to multicultural and multiracial communities can be observed and elucidated more generally in a global context.[2]

I documented the experiences of the children, teachers, and parents through in-depth interviews and participant observation in the two schools, and through a general "reflection-in-living" (see Schon, 1990, 1994) within the village. The interviews were unstructured and as open ended as possible, allowing for the voices to emerge. The specific details of the project were worked out collaboratively with the school directors, teachers, parents, and children in Neve Shalom/Wahat Al-Salam. The participants shared with me their stories about why they decided to live in this village, about the dreams that they had for the children's future, about both their great satisfaction with and various reservations about the school, and about the delicate sense of hope they nurtured for peace in their troubled land. Tape-recorded interviews were used in addition to fieldnote gathering and extensive journal writing. These data form the basis of this research story and create portraits of the school and village as a dynamic, complex moral community.

In its aspiration to be a genuine bilingual/bicultural/binational learning environment, the village and its two educational institutions potentially provide a new and global dimension for exploring moral issues within the context of cultural and linguistic diversity and intergroup conflict. Although there has been substantial research on various aspects of language, identity, and intercultural relations in many parts of the world (see, for example, Cummins, 1989, 1996; Feuerverger, 1991, 1994; Lo Bianco, 1989; Ogbu, 1978; Samuda, 1986; Wong-Fillmore, 1991), there has been very little work on the specific consequences of bilingual/bicultural programs in which children from majority and minority groups learn together against a larger backdrop of intergroup conflict. It is also difficult to find qualitative research that focuses on a social grouping in which the residents are actively dedicated to issues of conflict resolution and peacemaking in their daily lives (see Neve Shalom/Wahat Al-Salam in Dolphin, 1991; Rosenberg, 1991; and Simon, 1997). This chapter investigates the social and psychological complexities of moral development through this specific educational experience. It offers a narrative of the peace education initiative in this Jewish-Palestinian elementary school from the perspective of everyday moral issues and involves personal and professional accounts of teachers' and students' lives.

"Moral experience" as used here refers to the "lived experience" (Dilthey, 1910/1977, in Tappan & Brown, 1989) of my participants as they are confronted with everyday situations filled with moral conflicts, ambiguities, and dilemmas. I focus on giving meaning to their "lived experiences" by presenting them in narrative form. There is a growing understanding of narrative as a powerful way of giving meaning to lived experiences (see, for example, Mishler, 1986; Polkinghorne, 1988; Sarbin, 1986). This theoretical approach is congruent with Carol Gilligan's (1982) focus on the analysis of moral voice and development by using narrative as a vehicle to examine conflicts and their possible resolution in interpersonal relationships (in Tappan & Brown, 1989, p. 199). Mark Tappan and Lyn Mikel Brown (1989, p. 182) note that narrative is central to the study and the teaching of morality, and that authorship of moral choices, actions, and feelings develops a sense of moral sensibility. Indeed, the deepening crisis in American schools and society (Kozol, 1991, 1996, 1999) is obliging educators to explore educational programs that encourage moral development in their students through narrative.

The theoretical underpinnings of this ethnography are consonant with interpretivists such as Clifford Geertz (1988) and Norman Denzin (1988), who offer an understanding of theory not as explanation or prediction but as interpretation or the act of making sense out of a social interaction. Indeed, they see theory building as focusing especially on the "lived experience" instead of abstract generalizations. According to Corrine Glesne and Alan Peshkin (1992, p. 19), "the 'lived experience', originating in phenomenology, emphasizes that experience is not just cognitive, but also includes emotions. Interpretive scholars consider that every human situation is novel, emergent, and filled with multiple, often conflicting meanings and interpretations." As Ruth Behar (1996, p. 174) puts it: "In my view it isn't an accident that the effort to engage with the emotions in current anthropological and feminist writing follows upon Freudianisms, structuralisms, and poststructuralisms. I think that what we are seeing are efforts to map an immediate space we can't quite define yet, a borderland between passion and intellect, analysis and subjectivity, ethnography and autobiography, art and life."

This book aims to give the participants a voice and to construct meaning for their emotionally as well as intellectually vulnerable texts. I searched for the patterns and narrative threads that would weave together their lived experiences of moral dilemmas into a collective story. As participant-observer, I was concerned with the interaction between personal life histories and the shaping of moral assumptions about the teaching-learning experience in relation to cultural and linguistic diversity, and to a situation of conflict between two peoples in a land which they must learn to share. These are some research questions that guided my inquiry:

1. What perceptions of the conflict and more generally of the world do these teacher/educators bring to the classroom, and how do these perceptions interact with those of the students in the class?
2. How do these people envision themselves and their respective identities as Jews and Arabs caught in a very complex human struggle?
3. How are these views enacted in their school curriculum choices and communication within the classroom?
4. Does the school, in fact, incorporate an egalitarian bilingual/ bicultural/binational philosophy into its curriculum?

Narratively speaking, our implicit or even tacit cultural and historical life experiences have a tremendous impact on those of teaching and learning. "These culturally and socially embedded metaphors have a powerful shaping influence on the way in which teachers come to know teaching" (Clandinin, 1988, p. 9). I again draw on Henry Giroux's (1995, 1998) theoretical notion of "border pedagogy," which encourages teachers and students to reconceptualize the interaction between dominant and subordinate groups and thus transform their own relationships. My observations in the school and my conversations with my participants affirm Giroux's (1991, p. 509) claim that "[cultural] difference in this case . . . opens the possibilities for constructing pedagogical practices that deepen forms of cultural democracy that serve to enlarge one's moral vision." It is important to emphasize that this village and its educational programs wish to go much further than providing a remapping of the pedagogical landscape; their purpose resides in the powerful hope of ultimately moving toward the notion of coexisting homelands and wholeness and to bring self and identity together within particular discursive configurations in the homes and classrooms of this geographical space called Neve Shalom/Wahat Al-Salam. Adrienne Rich (1986, p. 212) observed that "a place on the map is also a place in history."

This village is not an idyllic place in memory or fiction; it is situated in our everyday reality and in our consciousness which is never fixed, just as the boundaries of our external and internal worlds are constantly shifting according to historical, social, and personal conditions. It is a provocative place—both pedagogically and epistemologically—in its interrogation of the meaning of national identity and sense of belonging in Israel. Therefore, the moral discourses that emerge through the conversations in this chapter respond to the interior psychological tensions and transformations that take place in the interstitial space among national identity, language, culture, religion, and tradition.

Between Aesthetics and Rigor: An Interactive Methodology

This book is based on a strong interactive relationship, between myself as researcher and the participants, developed through dialogue and conversation. Thus, its research approach used a variety of qualitative methodologies. Case study and narrative methodologies were adopted in order to document the construction and reconstruction of the meaning of teaching and learning from a moral perspective for the individual teachers, students, and parents in the specific bilingual/bicultural/binational village school setting. Research is therefore seen as a social process but also reflexive, as it is focused on the individual researcher. As participant-observer in everyday classroom activities, I explored the dynamics of power and identity and of cultural and linguistic difference and equality. Various qualitative methods of research (Clandinin & Connelly, 1995, 1999; Eisner, 1991; Eisner & Peshkin, 1990; Hopkins, 1987; Hornberger, 1990; Huberman & Miles, 1984; Glesne & Peshkin, 1992; Schon, 1991; Yin, 1984) were used to focus on how the curriculum and pedagogical strategies in the school have been reconstituted in such a way that they can offer, as Maria Torrez-Guzman (1992) explains it, "cognitive empowerment," allowing students to become critical thinkers in dialogue with their teachers.

I chose a narrative approach in order to give voice to the moral/educational initiatives that these villagers are creating. Carol Witherell (1991, p. 239) states that we "as educators are inescapably involved in the formation of moral communities as well as the shaping of persons." I quote Maxine Greene's statement adapted from Toni Morrison's novel *Beloved* (1987) to emphasize that "moral education requires becoming friends of one another's minds, even, perhaps especially, when the 'other' is 'stranger'" (in Noddings & Witherell, 1991, pp. 238–9). In this narrative process all participants were encouraged to reflect on their own personal philosophy on intergroup relations *vis-à-vis* the teaching and learning experience. The emphasis is on "thick" description, on process, and on the natural setting (the classroom, the home, the village) as the source of data (Geertz, 1984, 1995; Janesick, 1991). Geertz (1995, p. 117) captures the exploratory sense of it fully when he states that ethnographic research planning is "hardly . . . a straightforward matter . . . *'on s'engage, puis on voit,'* plunge in and see what happens."

This chapter focuses on the aesthetic of the moral development taking place in this village and the evolving relationship between myself as researcher and the villagers as my participants. John Dewey (1934, 1958) underscored "the need not only to capture the cognitive, social, and affective dimensions of educational encounters, but also to find frameworks and strategies for representing the aesthetics of teaching and learning. . . . More recent scholars have cultivated this fertile ground and merged the realms of art and science in an effort to . . . speak about things that resist reductionism and abstraction, in an effort to challenge the tyranny of the academy, and in an effort to build bridges between theory and practice, research and action" (in Lawrence-Lightfoot, 1997, pp. 6–7). Sara Lawrence-Lightfoot's (ibid., p. 3) notion of "portraiture" also influenced the construction of this book. She uses this term for "a method of inquiry . . . that seeks to combine systematic, empirical description with aesthetic expression, blending art and science, humanistic sensibilities, and scientific rigor. The portraits are designed to capture the richness . . . of human experience in social and cultural context, conveying the perspectives of the people who are negotiating those experiences."

The interviews I conducted are indeed like the portraits which are shaped through dialogues between the portraitist and the subject, each one participating in the drawing of the image. The encounter between the two is rich with meaning and resonance and is crucial to the success and authenticity of the rendered piece (ibid., p. 4). Indeed, the interaction between the two voices often seemed like a delicate *pas de deux*—the words similar to dance steps or brush strokes creating an artful rendering of the dynamic and everflowing lived experiences of each participant and myself. My work is congruent with Joseph Featherstone's (1989) notion that the "portrait creates a narrative which has an explicit human impulse to embrace both analytical rigor (a perspective that is distant, discerning, and skeptical) and community building (acts of intimacy and connection) . . . which give voice to a people's experience" (in Lawrence-Lightfoot, 1997, p. 10). My intent is to contribute toward an understanding of the moral complexities of a collective teaching/learning enterprise dedicated to equality and cooperation within the larger context of social and political conflict in the wider society.

Moral Dilemmas within a Sociohistoric Context: The Dialogic Relationship between Justice and Care

The moral climate of schools has been a significant issue in education since ancient times (Johnson, 1987). The belief that American schools, for example, should be moral communities was stated explicitly in 1918 by the National Education Association. The type of didactic ethical instruction popular at the time, however, was claimed to have little effect on moral development in a series of studies by H. Hartshorne and M. A. May (1928–1930). In the 1940s, there was an increase in the emphasis on citizenship education as highlighted in social studies curricula (Sockett, 1993). In the 1960s, the curriculum reform movement brought issues of public education to the foreground of academic research. In the turbulent years of the 1960s, the rise of the civil rights movement, the Vietnam War, and the feminist movement all helped to create a sense of moral relativism which, under the social circumstances, made teaching moral values seem unfeasible in schools. Eventually a paradigm for moral development and education did emerge on the contemporary North American scene. It was a cognitive/developmental approach based on the work of Jean Piaget, on a view of justice from a Kantian perspective, and also to some extent on John Dewey (Kohlberg, 1981, 1984; Mosher, 1980; Selman, 1980). This approach claimed that moral development uses reason in order to solve moral dilemmas.

This paradigm, developed by Lawrence Kohlberg, ascribed to the democratic principles of discussion and cooperative problem solving. It incorporated the community meeting as a salient symbol of a democratic society where everyone has a say in making decisions that build a "spirit of community." In their evaluation of the "just community approach," F. Clark Power, Ann Higgins, and Lawrence Kohlberg (1989) indicated that this experience allowed students to cope more successfully with everyday, true-life moral problems in their schools. This notion was influenced by Emile Durkheim's claim (1925, 1973) that the school is a "transition institution between the family and the wider society." There, students need to develop what he called the spirit of altruism or attachment to the group. Through participation in a just community school, students receive an intense and concentrated form of social experience that encourages them to examine the quality of their relationships and their responsibilities to each other and to the group as a whole (Power, 1988, p. 199).

Kohlberg argued that the classroom atmosphere is crucial to moral development in the sense of students having the opportunity to make meaningful decisions in school as a means of self-empowerment. The "just community" school developed by Kohlberg emphasizes not only democratic principles but also the notion of *gemeinschaft* community with the ideals of group solidarity and a commitment to care and responsibility, which promote a sense of integration and unity (Power, Higgins & Kohlberg, 1989). This approach to schooling was derived from the practice of a democratic communal education model that he witnessed on an Israeli kibbutz (Kohlberg, 1971). What the kibbutz represented to Kohlberg, which was then incorporated into the "just community" model (1966, 1985), was the emphasis on a collective or shared consciousness representing the norms and values of the group and thus creating a strong basis for moral development and responsibility. The village of Neve Shalom/Wahat Al-Salam may reflect in some important respects a "just community," but there are also significant differences. For example, the villagers do not share the same religious and cultural values and norms; nevertheless, they do ascribe to similar underlying beliefs in equality and justice. In other words, there appears to be a collective consciousness about peaceful coexistence and respect for both the Palestinian and Jewish identities. Nevertheless, moral dilemmas arise frequently among individuals due to the intergroup conflict in the wider society which influences their daily lives in a myriad of ways.

It appears, however, that these complex emotional issues cannot be studied solely through cognitive development theory but rather through a new focus on a different methodology of interview and interpretation. Gilligan (1982) claims that a different development pattern could emerge when thinking is "contextual and inductive rather than formal and abstract." According to Gilligan (1982) and Gilligan, et al. (1988), there are two different moral voices or ways in which to resolve moral issues—justice and care—and there is a dialogic relationship between the two. Tappan (1991) elaborates on this notion by putting forth the view of "an ongoing inner moral dialogue between justice and care. The dialogue between the voices goes back and forth—the 'justice' voice speaks the language of fairness and equality and advocates one solution . . . while the 'care' voice speaks the language of relationship and responsibility, and advocates another solution . . . [people] frequently oscillate from one voice to another when responding to and resolving problems, conflicts, and dilemmas in their lives" (pp. 248–249). The harmony of the intertextuality in this dialogue underscores what Julia Kristeva (1999) regards as, not only in reference to Mihail Bakhtin but also to Hannah Arendt, ". . . a quest for shareable meaning. The political or social life is inseparable from the story; it is an activity as praxis. It is not a finished work; it is a [problematic] story, and . . . it is the fragility of human affairs that stirs us to action."

In Neve Shalom/Wahat Al-Salam these multilayered moral voices are constantly being played out and corroborate Kristeva's notion that social redemption is found in action, and that human diversity is in fact a necessary condition to action; this, however, is also a fragile affair. "It is a collective construction," Kristeva claims, *"un sujet en procès."* Edward Said (2000)[3] claims that "[education] must be worldly, it must be invested politically. Controversy is what the intellect is all about. Life is about not giving up; it is about fighting for less pain and evil; it is an everlasting effort—a resistance to pervasive ideas, cliches. . . . We need to find the actual truth that may be hidden; the concealed injustices . . . to make trouble when passivity is expected. . . . Education must go on." In the village school, the Jewish and Arab teachers are constantly negotiating the curriculum collectively, especially in the case of history, social studies, and current events.

Both the theoretical approaches of the reasoned "just community" and the vital process of the narrative action are significant when examining the moral development at Neve Shalom/Wahat Al-Salam. First, Kohlberg's notion of the just community, with its emphasis on building a sense of *gemeinschaft*: Community here is a "normative concept that entails a valuing of the ideal of group solidarity and a commitment to norms of care and responsibility that promote this sense of unity" (in Power, 1988, p. 198–199). Second, Gilligan's research, which uses a narrative approach in the study of moral development and moral education (Gilligan, 1982, 1988; Gilligan, Brown & Rogers, 1990) encourages us to feel the desire within us to tell our stories in order to share and interpret our contemporary inner lives as well as the lives of our forebears so that we can educate one another, and in so doing attempt to create a moral community that imagines as well as reasons.

Moral Development through Narratives of Lived Experiences

The discussion that follows explores the process of narrating stories of moral development and thereby authoring one's moral lived experiences and ultimately taking responsibility for action. There are several meta-themes explored in the narrative structure of this study:

- The commitment of the participants to confront the central question of Jewish-Palestinian coexistence on a grassroots level within the village and school;
- The school as a microsociety and as a moral community that can be used as a role model for conflict resolution and peacemaking;
- The village as a symbol for creating a dialogue between Arabs and Jews in Israeli society and in the larger Middle East arena— negotiation and compromise in an atmosphere of moral complexity.

My imagination as an educator and researcher was immediately captured by the stories that two of the educators, Anwar and Bob, began to tell about the history of the village and its people and school on the first drive from Jerusalem to the Neve Shalom/Wahat Al-Salam. Elliot Mishler (1986, p. 75) explains that "telling stories is a significant way for individuals to give meaning to and express their understandings of their experiences." More specifically, Michael Connelly and Jean Clandinin (1990) express this idea in the statement that "education and educational research is the construction and reconstruction of personal and social stories; learners, teachers, and researchers are storytellers and characters in their own and others' stories." My intent was to, in Maxine Greene's words (1983, p. 388), "communicate a sense of their lived worlds." I agree with Geertz (1973) and Lawrence-Lightfoot (1997) that "in the particular resides the general . . . [we] seek to document and illuminate the . . . detail of a unique experience or place, hoping that the audience will see themselves reflected in it, trusting that the readers will feel identified" (p. 14). My desire was to present a picture that conveys the tough moral struggles that confront these individuals on a daily basis. Their lives are, in fact, a microcosm of the Jewish-Palestinian dilemma.

Conversation: A Tool in Data Gathering

Conversation became one of the most successful data-gathering tools during my sojourns. My experiences concur with Connelly and Clandinin (1994) and Elliot Eisner (1991) that listening constitutes a salient part of conversation. These conversations with my participants were a metaphor for the teaching/learning relationship. It is important to note that the specific cultural mind-set of the villagers set the tone for the various approaches that I adopted. It was necessary for me as the researcher to be flexible at all times. An example of the cultural differences that hampered my research work at the beginning of my first visit will demonstrate how easily misunderstandings can arise as a result of a mismatch in cultural norms. The following is one of my journal entries in the first days of the sojourn:

> *I am so exhausted, it's hard to describe it. Everything is happening so fast and emotionally I feel as if I'm on a roller coaster. I am stunned by how hard these people are trying to break through the Jewish-Arab impasse. There is an amazing sense of goodwill and sharing that permeates the whole village. But right now I want to mention how frustrated I've been—trying to interview some of the people. Every time I try to set up an appointment, I am faced with a very noncommittal attitude. And yet I feel that they are very pleased with my research project and with my being here. I've been invited to dinners and am having amazing discussions with many people. But the minute I try to formalize a time for an interview I'm staring at a blank wall. And yet I know they feel comfortable with me. Maybe I'm trying to go too fast! . . . Oh gosh, I just realized what the problem is! I've been superimposing my own values onto their values. They perceive making "appointments" as distant and unfriendly. . . . I think I've just worked out something important here. I will have to discard this North American urban approach and just go along with their rhythm. I will have to stop being in a hurry and just listen.*
> (December, 1991)

I began to realize that I had to slow down and allow the voices of the villagers to emerge at their own pace. I had to have faith in the fertility of the participant-observation process. In order to optimize data collection, I had to let go of my own researcher needs and put those of my participants first. They had to get to know me and I needed to live fully in the moment. I decided to cast a wide net and began to simply enjoy being in this community. My most interesting data emerged out of very ad hoc situations. I would be walking along the road en route to someone's house or back to my room for some rest; I would see a villager and we would begin to talk. Spontaneously we engaged in conversation about the school and the *raison d'être* of the village in general. Conversations around dinner tables in people's homes and in the school staff room provided gold mines of information. These conversations were a collective, interactive process in which we would learn how our individual life stories had been shaped by our specific families and social histories. It was when the tape recorder was not running that often I gained the most valuable information. On these many occasions, I would reconstruct the conversations through notes that I wrote when I returned to my room.

The data were shaped by and evolved out of the relationships I formed through interaction with all sorts of people in the village. The conversations continually pointed to the underlying tension of differing cultural, linguistic, historical, and religious systems—many frameworks of meaning in competition with one another. What emerged, too, from my encounters was the significance placed by the villagers on interpersonal relationships as a means of conflict resolution. The people reflected a sense of belonging to a community which articulated clearly the expectations for peace and equality between Israeli Jews and Palestinians. My conversations revealed a group of people involved in the transformation of individual as well as collective consciousness; a society with a commonality of purpose toward mutual understanding. Power (1988, p. 203) explains that "this shared consciousness represents the authority of the group and is the real agency of moralization." Through conversations with the participants, I gained a glimpse of how these people are constructing meaningful lives through their common goal of peacemaking, but also how problematic the enterprise really is.

Stories of Moral Dilemmas

As participant-observer, I saw how the teachers were facilitators in the moral development of themselves and their students. During the interview process, I explored Giroux's notion (1988, p. 167) of teacher development as a "cultural politics that defines teachers as intellectuals who will establish public spaces where students can debate, appropriate, and learn the knowledge and skills necessary to achieve . . . individual freedom and social justice." The underlying message at the Neve Shalom/Wahat Al-Salam school in terms of teacher development was the constant need among the participants for negotiation, discussion, dialogue, and change in terms of what is "right or wrong" for curriculum development and classroom instructional practices. This theory was often very difficult to put into practice, however. The discussions were frequently heated and difficult; I was witness to a great deal of "moral negotiation" among the teachers and students. On a cognitive level, what emerged as sacred was to present each side of the story, unresolved conflicts and all. On a deeper emotional level, the situation was much more complicated than that. The narratives that follow explore the complex nature of the participants' moral responses to one another and to themselves. Excerpts of stories from various teachers and students are presented in order to better understand their moral experiences and their moral development. Later, we will examine more closely the multilayered issues discussed through the telling of stories from the participants' lived experiences. Due to the sensitive nature of some of these discussions, most of the names in this section are pseudonyms. When the name is real, the first and last name of an individual is given.

One teacher describes the delicate *pas de deux,* discussed earlier as essential in sorting out competing value systems of both groups and thus bringing equity into the history and social science curricula. He explains the risk taking that is involved in this endeavor and the benefits of shared decision making which lead to shared ownership of the curriculum:

> There's a lot of interaction between me and Ibrahim [a Palestinian teacher] regarding how we look at historical symbols. For example, the Israeli War of Independence of 1948 is obviously not looked upon as independence for the Palestinians. Language is so powerful. We have to present both points of view and that's what we're grappling with. We've gotten into some harsh disputes, sometimes noisily, sometimes in silence. It's such a delicate process. But we're moving forward and then you see the flash of a breakthrough and what a great feeling. It's all worth it because we're trying to give our children a better future. The children are being presented with both the Arab and Jewish perspectives. Many times we can't resolve issues but at least we're facing the problem—which at least allows the children to reflect on these problems in a more balanced way.

The narratives below are intended to provide a picture of various moral dilemmas that have no easy solutions, and as such have significant implications for moral education from a larger perspective. These stories ask us to reconsider our "ways of knowing" (Belenky et al., 1986) by illuminating very complex issues of human conflict. Sometimes, as George Marcus (1998, p. 73) suggests "[moral] collisions take place" and we feel what we feel in accordance to who we are and where we come from. Is it morally wrong to remain faithful to the memory of our respective histories? The following narratives push our thoughts to new levels and new extremes.

Avi, a Jewish teacher who lives in the village, describes a moral conflict that enveloped the whole village during the Persian Gulf War in January, 1991:

> The Gulf War affected the village in a very deep way. I think it was one of the very few times that you could feel a difference between the Jews and Arabs here. It polarized the community in a very unsettling way. Since I've been here (approximately ten years) I don't remember a more difficult separation emotionally. Of course it's never absolute and not everyone was polarized. But it did open up some deep splits. What surprised me most was that although we were all under the same threat [of being bombed by Iraq] and we were all anxious and frightened and living together and helping each other in the bomb shelter, I felt the Arabs were not as scared as the Jews. There was a difference in the feeling of threat. That's what I think—I mean we were all in this together—but it was different. Underneath it all, I think the Arabs still saw Iraq as an Arab

country, and they reacted differently. We had discussions about this and they were very helpful and meaningful. We're still working through it.

Avi explained that, morally, the issue was difficult to resolve because doubt had been planted in the minds of many of the people in the village. An emotional rift had been created which needed repair:

> We talked about the fact that naturally the Arabs will identify with their people in other countries in the Middle East but it left some of us feeling let down and worried. The Jews saw Saddam unequivocally as a mad dictator who was bent on destruction, but many of the Arabs were ambivalent because after all Iraq was an Arab country and their identification is with the Arab world. In all fairness many Arabs in the village were just as against what Saddam Hussein was up to as the Jews were. Nevertheless, it brought up such complicated emotions that we are still working on and showed clearly that we are two different peoples with different histories and cultures. But that doesn't mean that we can't learn to live in peace. And the arguments didn't bring about clear divisions among Arab versus Jew: Many Jews disagreed with one another and it was the same for many Arabs among themselves. It is important to mention that.

This kind of moral reasoning based on narrative provides Avi and the other participants the opportunity to author their own moral perspectives and in this way it encourages a sense of responsibility for action. Bakhtin (1986, p. 147) claims that the search for one's own (authorial) voice needs to "be embodied, to become more clearly defined . . . to cast off reservations . . . not to remain tangential [but] to burst into the circle of life [and] become one among other people."

Osamah, who grew up in a small Arab village in the north of Israel and who lives in Neve Shalom/Wahat Al-Salam and works in Jerusalem, explained the Gulf War conflict this way:

> The Gulf War was unfortunate in one way, but clarifying in another. It pointed to the fact that Jews and Arabs in Israel do live separate lives culturally, religiously, [and] politically. Our identities revolve around different symbols and different values and I think we have to be honest about that. As Arabs we have always felt isolated within the Israeli society, marginalized in many ways. So we certainly do not want to lose our ties with the rest of the Arab world. Our reaction to the Gulf War was more a question of retaining some thread to other Arabs. It doesn't mean we necessarily agreed with Saddam Hussein's policies. But naturally we are emotionally involved with the people in Iraq as Arabs, just as Jews would be involved with other Jews in different parts of the world. But living in this village teaches me daily that having different allegiances is not necessarily a bad thing as long as we have certain social and personal

values that are based on sound moral principles. Maybe that's easier said than done. But we must teach our children to learn to respect each other's differences. It's the issue of trust which is most difficult.

Both Avi and Osamah reflect the psychological complexities inherent in the moral dilemma that emerged from the emotional "fallout" of the Gulf War. They both went on to say that all members of the village were encouraged to discuss these issues in ad hoc meetings. There were a great many ambivalent feelings that emerged and heavy arguments that followed but the most significant outcome was that the villagers were thrashing out the issues *together*. The teachers and school directors had to sit down and work out strategies in order to resolve these dilemmas with their students. Their approach is consonant with Gilligan's (1982, 1986) assertion that the affective dimension of storytelling and dialogue encourages moral decision making. The moral perspective of the participants informed their teaching on practical as well as theoretical levels. These moral issues were not simply "add-ons" to the curriculum but embedded within and a part of the everyday classroom life in the school.

The children were also greatly affected by the atmosphere created by the Gulf War and this issue became an explicit part of the class curriculum in all grades. Shuli, a third-grader, and Yaakov, who was in grade six, were two young boys who discussed some moral conflicts in terms of the Gulf War from their point of view:

> *Shuli:*   You know in our school some of the Arab kids said things like, "Go Iraq, go Iraq!" And the Jewish kids said that Iraq was wrong.

> *Yaakov:*   We argued about it in class all the time all during the war. Even with my best friend. He's Arab and he kept saying that Saddam is right and is the son of all nations. And the Jewish kids felt that Saddam was crazy and bad. But we stayed friends because our teachers talked to us about what was going on and told us that we both have a right to our opinions but that when everything is all over we still will live together and it's better to live together as friends.

Mohammed, a child from a nearby Arab village who was bussed to the Neve Shalom/Wahat Al-Salam school every day, explained why he sang the pro-Saddam songs:

> I sang the songs because the other kids in my village were singing them. They made me feel proud about being Palestinian and Arab. I didn't mean it to hurt my friends at the school who were Jewish. I don't think they understood how much better it made me feel about being Arab. I tried to explain it to them during our discussions with the teachers. It's hard because people were feeling angry and scared.

Zahra, a twelve-year-old girl who lives in another nearby Arab village and attends the Neve Shalom/Wahat Al-Salam school, was torn between two allegiances. She described her moral dilemma:

> In my village many of the kids got very excited about Saddam and shouted the slogans and sang the songs and I wanted to go along with them and be part of what my friends were doing. But at Neve Shalom/Wahat Al-Salam the teachers were telling us to see both sides of the problem. We have a class called actualia (current events) and both my Arab and Jewish teachers in the class talked with us for many days about trying to find peace and not war. They also explained how much better it would be if countries in the Middle East could be friends and not enemies. Not only are many Arabs enemies with Jews but many Arabs are enemies between themselves in different countries. But when I would go back home every day to my village some of my friends were mad at me because I was friendly with the Jewish kids. At least there were some of us from my village who go to the school so we stuck together. It made me very unhappy but I wasn't alone at least. And I decided not to shout those slogans or sing those songs. My parents wouldn't have wanted that.

Zahra's narrative and those of the other children tell an intricate tale of moral dilemma and development. They indicate the complex interrelationships in the lived experiences of the people involved with the Neve Shalom/Wahat Al-Salam school. As these participants explain, the issue of cultural identity and conflict of allegiance is an essential ingredient in the moral dilemma.

Another story of moral conflict in terms of identity formation and moral development was told by Ahmed, who teaches in the school:

> In the beginning I came here only to work. I was living in Jerusalem and was already married. I had been a student at the Hebrew University and became a journalist. I was getting tired of my journalist work and then I noticed an ad in the paper about the Neve Shalom/Wahat Al-Salam school needing teachers. It was 1988 and I worked there for two years and lived in Jerusalem. It was hard because I had to come by bus. It meant getting up very early and coming back very late every day. I was living in Arab Jerusalem (East Jerusalem) and there were events that forced me to decide where I belong. I knew these were my people, the Palestinians, but I didn't feel like I really belonged there. One morning when there was a general strike (as a result of the Intifada[4]). No one was working but I went to work at Neve Shalom/Wahat Al-Salam. It was very hard for me; I had to decide which side of the Green Line I belonged to. I had a little child by then and both my wife and I wanted to figure out a way to have our baby grow up in a good environment. So when they suggested to us to move to Neve Shalom/Wahat Al-Salam, we decided to do it.

Ahmed's narrative is filled with moral ambiguities and challenges. Embedded within his story is the sense of guilt in having to choose on "which side of the

Green Line" he belongs. His narrative becomes a vehicle for exploring the cognitive and affective dimensions of his moral decision to leave East Jerusalem and come to live in Neve Shalom/Wahat Al-Salam. It reflects his intellectual and emotional struggle in attempting to solve a crucial moral dilemma. In authoring his own moral story, Ahmed offers insights into his personal development that bring a sense of meaning and moral value to the situation. This authorship allowed Ahmed to acknowledge his own moral perspective in the midst of conflict and tension and to emerge with a sense of his moral identity and authenticity (Blasi, 1980):

> It was such a difficult choice (to leave East Jerusalem and move to Neve Shalom/Wahat Al-Salam) because I'm Palestinian but I have Israeli citizenship. That means—I don't know how to explain it—this feeling that you know they are my people, I belong to them, but because of the circumstances I have to move away from there and live in another place. I also realized that I was different from them because I was born and grew up in Israel and went to the Hebrew University. So that, even though we [Ahmed's neighbors in the West Bank] speak the same language and have similar customs, we grew up in different places and have different mentalities. I had so many long discussions with my neighbors and friends. We spoke about the way we were feeling and it became clear that even though we had so much in common we did behave differently in terms of political choices. This was hard to admit. I had to recognize the fact that there was a split in my identity. For example, I made a pact with myself that I would not be involved in any stone throwing (during demonstrations) at the Israeli soldiers. I was in solidarity with my neighbors but I decided not to take part in the violence. . . . This problem with identity for Israeli Arabs is very difficult. I think that Arabs even abroad now are beginning to understand this hard situation that we're in—that we don't feel like we totally belong in Israeli society but that we have different values from many in the West Bank.

It was through dialogue and reflection that Ahmed began to make sense of the moral and psychological tensions that had been thrust upon him. He began to shape his moral development by gaining ownership of his moral decisions on a gradual basis. The move to Neve Shalom/Wahat Al-Salam was a way of maintaining his Palestinian identity without having to reject his Israeli identification.

Abdul, a young Arab teacher who was new to the school at the time and commutes from Jerusalem, provides some insights into the special nature of the Neve Shalom/Wahat Al-Salam school in terms of Arab control over the curriculum and its implications for self-esteem:

> What I like about this school is that the Arabs have more responsibility over their own education. This is not the case in most other schools in Israel. And this is one of the big problems for Israeli Arabs in terms of issues of identity and for a sense of self-esteem. At least in the West Bank,

Arabs have their own school systems and universities. They have a clearer feeling of who they are, even with all the problems. Nobody is really looking at the problems that Arabs have in Israel proper. That's why Neve Shalom/Wahat Al-Salam is so special. It confronts that fact and tries to improve it and opens a line of communication. I get into a lot of arguments about it with the other teachers; we don't always know how to solve these problems but we're talking. That's so important. It means there's a chance for real change. It's also really good to see that the children are getting along well. They are given more opportunity to discuss their needs in terms of their language and cultural backgrounds.

Abdul explained that when there are disputes or arguments due to the political situation, the teachers don't "push it under the carpet." They discuss it with the children and listen to their voices. Allowing the children to explore moral issues through narrative encourages a sense of authority and responsibility. Nel Noddings (1984, 1991) claims that a good education must be based on caring relationships in terms of "how to meet the other morally," and thus opens a space for contemplation.

Ariela, a Jewish teacher from a nearby village who was also new to the school, expresses it this way:

I enjoy teaching here very much. It is good to have dialogue and to show us how things can work between Arabs and Jews. It is difficult but it works. There are so many emotions and years of hating and being afraid of each other. We have to learn not to blame each other. We have to try to live together side by side. If it's happening here, then it can happen elsewhere. The big thing is respect. That's what happens in this school and in this village. My ideas have become more open since I started to work here.

Ariela did, however, have to interact with people in her village who were wary of the philosophical principles of the Neve Shalom/Wahat Al-Salam school; for example, that it is preferable for Jewish and Arab children to be schooled together on an everyday basis. She told me that some of her fellow villagers were openly hostile to the idea. She was involved in a deep moral dialogue within herself and with these neighbors as far as arriving at the decision that her involvement in the Neve Shalom/Wahat Al-Salam school was the right thing to do:

It wasn't easy coming back home every day having to deal with some glowering faces. There are some in my village who feel that Arabs cannot be trusted and that they are all terrorists. So they see the school in Neve Shalom/Wahat Al-Salam as idealistically foolish at best and dangerous at worst. My feeling is that if they had had the opportunity of going to such a school maybe their attitudes would be more positive. I have been trying to discuss these issues with them and some are listening but others are too far away from the idea of the possibility of coexistence. What I find wonderful about the school is the hope that these attitudes can change with these Jewish and Arab children who are learning together side by side. They are being given the opportunity to see the situation in a different way on a more equal basis.

During my participant observation at the school, I often witnessed the transformative power in the discourse of caring, equality, and justice in each classroom within the context of team teaching and cooperative learning. These teachers' comments support Giroux's (1991, 1995) notion of difference, equality, and social justice. The Neve Shalom/Wahat Al-Salam school explores ways in which to offer students curricula that will enable them to "make judgments about how society is historically and socially constructed, and how existing social relationships structure inequalities around racism, sexism, and other forms of oppression" (Giroux, 1991, p. 508). Joel, for example, reflected on these issues as they relate to the current events classes:

> I originally taught that class with Salim [who is now one of the directors of the school] and we'd just both sit together and try to thrash it out. It doesn't mean that you don't get differences of opinion and that it's clear sailing. It's actually very hard but there's the significance of the fact that you have a Jewish and a Palestinian teacher trying to face the issues honestly and above board. For example, after a terrorist attack that happened one morning in Jerusalem, Salim was directing the class and he brought out the issue of who profits from this type of activity. He said how it just increases the hatred and gives more power to the right-wing groups. The fact that an Arab teacher said that obviously meant something. It has an effect on both the Jewish and the Arab kids in the class. It opens up a line of communication, of real dialogue.

The daily events and interactions that take place at the school present a practical embodiment of the thesis that "educating for difference, democracy, and ethical responsibility is not about enshrining reverence in the service of creating passive citizens. It is about providing students with knowledge, capacities, and opportunities to be noisy, irreverent, and vibrant" (Giroux, 1991, p. 509). The teachers at Neve Shalom/Wahat Al-Salam speak to the necessity that students understand how cultural, ethnic, racial, and ideological differences enhance the possibility for dialogue, trust, and solidarity. They stress, as he does, the development of pedagogical contexts that "promote compassion and tolerance rather than envy, hatred, and bigotry, and that provide opportunities for students to be border crossers" (ibid., p. 508). This idea of "border crossing" is a pedagogical approach that is being practiced on a daily basis in Neve Shalom/Wahat Al-Salam; it provides a new way of reading history as a way of reclaiming power and identity (Aronowitz & Giroux, 1991). During my first visits to the village, the two codirectors of the school were a Jewish woman, Ety Edlund, and a Palestinian man, Anwar Daoud. They both live in the village with their families. The teamwork they displayed is heartening. This school had been Ety's dream for many years and she was a key player in its development:

My husband and I met in Israel and then we spent some time in Sweden because he is from there. I then learned about this village and we decided when we got back to Israel to move here. My dream was to open a school in the village and it is incredible that this dream has come true, and that it is not only growing but that children from Jewish and Palestinian villages outside of the village are now attending the school. Sometimes I can't believe that it is really happening! What is really exciting now is that the school is being formally recognized by the Ministry of Education, which means that we will be hopefully getting some funding in the future and input from them. Up until now we have been basically ignored. It gives a sense of normality and legitimization to the school—which was missing up until now. Also, we have hired some new teachers this year and they are excellent. There's a sense of "getting along" and things are going very smoothly because of that.

Anwar explained the role that the school plays in enhancing a positive sense of identity for its students and commented on the moral development that is embodied within the daily educational discourse in the classes:

The Arab children who come to this school feel so much better about themselves. They feel a sense of equality here with the Jewish students. It really is a wonderful thing. There are very few places where this happens on a formal and everyday level. In most cases Arabs feel very marginalized within Israeli society. In this school the children are able to share their stories and their experiences, their fears and their hopes. I think this school and this village is the hope for the next generation. There are all sorts of examples I can give you that would show how difficult moral issues are treated in the daily class lessons. The students and we the teachers live these problems all the time and they are there in every aspect of our teaching and learning.

The children also had many opportunities for moral reflection and deliberation. They were encouraged to examine and communicate their views of a situation and to encounter those of their classmates. These classroom approaches reflect the words of Dewey (1909, 1975) as quoted by Harriet Cuffaro (1995, p. 54): "We need to see that moral principles are not arbitrary . . . that the term *moral* does not designate a special region or portion of life. We need to translate the moral into the conditions and forces of our community life, and into the impulses and habits of the individual."

I spent my first morning in the grade-one class. The teacher lives in a nearby Arab village and commutes to the school every day. She is a natural teacher and all the children love her. She explained to me how important it is for a teacher to see the children first, not their cultural backgrounds:

You must see them with open eyes for the special qualities they have inside them. You must give them a chance to show you their unique [selves]. And then I deal with whether they are Arab or Jewish, but only after we really get to know each other. I try so hard to keep an open mind. Nobody says it's easy. But it makes such a difference.

In her class, the children were collectively preparing their songs, poems, and stories for the Christmas party that was fast approaching. The atmosphere was festive and industrious. In this class Hebrew and Arabic were being spoken simultaneously. The children, guided by their teacher, were crafting themes revolving around war and loss and a hope for peace and normality. The class activities and discussions reflected the actual experiences that the children must deal with in their everyday lives. Their contributions to the curriculum were evident in this lesson. In fact, the teacher and her students shared in the development of the lesson and thus participated in the construction of knowledge and understanding of difficult moral issues within the larger sociopolitical context in which they were situated. A number of children recited this poem in Arabic, Hebrew, and English:

> *I am a child with something to say*
> *Please listen to me*
> *I am a child who wants to play*
> *Why don't you let me?*
> *My toys are waiting for a chance*
> *Give us a chance*
> *Please, please give us a chance!*

What was remarkable about this presentation was that the children, Jewish, Moslem, and Christian, were singing in unison for peace and understanding: "We don't want guns, we want music and feasts and gifts from Baba Noel on this holiday." There was magic in this classroom. Suddenly I felt as if I was in a sacred place. At that moment, I knew I didn't want to be anywhere else on Earth. I thought of how in Judaism, the Torah (the holy book) explains that each and everyone of us has our own distinctive contribution to make in order to help "repair the world." This is termed *Tikkun Haolam* in Hebrew; it is a very empowering idea in its call to action on Earth. Idealistically, Neve Shalom/Wahat Al-Salam embodies this philosophy, which allows every human being to feel that they can and will make a difference, each according to their own special talents and nature.

I was impressed with these children chattering away in Hebrew and Arabic, helping each other with their lessons, laughing together, playing together. I looked at the teachers, Arab and Jewish, planning and teaching lessons together, examining each other's points of view on some very thorny issues in history and current events. I witnessed the healing power of singing, story writing, artwork, music, and drama in the classrooms and I, as researcher, tried to live up to Dewey's notion that "to envision and document the artfulness of good education, one requires a joining of aesthetic and empirical approaches, merging rigor and improvisation." This little village school embodies a moral community where moral education focuses on the shaping of the self and the development of identity and equality. There is a profound motivation to act morally. Giroux (1991, p. 507) views "schools as deeply implicated in forms of discourse, social relations, and webs of meaning that produce particular moral truths and values." This philosophy also concurs with Tappan and Brown's (1989) claim that such an educational endeavor can be called a poststructuralist or postmodern approach to moral development and moral education and provides a new vision of the relationship between developmental psychology and education. This vision—still in its nascent form—seeks to use education less to facilitate development along a hierarchical progression of structurally defined stages, and more to enable each student to resist and overcome social and cultural repression, and hence to authorize his or her own moral voice (p. 200). In the Neve Shalom/Wahat Al-Salam school, a sense of moral responsibility toward constructing knowledge and relationships for coexistence and peacemaking informs all aspects of classroom activity.

The Christmas Party: Exploring Interfaith Understanding

The Christmas party took place on the last day of school at the end of the term during my first sojourn in the village. This event exemplifies the moral enterprise in which these people are engaged on a daily basis, both personally and professionally. The narrative below attempts to draw a picture and interpret the details of the gathering from my personal and professional perspective as researcher and observer. I follow Geertz's advice when he claims that "what is needed, or anyway must serve, is tableaux, anecdotes, parables, tales: mininarratives with the narrator in them. . . . Field research in such times, in such places, is not a matter of working free from the cultural baggage you have brought with you as you enter, [as if you are] without shape and without attachment, into a foreign mode of life. It is a matter of living out your existence in two stories at once" (1995, p. 65, 94). In his earlier writing, Geertz points to the "imaginative tableau," the ethnographic work as painting a likeness; in spite of the importance of creativity and imagination, the underlying goal of the interpretation is to attend to the details of social reality and human experience: ". . . we must measure the cogency of our explications, but against the power of scientific imagination to bring us in touch with the lives of strangers" (1973, p. 16). The following excerpt is from my journal entry about the school party.

> *The Christmas party was scheduled to begin at 5 P.M. in the kindergarten; and 6 P.M. in the elementary school. I was told that it would be special because many parents would be meeting each other for the first time. This*

is because this is the first year where children fron
Shalom/Wahat Al-Salam are attending the school.
growing and that is such a positive sign. By 4:00 in
whole village was buzzing with anticipation. I had h
nap before the parties but the euphoria was contagio
over to Bob and Michal's place and helped them dres:
daughters. They looked like two little dolls in pink an
the kindergarten at 4:45 P.M. and it was already a mob
had prepared me for what I was about to witness. Pare   *were taking
their first steps towards one another and friendship. In most cases, I could
not tell who was Jewish and who was Arab, except, of course, for those
who wore traditional outfits. Some held back shyly; some moved forward
easily in the crowd. Everyone sensed that they were part of something
very special.

My eyes fell on an Arab woman in her hijab sitting with a lovely little
baby on her lap. Right next to her was a Jewish woman, also sitting with
a little child on her lap [Figure 2–1]. They began to chat about their
children in the kindergarten. "This is what peace is all about," I
remember saying to myself. I was disgusted with the world's media for

Figure 2–1   Two mothers, one Palestinian and one Jewish, sit side by side at the
school play, with their younger children on their laps. (Courtesy of the author.)

ocusing on the negative and on distortions and sensationalist *anipulations*. Why do we never hear about these peace efforts?

A hush fell over the crowd as the two kindergarten teachers entered the room and began to narrate the Christmas story in Hebrew and Arabic. As the story progressed, the children entered in their costumes. "Miriam", "Yosef" and "Yeshua," the baby in Mary's arms, emerged from the side. Little five-year-old "Miriam" was breathtaking in her white cape and headcovering, hugging her little baby doll all covered up in a blanket [Figure 2–2]. Then the innkeeper; the stable with the animals; the three wise men; angels; and so it went. Each child had a little piece to say. Their brothers and sisters in the audience along with their parents looked on proudly. It was a boisterous, happy crowd. My eyes filled with tears. Here in this little village not very far from Jerusalem—a place little known to the rest of the world—was the true spirit of Christmas: Jewish and Arab children performing the Christmas story in their classroom with their families sitting side by side in the audience. Here was the Christmas message as it had been originally meant: good will to all humanity (Christians, Jews, Moslems, EVERYBODY!) I snapped my photos but the

Figure 2–2 A little girl ready to play the role of "Miriam," holding the baby "Yeshua" (a doll), in the school play. (Courtesy of the author.)

scene was blurry in front of my watery eyes. I don't think anyone noticed my tear-stained face as we all moved out toward the elementary school. Every one was busy in friendly conversation.

There were many more parents in the large elementary hall. More lively conversation. Many of the parents from the neighboring villages knew who I was because their children had come home talking about me over the past week. The atmosphere in the room was so congenial. The two school codirectors welcomed the parents and described the evening program. Suddenly the lights were [turned off] and in the darkness the children began to approach the front of the room with candles. The girls were dressed in splendid pale-colored dresses, some chiffon or satin or lace. They had large bows or flowers in their hair. Most of the outfits had been sewn by their mothers. The boys looked neat in freshly pressed pants and shirts. They were all so magnificent. The image that came to my mind was that of a beautiful ballet [in which] each dancer knew his or her role and performed gracefully. The whole audience was transfixed. There was music and song and dance and story. I wished that the evening would never end. I felt like a child in a candy shop, tasting all these goodies. The presentation ended with a dramatic entrance by none other than Baba Noel, who distributed gifts to all the children. I will never forget the bilingual and bicultural laughter and good cheer that evening.

I remember saying to myself during the flight back to North America, "Perhaps this little village in Israel has the potential to become a model for conflict resolution and peacemaking." I came away from that first sojourn in this little "oasis" with a sense that there is no possibility of achieving peace without facing the ravages of war. Indeed, the power of narrative may lie in allowing the suffering of the "other" to become part of our own consciousness, part of how we perceive the world. Perhaps it is only through the telling and retelling of stories of war, trauma, and violence that a liberation and transformation toward global emotional recovery can take place—a "narrative rebirth . . . where the public space becomes a space of differences" (Kristeva, 1999). Indeed, in a village such as Neve Shalom/Wahat Al-Salam in which there is a sense of safety and goodwill, the sharing of stories of pain can transform feelings of fear and hopelessness into those of compassion and reconciliation. At least they are trying.

Conversations with the Schoolchildren

All children in Israel possess a heightened awareness of cultural difference and inter-group conflict and violence, due to the ongoing struggle between Jews and Arabs. What sets the children who attend the Neve Shalom/Wahat Al-Salam School apart from most other children in Israel is the possibility for them as Jews and Arabs to learn together in bilingual/bicultural classrooms on a daily basis. The children who come to school from outside the village are encouraged to talk over their fears of each other in open dialogue. The teachers are constantly discussing issues of conflict and possible resolution in the staff room and in staff meetings, and the two codirectors of the school play a major role in being available to their teachers to help with problems. The children learn to work and play together and to examine their respective cultures, histories, religions, and languages within a context of safety, trust, and friendship. Their cultural space resides in many contexts: literature, social studies, history, music, mathematics, and language arts, and is understood to be a contested space with differing and often conflicting viewpoints. In such a place dialogue is envisioned as a necessary way to authentic collaboration, reflection, and negotiation (Kaiser & Short, 1998).

The teachers enter this cultural space as facilitators who are expected to nurture and protect the authenticity of the collected visions and stories written for and by the children. Replicating old norms and hegemonic ideologies and living within narrowly defined value systems do nothing to further the arduous but beneficial work of "teaching to transgress" (hooks, 1994); in fact, to engage in a pedagogy of freedom one must widen the existing cultural and moral space into one where both Jews and Palestinians are respected for their own national aspirations. In Neve Shalom/Wahat Al-Salam, children's voices are heard, acknowledged, and deemed worthy to express their subjective histories. The pedagogical strategies are in concert with the ideas of educational theorist Terry Eagleton, as quoted in bell hooks (1994, p. 59): "Children make the best theorists, since they have not yet been educated into accepting our routine social practices as 'natural,' and so insist on posing those practices and the most embarassingly general and fundamental questions regarding them with a wondering estrangement which we adults have long forgotten. Since they do not yet grasp our social practices as inevitable, they do not see why we might not do things differently." In my interviews with some of the children, they discussed their feelings about sharing and learning together in the school. They reflected on the Hebrew-Arabic bilingual program, on the specific sociopolitical climate in their war-torn country, and on their personal relationships with one another in and out of the village. They demonstrated a great sense of pride in their school. One grade-six boy said:

> I think this school is a very good idea. Because it's where we learn to know each other and to learn Arabic as well as Hebrew. . . . We learn to live together and not be separated and have wars and stuff like that. . . . There is a desert of war in our country and here we have—how do you say it—an "oasis of peace." That's what Neve Shalom/Wahat Al-Salam" means in English.

A boy in grade four explained the ease with which he is learning both Arabic and Hebrew:

> Many kids that I know who don't go to this school don't learn Arabic the way I do and they find it harder to read and write than Hebrew; it's more complicated for them. But because I'm learning it every day as much as

I'm learning to read and write Hebrew it's much easier. Also there are Arab kids in my class who help me when I get stuck on something. And I can help them with Hebrew. Some of my friends who don't go to this school can't imagine that this works so well. They can't imagine speaking and reading Arabic so easily. Also we have Arab teachers here and they don't.

A grade-five girl who lives in the village makes explicit the need for intergroup relations in order to dispell fear, hatred, and prejudice:

It's a terrible thing to say bad things about people, especially when you don't know them. Like people say bad things about Arabs but that's because everybody is afraid. We have a lot of wars here and sometimes people get hurt or killed by terrorists. And that makes many people hate each other. I have so many friends who are Arabs and so we're not afraid of each other and we don't hate each other at all. But that's because we live here together and we know each other. I don't know what would happen if I lived in Jerusalem or Tel Aviv or something.

A little grade-four girl explores considerations of caring and concern for intergroup relationships. She discusses how daily "border crossing" from [an Arab village] to Neve Shalom/Wahat Al-Salam allows for the creation of new responses to cultural differences and conflict. She also expresses her pleasure in the greater intimacy of the smaller school:

I come into this school every day by bus from [an Arab village]. I like the school here because there aren't so many kids in each class. The teacher has more time for us. I don't feel left out or ignored. I really know how to read and write Hebrew and when I go back to my village, I can't help but show off to my friends. I have Jewish friends because I go to school here and I like them the same way I like my Arab friends. The kids in my village who don't come to this school don't understand that. They think the Jews want to take away their homes. They don't realize that the Jews are just as afraid as they are. It's a real mess. When I'm in Neve Shalom/Wahat Al-Salam I feel different than when I'm in [my village]. I mean I feel special.

This grade-two boy illustrates the value of the bilingual/bicultural education that he is receiving. He explains how he is being taught an understanding and appreciation of his own Jewish heritage and a respect for the Moslem and Christian traditions. His words indicate an education toward a sense of community within a framework of diversity:

We learn about all the holidays of Christians, Jews, and Moslems. I like that because I get to understand other ways. But I celebrate my own holiday and learn to be Jewish but I know that you can't laugh on certain holidays, like when they celebrate Mohammed and you don't want to hurt them. You have to respect what they do. Like when they fast on

Figure 2–3   Two students in the central school hallway in the village of Neve Shalom/Wahat Al-Salam. (Courtesy of the author.)

Ramadan. You don't want to show them your food during the day or it will make them feel bad.

A grade-five girl who lives in a nearby Jewish village discussed her changing attitude toward Arabs now that she attends the school in Neve Shalom/Wahat Al Salam:

I find that since I'm at the school, I am less afraid of Arabs. Until now I used to be very afraid of them because of the wars. . . . In our current events classes we have an Arab teacher and a Jewish teacher and so we have more of a chance to hear the Arab side. I'm still learning to speak Arabic and so the teacher translates what I don't understand. . . . My best friend in [a Jewish village] where I live doesn't know Arabs the way I do. She's a lot more afraid.

An atmosphere has been created in Neve Shalom/Wahat Al-Salam in which differences can be appreciated and respected instead of feared (see Figure 2–3). Another girl continued:

In this village the children have respect for themselves and for one another, and for their different religions. That person is your enemy [referring to Arabs] not because you don't like him or her but because your people and her people are at war. But what I learn here is that we are all humans and we have to learn to get along. . . . This hatred is something to be ashamed of. Here we try to repair the hatred. Countries are always in competition with each other. They don't share anything. I think most people want peace in this world. If only Neve Shalom/Wahat Al-Salam could be the capital of the world!

One grade-six boy expressed it this way:

Many Arab families have more kids than Jewish families. But they love the same kinds of things we do. They love to play and watch television. We love to play and watch television. They're no different; they're people—like we are. We're alike. There's no such thing like I'm worth more than other people. If someone is better in mathematics, for instance, it's not because he's Jewish. Some Jews are good in mathematics and some Arabs are good in mathematics. I don't like people who think they are better and worth more than others.

It's like the Nazis. They thought they were better than everybody else and they thought the Jews were the worst. They killed the Jews because they said they were bad. My grandparents have friends who were in that Nazi war. . . . There is war in the territories. People killing each other. I think the best place to live in all of Israel is here in Neve Shalom because, here there's peace between the Arabs and the Jews. We live together but we keep our own religions.

These children are creating new realities, new expressions, and new images which give voice to a new collective consciousness of coexistence and hope for peace. By being given opportunities to reflect on their experiences in their classrooms with their teachers and with themselves, they have become aware of an educational discourse that is based on discussion and cooperative problem solving. Their teachers serve as role models in this respect.

The Specter of the Holocaust

Probably the most unexpected finding that emerged from my first visit to the village, which became more apparent on subsequent research trips, was the underlying and unresolved pain of the Holocaust which impacts on Jewish-Palestinian relations in a myriad of subtle and not-so-subtle ways. What became apparent quite early on was the centrality of the Holocaust in the shaping of the collective Jewish-Israeli consciousness. The conversations I had with many of the villagers indicate how the specter of the Holocaust lies hidden within the Jewish-Palestinian conflict and in some cases creates an impasse that neither Arab nor Jew can overcome. The grade-six boy who spoke in the excerpt above alludes to the "victim/victimizer" problem (Bar-On, 1991). This child understands that Jews in World War II were in the victim role and that, in a different sense, Palestinians are in the victim role in the present conflict. He explains that the Jews are not perpetrators in the same way that the Nazis were. This is a conflict focusing on territory and not on an ideology of racial purity that had as its formal agenda the objective of annihilating all those who did not fit the Aryan mold. There is a difference. The boy's father, whom I also interviewed, denounced those who compare Israeli Jews to the Nazis:

> I know some people are saying that the Jews here are treating the Palestinians like the Nazis did the Jews. But that's not exactly true. I mean there's a lot of craziness going on but partly it's because both people (Jews and Palestinians) got caught in this trap of needing this same land. They are both victims really. I think that many Palestinians don't understand how Jews feel about what happened in World War II. If my parents hadn't come to this land before World War II, they would probably have been killed by the Nazis, and my family and myself would not be here today at all.

The trauma of World War II is now considered as the watershed of this century. In their introduction, Shoshana Felman and Dori Laub (1992) discuss it as *"a history which is essentially not over,* a history whose repercussions are not simply omnipresent (whether consciously or not) in all our cultural activities but whose traumatic consequenses are still evolving (Eastern Europe and the Gulf War are two obvious examples) in today's political, historical, cultural, and artistic scene, the scene in which we read and psychoanalyze, and from within whose tumult and whose fluctuations we strive both to educate and write" (p. xiv). Their book was essentially written for an American audience. How much more relevant is this issue of trauma for the Israeli scene! David Shipler (1986) in his Pulitzer Prize–winning book, *Arab and Jew,* explains, "very few Arabs seem to know much about the Holocaust. Its full horrors rarely seem to penetrate. It goes unmentioned in the Jordanian curriculum that governs teaching in West Bank schools, for example, and it is skimmed over quickly in the Israeli schools for Arabs. Even the best informed and most sophisticated and moderate of the Palestinian Arabs cannot bring themselves to gather the experience of the Holocaust into their understanding of the Jews. That essential feel for the trauma, the tragedy, the aloneness of the Jews in that dark period is simply missing from the Arabs' sense of history and from their grasp of the present. And therefore they cannot understand Israel. They cannot understand the fierce sensations of vulnerability, the lusty devotion to military strength, the stubborn resistance to international criticism, the waves of guilt that soften the core of the hardness. They cannot comprehend the gnawing fear of powerlessness that grinds beneath the arsenal of tanks and planes, the lurking conviction that it could happen again, and that again the world would look the other way" (p. 339).

I grew up in the aftermath of a catastrophe—one like no other in the long history of persecution of the Jewish people—and I certainly identify with Shipler's analysis and also with Saul Friedlander's (1988, p. 43) assertion that "for the community of the victims, and for others as well, the Nazi epoch and the Holocaust remain an unmastered past."[5] This discussion is developed more fully in Chapter 4, in which the participants in a "School for Peace" workshop confront this "historical unspeakability" (Felman & Laub, 1992) and thus attempt to pierce open the denial and reticence around the magnitude of this event on the collective psyche—both for Jews and for Palestinians.

Concluding Remarks

From its very beginning, this reflective inquiry is a shared experience which intends to validate all participants (including myself as researcher) and empowers us to explore the meaning of moral community within the context of the Neve Shalom/Wahat Al-Salam elementary school. I intended to explore the ways in which discussion, moral negotiation, and collaborative decision making formed a basis for creating a spirit of community within the village and in the school and to explore the ethos of the school as embedded within the larger social organization of the village. I wanted to describe the interconnected settings of school and village as a moral community within a larger sociopolitical setting of intergroup conflict. When I returned to the village for a visit in the spring of 1993, I was impressed to see a larger number of children in attendance at the school. The atmosphere was robust and cautiously optimistic in view of the peace initiatives, which were just beginning. In January 1994 I received some correspondence from several participants on their first reactions to the signing of the Israeli–Palestinian peace agreement:

It is difficult to describe my feelings in these days. I waited with my family and my friends and with thousands of Israelis and Palestinians who love peace (with compromise) for this historic moment when the two peoples would recognize the national rights of each other. For many years each side ignored and even denied the right of existence to the other, and now we are living the dream. . . . I expect many troubles and many difficulties on the way to achieving peace. (Arab male participant)

When I first heard about the peace agreement, I couldn't believe it at first and thought it to be only rumor. Then I became hopeful and happy, and suddenly very afraid, as if this peace agreement is a small baby surrounded by so many dangers and people who will try to kill him. (Jewish female participant)

The experience of seeing walls so heavily guarded suddenly collapsing in front of one's eyes is almost surrealistic. The rays of hope which come from plans for peace are dimmed by the extremists who cling to fanatical ideas which will only bring despair. Don't let [this ray of light] be only a dream. (Jewish male participant)

The village and its school as a moral enterprise appear to reflect the need for bringing about an understanding of the "self" in relation to the "other" in terms of Jewish and Palestinian conflict resolution. It is this quest for understanding between the two cultural/national groups and for awareness of the complexity of the Jewish-Arab issue which is at the heart of the peaceful coexistence between the villagers. In allowing my participants to share their multiple voices with me, I struggled to understand the moral dilemmas and complex interrelationships in their lived experiences. Here are excerpts from correspondence from the two codirectors of the school in 1994:

> *For the first time after nine years of working with the children of the two nations, I have the feeling that we are no longer alone in the battle. I can see this even in the eyes of the children in the school. Those who attend from outside the village no longer feel at odds with their friends at home. . . . There are many cities in Israel where Jews and Arabs live together. More than ever I believe [our school] can be a model to be emulated there. . . . By playing together and exchanging knowledge . . . they can come to understand each other's traditions and culture. These children will grow into ambassadors and promoters of peace.* (Jewish female codirector)

> *The children who have been here longer better understand the meaning of the agreement and realize it is only a beginning and that many obstacles lie ahead. . . . We have a policy of linguistic equality in the management and teaching staff of the school and of numerical equality among the students. Outside the village it is very rare to find an Arab managing Jewish workers. In the school we always try to draw the connection between what happens here and what happens outside.* (Arab male codirector)

In a short report written in August 1994, the directors discussed some of the problems they are facing in terms of their educational objectives for Jewish-Arab coexistence. Briefly they identified three major points: 1) the need to address the issue of equality in the bilingual program, 2) the interest of the school to families outside the village and parental involvement, and 3) the need for more funding from public and private sources. First, in their attempt to give the two languages (Hebrew and Arabic) equal weight in the school curriculum, they constantly struggle against the asymmetry of the two languages in Israeli society.

> *The common language between Jewish and Arab teachers is Hebrew, and the dominance of Hebrew in [the wider society] creates a situation in which the Arab children learn Hebrew far more quickly and easily than the Jewish children learn Arabic. The Jewish children acquire a working level of Arabic, but on the playground the Jews and Arabs will almost always speak to each other in Hebrew. In the coming year we will address this problem by introducing more of a "corrective balance." The children*

will be expected to work with each other in more formalized language learning sessions (for example; language labs, computer language programs, and so on).

Chapter 3 discusses the issue of asymmetry between Hebrew and Arabic in more detail.

A second problem the codirectors identified was the fact that outside of Neve Shalom/Wahat Al-Salam the interest in the school remains higher for Arab families than for Jewish ones, saying, "The school will attract Jewish families with a strong ideological incentive, but ideology is not always enough. State-supported public schools require no tuition fees and present our school with serious competition." In some cases the small size of the school and its distance from certain villages become a major obstacle, especially for the older children who feel that their circle of friends becomes too limited. It turned out that the children of a certain village made a group decision to continue on to a larger and more established junior high school five minutes away from their homes. What the directors suggested, in order to deal with these situations, is to encourage the parents from the other villages to become more involved in the school's educational content by setting up social events for the families of the various villages. They did have a very successful picnic that spring and began planning more informal programs for the following academic year. These events have become a more prominent part of the school year.

Third, due to the fact that this is a private school very much in uncharted waters in terms of its bilingual/binational philosophy, it was looked on with some uncertainty by the Ministry of Education. Nevertheless, the Ministry took a very important step in 1994 by deciding that it would fund 50 percent of the cost of each child up to the fifth grade, not including transportation. Although this was a sign of real progress, it was still regarded as far from adequate. Therefore, this school survives in part on the basis of private fundraising, which is a collaborative effort of individuals from some European countries and North America who believe in this model of Jewish-Arab coexistence. Another interesting recent development was that the directors of the school had been invited by the Ministry of Education to attend monthly meetings of all directors of schools in the Jerusalem regional area. This was a very significant step forward in terms of providing the Neve Shalom/Wahat Al-Salam school a greater sense of legitimacy within mainstream Israeli society.

A terrible tragedy befell the village on February 4, 1997. One of the sons of the village, Tom Kitain, was killed in a helicopter crash, along with seventy-two other young Israeli soldiers, during military service in South Lebanon. Reporters from the media came to the village to cover the funeral. They wondered how the Palestinians would react to the moral dilemma of whether they should attend an official Israeli Armed Forces funeral. Palestinians are on principle against the presence of the Israeli army in South Lebanon and the Occupied Territories in the West Bank, and it has been considered anathema for a Palestinian to be involved with any event sponsored by the Israeli Armed Forces. But what the reporters found were Jews and Palestinians standing side by side at the village cemetery in their grief for the accidental death of one of their children while the military rabbi recited the Kaddish.[6] Friendship and neighborliness transcended the Jewish-Palestinian conflict. When Tom's parents wished to establish an official memorial for their son within the village, however, they were met with opposition by some villagers who perceived that this act would be a legitimization of the Israeli army's treatment of the Palestinians. The incident created a very painful rift among the villagers, which has not yet been resolved. It remains as an open wound and only reinforces the reality that what happens in the village is very much informed by what takes place outside of it in the wider society. Such moral complexities are overwhelming, especially with setbacks to the peace process, and yet these individuals continue to have the courage to keep on living in peaceful coexistence in their village.

During my 1997 sojourn, which took place four months after this tragedy, I realized with deep sadness that in spite of this community's enormous efforts toward peace, it is still not able to escape the grim reality of the Jewish-Palestinian dilemma, which engulfs the whole of Israel. Furthermore, with ongoing obstacles to the peace process, I was very aware of the constant social and political tensions that haunt the villagers, and the moral negotiation that continues at all levels of discourse in the community. I was struck by how the villagers were constantly negotiating the space between the tensions of competing national aspirations and their personal attempts at coexistence and goodwill in spite of both the emotional crisis in the wake of Tom's tragedy and the faltering negotiations in the wider political arena.

In the educational realm, however, things began to take a turn for the better. In 1998 the Ministry classified this school officially as "experimental" and began to offer more funding as a result. Hundreds of schools in Israel had applied for this status; this school was one of only two elementary schools to be accepted. In the words of the codirector: "It means that the Ministry is prepared to explore our methods to see what can be learned from them and what can be applied elsewhere in the country. This has been our dream from the outset" (village newsletter, January 1998).

In 1999, with a new prime minister who had declared his commitment to the peace process, I began to receive more hopeful e-mail messages from my participants. The director wrote, "The 1999–2000 school year got off to a bright start with some 250 students enrolled in the kindergarten and elementary school—a 20 percent increase over the previous year. These include forty-eight new students who had to be selected out of eighty applicants. In order to accommodate the increased enrollment, we had to complete a new classroom. The new bright and airy classroom was constructed in such a way that it blends nicely into a corner of the existing school building. The school also absorbed six new teachers" (September 4, 1999).

During my sojourn in November and December 1999, I had a chance to see the new construction and to meet the new teachers. What struck me was how established the school looked. It was no longer in its infancy. Another highly significant event happened during this visit. The decision was taken by the Abbot of the Latrun Monastery, Abbé Père Paul Sauma, to offer to the villagers as an outright gift the land that had originally been leased to them. This was a monumental development, which came about as a result of very skilled and delicate negotiations that the then mayor of the village, Rayek Rizek, conducted with the Abbot. I had the opportunity to interview Father Paul at the end of my visit, which I describe in chapter 5.

I have tried in this chapter to present some examples of a collective moral dialogue—both heartening and excruciating—which has been weaving its way into the lives of each individual and into the very fabric of this community. It may very well be the case that this school and this village have an important role to play in the moral education of culturally diverse communities in conflict, not only in other parts of Israel, but also in the international arena, especially with the deep setbacks to the peace process and heightened violence in the Occupied Territories in October 2000. The ongoing quest for peace and equality, evidenced through their personal, social, and educational activities, provides the villagers with countless opportunities to interpret and contemplate their cultural and historical destinies. Their stories are simple and complex, ordinary and extraordinary, mundane and heroic, foreign and familiar, full of tension and pain but also full of hope. I am honored to have been among them. When I asked some of the children in the school what they would like me to tell others about their way of life, they responded with these words:

> It is very easy to call people names and to hate them. But when you begin to live with them and go to school with them and play with them, then you realize that, even though they may have different customs and beliefs, they are really very similar in many ways. You have to find a bridge and meet them halfway.

Endnotes

1. The term "moral edifice" is attributed to Peter Applebaum, in a different context.
2. Some of this chapter's material appeared in *The Journal of Moral Education*, Vol. 24, No. 2, 1995, under the title "Oasis of Peace: A Community of Moral Education in Israel" (pp. 113–41).
3. This excerpt comes from a speech Edward Said gave as recipient of an honorary degree at the University of Toronto Spring Convocation, 2000.
4. The Intifada is an uprising by the Palestinians against the Israelis in the Occupied Territories. It began in 1988.
5. As Friedlander (1988) suggests in his article, "Trauma, Transference, and 'Working Through,'" "today, almost fifty years after the events, no mythical framework seems to be taking hold of the Jewish imagination . . . as when in the wake of the expulsion from Spain [in 1492] it embraced the mythical symbolism of the Kabbalah. Nor does the best of literature and art dealing with the Shoah (Hebrew for Holocaust) offer any redemptive stance. In fact, the opposite appears to be true" (p. 43).
6. Kaddish is the Jewish prayer of mourning for the dead.

The Pedagogy of Peace:
Language Awareness in the Neve Shalom/Wahat Al-Salam Elementary School

If you wish to promote peace, begin with the children.

—Mahatma Mohandes Gandhi

Emancipatory Discourse: "Border Crossing" and Peacemaking

One of the greatest challenges in Israeli society is to overcome the fear and enmity that have evolved through the years of war between Jews and Arabs.
One of the Jewish parents very eloquently expressed her hope, shared by all
those connected with the school: "We want our children to learn in friendship
and joy, not in conflict and sorrow." In order to make friends with "the
other," as the residents of this village are doing, we must confront the "other"
in the deepest part of our souls, in the psychological no-man's-land where the
"foreigner" lurks—"he is the hidden face of our identity, the space that
wrecks our abode, the time in which understanding and affinity founder"
(Kristeva, 1991, p. 1).

In this chapter, I examine how the participants acknowledge the "foreigner" whose language, culture, values, and traditions are different and who
competes for the same geopolitical space. The possibility of collaboration instead of competition and hostility is being opened; the hegemonic discourses
and institutions are being challenged, and transformative intergroup and interpersonal dialogues are being created. What immediately caught my attention
when I began my visits to the school was that what these individuals were in
fact doing was imagining a new way of life, inventing a new educational story
by creating a curriculum with narratives (both Jewish and Palestinian) of home
and displacement, of borders and crossings. Above all, theirs is a quest for authenticity in search of a peaceful future for their children. The words of bell

hooks (1991, p. 9) speak to this situation: "To imagine is to begin the process that transforms reality." The Neve Shalom/Wahat Al-Salam elementary school thus becomes a site of cultural encounters and a network of negotiations and reconciliations. Behind the idea of the "binational space" of the school lies the anguish of oppression and dispersion, the fear of terrorism and incarceration, the memory of genocide and the agony of annihilation—all caught in the dream of devising an open discourse that will incorporate the linguistic, social, and psychological needs of both peoples.

This complex discourse of cautious hope with its promise of a better world was both overwhelming and fascinating. It illuminated my research journey and my writing, as well as the sharing of my own narrative with those of my participants in this extraordinary village. Max Van Manen (1990) explains that "we gather other people's experiences because they allow us to become more experienced ourselves." Michael Connelly and Jean Clandinin (1990, 1995, 1999) support this view and claim that narrative refers to the process of making meaning of experience by telling stories of personal and social relevance. Indeed, by presenting sketches of the language experiences of some of the students, teachers, and parents connected with the school, I discuss how language awareness operates in the school curriculum to create an educational system that is based on the principle of egalitarian coexistence between two nations; that is, the Jews and the Palestinians.[1] In this way we will explore the concept of language awareness in relation to the educational goals and activities of this binational/bicultural/bilingual school within the larger context of Israeli society.

Theoretical Considerations

Language awareness is defined as "a person's sensitivity to, and conscious awareness of, the nature of language and its role in human life" (Donmall, 1985, p. 7). Language awareness can be divided into five interrelated categories: (1) affective (for example, attitude formation), (2) social (improvement of intergroup relations), (3) power (choice in language acquisition and use), (4) cognitive (intellectual improvement), and (5) performance (enhanced proficiency). In this chapter, I concentrate, for the most part, on the affective and social domains of language awareness as they are embedded within the formal and informal structures of the school and more generally within the broader social and cultural system of the village. We will examine how language awareness plays a major role in this school in its overriding commitment to fostering an emancipatory discourse of education based on conflict resolution and peacemaking.

This alternative discourse underscores the need for a radical reconceptualization of Jewish-Arab relations in education and in Israeli society in general, and as such contests the dominant-subordinate power structures in the wider society. Eric Hawkins (1984, p. 6) claims that by developing language awareness in the classroom, ". . . we are seeking to arm our pupils against fear of the unknown which breeds prejudice and antagonism." I also agree with Norman Fairclough (1993), who claims that both macro and micro power factors operate in a given discursive context, and Chris Jenks (1991), who claims that by contesting hegemonic practices and raising critical language awareness in classrooms, we are liberating ourselves as teachers and our students from a dangerous narrowness of vision. David Corson (1999, p. 160) emphasizes this notion: "When teachers encourage students to reflect critically on the language practices used in the school itself; it is a clear statement that this is the way teachers would like the world of discourse to be outside the school. By looking at real acts of emancipatory discourse in the school's setting, rather than at vicarious examples, students become empowered by the activities." Tony Adams and Witold Tulasiewicz (1993, 1994) agree that language awareness is crucial in a multicultural society as a means for effective communication enabling enhanced instrumental use of language, as an emancipatory vehicle for asserting one's identity without clashing with that of others, and as a tool for understanding others by developing linguistic sensitivity.

These notions are congruent with the social philosophy put forward by the critical theorist Roy Bhaskar (1986, 1989) in his reflections on language, power, and human emancipation. Briefly, his argument is that emancipation occurs when we make the move from unwanted to wanted sources of determination by changing the relations between human action and structural context. He proposes a "much more subtle and complex view of society in which human agents are neither passive products of social structures nor entirely their creators but are placed in an iterative and naturally reflexive feedback relationship to them. Society exists independently of our conceptions of it . . . yet it is dependent on our actions, human activity, for its reproduction. It is both real and transcendent. . . ." He fully accepts the hermeneutical and postmodernist position that the production of knowledge about society is a part of the entire process of social production, that it is a part of its own subject matter and may transform the subject matter (Davies, 1999, p. 18–19). In terms of schooling, Bhaskar's philosophy can be translated into language policies that give the culturally disadvantaged the right to determine and shape their own curriculum based on equality and power sharing. His theoretical notions offer us the makings of pedagogy suffused with aesthetic sensibility and egalitarian conscience.

One example of a school that fosters such an ideology is a multilingual/multicultural primary school in Auckland, New Zealand, which encourages pluralism and empowerment for aboriginal children through a language policy across the curriculum. (For a more detailed discussion, see Cazden, 1989; May, 1994.) Such attempts at genuine bilingual/bicultural education are relatively few and far between. Neve Shalom/Wahat Al-Salam is also a maverick school in its dedication to language and cultural inclusiveness, but it operates on a much more difficult frontier—that of open conflict between its two linguistic/national groups. The school attempts to weave into its tapestry of academic subjects the threads of both Jewish and Arab/Palestinian perspectives in Israel in order to transcend the profound problems of marginality, belonging, and conflict. This school and this village invite us to traverse a mirror of turmoil between both peoples and to touch the soul of their struggle. The school's philosophy states unequivocally that maintaining personal, social, national, and linguistic identity is of utmost importance. Its mission is to create national identities informed by moral vision and social ethics in order to provide an understanding of what it means to become active and critical citizens in a diverse, pluralistic Israeli society against the backdrop of conflict.

Language educators and researchers agree that it is essential to develop appropriate pedagogies that respond to the diversity of the social contexts in which the learners are situated. (See, for example, Cummins, 1994, 1999; Corson, 1993, 1995; Delpit, 1992; Krashen & Biber, 1988; Garcia, 1994; Goodman, et al., 1987; Spolsky, 1989; Trueba, 1989; Wong-Fillmore, 1991.) We must explore the need for rethinking and reshaping an understanding of language awareness as a social phenomenon fundamentally linked to learners' sense of identity and self-worth within their communities as well as to notions of national belonging. For Arab students in Israel (and, in fact, for all students who perceive themselves to be in a subordinate position in their societies), it is important that their values and culture be represented within the mainstream curriculum, and especially within the texts that they read and write. (See, for example, Abu-Rabia & Feuerverger, 1996; Mari, 1985; Shohamy, 1993; Spolsky and Shohamy, 2000.) The Neve Shalom/Wahat Al-Salam school distinguishes itself in the way in which the dominant versus subordinate status of Arab students is contested within the structures and discourses of the school. The critical awareness of the asymmetry between Hebrew, the dominant language, and Arabic, the principal minority and second official language in Israel, underscores all classroom activities. The attempt to redress this imbalance focuses on interior psychological transformations within the students and teachers as a way of changing their worldview in the school and in the village, and ultimately in mainstream society.

Complexities of the Hebrew-Arabic Asymmetry

The words of the school co-director describe the importance of language equality:

> Language is the essential tool for communication and learning. At this school, and from the preschool onward, the children who live in this village hear both languages, Hebrew and Arabic, and they begin to speak both in kindergarten. When they arrive in the first grade, their ears are already attuned to both languages. They learn to read and write both languages, side by side, literally and figuratively.

I was witness to a collaborative educational conversation that offered the possibility of relationships among student and teacher, student and student, and teacher and teacher that honored their differential social, historical, cultural, and religious narratives as well as the complexities of understanding and interpreting the languages that they inhabit and the limits that those languages place on them. According to Martin Heidegger, "it is in language that we dwell, construct, and extend our realities" (as cited in Chambers, 1994, p. 133) but to Jacques Lacan the *reél* "constitutes that space left unmarked by language or signs." It is in these paradoxical notions that we may be able to address the issue of borders, exile, homeland, and the intersection among them. My work as ethnographer is ultimately to interpret what I observed in the school and what I heard in the conversations with my participants in their search for meaning within the complex layers of the sociopolitical discourse in Israel. What emerged clearly is that, fundamentally, the discourse is not merely about a majority group versus a minority group. Through the dialectic of interviewer and interviewee, I began to understand that it is a much more complicated issue than the usual hegemonic one, because what we have here is a minority within a regional minority.

For the Arab Israeli, Hebrew is perceived to be the language of the oppressor; nevertheless, Hebrew is demographically only a minor language in the Middle East, without much international importance. Therefore, the lines of power and language are negotiated very differently within the physical reality of Israel as compared to outside of Israel in the Middle East and elsewhere. Certainly, within Israel this sociolinguistic phenomenon disrupts and thwarts Palestinian identity formation and complicates the issue of production and consumption of Arab/Palestinian culture in a broader sense. If the Palestinian Israeli is able to reach across both linguistic and national borders through literary articulation in Hebrew as well as Arabic, however, he or she is neither at home nor in exile, but in a curious space of "in between," which can paradoxically become a place of power. This border zone and the hybrid text that it creates gives voice to the border dweller (Potok, in Barkan & Shelton, 1998). The Palestinian Israeli who becomes literate and literary in Hebrew is more advanced than the Jewish Israeli who (as a general rule) has not mastered Arabic to any great extent and thereby loses a certain sense of superiority. Such situations are rarely of concern in mainstream Israeli society, but for those on the "borders," such as the villagers at Neve Shalom/Wahat Al-Salam, it becomes a salient issue. Most of the Jewish villagers are not nearly as fluent or literate in Arabic as their Palestinian counterparts are in Hebrew. Suddenly the dominating majority and the dominated minority have changed positions. On my most recent sojourn to the village, for example, I witnessed the discomfort at a teachers' staff gathering when the suggestion was made that some of the meetings should be conducted in Arabic rather than Hebrew. The Jewish Israeli teachers suddenly felt threatened because only a few of them would have been able to handle this new sociolinguistic reality. They were well aware of the lack of equality in the situation but they countered that, given the realities of their ages and very busy lives, it would be practically impossible for them to catch up and become as fluent in Arabic as the Palestinian teachers were in Hebrew. They did acknowledge that they were, unfortunately, products of a school system that did not promote good learning of Arabic—or other minority languages for that matter.

One Palestinian teacher explained it to me as follows:

The Jewish Hebrew speakers were really rather stunned by this sudden loss of status in the meeting. It must have been a bit of a shock for them, even though their hearts are in the right place and they want bilingualism for their children. But I guess they feel it's too hard for them to really learn Arabic in earnest at this time in their lives. I can't blame them. It would be hard for anyone to learn another language, if you don't have to. That's what it's all about: Arabic being the minority language and therefore not necessary for getting ahead in the mainstream society. That is one symbol of our (Palestinian) sense of inferiority. At least what is good about this village is that they want to change it in the next generation with their children. But we [the Palestinian teachers] are saying: Let's change it now in our meetings; at least a bit. It is difficult but it is again a symbolic gesture. If we want to be role models, let's start with ourselves, no?

Schools need to be viewed in their historical, societal, and relational contexts. The construction of teaching and learning is, in fact, a relational act and therefore a discourse of empowerment needs to be created out of the historical, social, linguistic, and cultural realities that are the bedrock of the forms of knowledge and meaning that teachers and students bring to school. Reciprocity is important. Reclaiming voice is important. Retelling and comparing stories are important. These activities, however, are not enough in themselves, and therefore need to be positioned within a larger social and intellectual perspective. In this regard, the school at Neve Shalom/Wahat Al-Salam can be located within the Freirian framework of a moral and political project that links the production of meaning to the possibility for human agency, democratic community, language reform, and transformative social action (see Paulo Freire, 1970). In this school the use of both languages has become emblematic of egalitarianism and mutual understanding both in formal and informal school activities. This reflects Roger Simon's (1992) assertion of ". . . a view of human agency reconstructed through forms of narrative that operate as part of a pedagogy of empowerment . . . centered within a social project aimed at the enhancement of human possibility." This pedagogical approach reinforces Freire's (1970) claim that all critical educators are also learners, but where is the Neve Shalom/Wahat Al-Salam school situated within the larger educational system of Israel? The following section addresses this question.

The Israeli Educational School System: A Brief Overview

In order to familiarize the reader with the complexities of the Israeli school system, I include here a brief sociohistoric overview. The modern Israeli educational system began about fifty years before statehood and shares many similarities with other national school systems in developed countries. Its uniqueness, however, derives from the specific project of Jewish revival over the past 150 years and its geopolitical situation in the Middle East, from the genocide of the Holocaust which intensified the need for Jewish statehood, and from the successive waves of immigration that have taken place from that time to today. It is outside the scope of this book to discuss in detail the daunting challenges facing the Israeli educational system in absorbing a population as multicultural, multilingual, socioeconomically diverse, and conflictual as exists in this tiny country. As a result of this national, religious, and linguistic pluralism, the educational system is divided into two main separate systems: Jewish and Arab (Mari, 1978; Iram & Schmida, 1998). In addition, even within the Jewish population there are deep divisions between religious and secular Jews as well as between Ashkenazim (Jews from Eastern and Central Europe) and Sephardim (Jews from the Mediterranean and Arab/Moslem countries) (Ben-Rafael & Sharot, 1991).

Within the mainstream (Jewish) population, the Israeli educational policy from the beginning has encouraged a "melting pot" approach. The goal is for all citizens to become "Israelis" as soon as possible, and acknowledge the primacy of Hebrew regardless of their home culture and language (Nakoma, 1983; Shohamy, 1993). Indeed, until very recently, the Israeli curriculum did not focus on the maintenance of the cultural heritage and language of immigrants arriving from all parts of the Diaspora. This was in keeping with the official national (Zionist) policy of the "ingathering of the exiles" and the consolidation of the Jewish people in Israel as embodied in the constitutional Law of Return of 1950 (Eisenstadt, 1967; Elazar, 1985), according to which every Jewish immigrant is entitled to Israeli citizenship. In fact, the need and the will to absorb Jews from the various exiles of their dispersion—particularly as a result of the plight of the survivors of the Holocaust after World War II—was the *raison d'être* for the establishment of the state of Israel in 1948 (Iram & Schmida, 1998).

One of the overarching goals of the Israeli educational system in the early years of statehood was to eradicate the negative connotations of Diaspora Jewry—symbolic of the Nazi destruction of European Jews during World War II (Urofsky, 1976; Gordon, 1995). Hand in hand with this objective was the responsibility of integrating immigrant children into the social fabric and cultural norms of the new society—first and foremost through teaching the Hebrew language, which was and remains a metaphor for Jewish nationalism and cultural integration. The Jewish settlers of modern Palestine under the British Mandate began the process of immigration in the late nineteenth century and came mainly from European countries with Western cultures. The survivors of the Holocaust also came from Europe. The wave of immigration in the early 1950s of Jews from Arab/Moslem countries in the Middle East and North Africa (Iran, Iraq, Yemen, Morocco, Tunisia, and Algeria), however, created new social challenges. Many of these Sephardim or Oriental Jews had large families and were not formally educated; they were thus ill equipped to face the modern, urban, and industrially oriented society that Israel was aspiring to develop. Consequently, there emerged a socioeconomic gap between these Eastern Jews and their more Western counterparts, the Ashkenazim (Peres, 1976; Smooha, 1978) which became evident in the school system by the fact that the Oriental students lagged behind in terms of occupational and social standing.

In the mid-1960s when this problem of disadvantaged student populations became salient, a policy of social integration was instituted and was defined as the bringing together of all students into a common system, regardless of ethnic origin, socioeconomic level, intellectual talents, and areas of interest, which placed them in heterogeneous schools and integrated classrooms. In spite of awareness of the importance of this policy, its implementation in the school system lagged behind due to a plethora of political, demographic, and financial reasons. (For more details, see Iram & Schmida, 1998.) Basically, the language and cultural heritage of the Oriental groups was not valued in the school system; this created a deep schism in Jewish Israeli society. In the early 1970s the social tension and ethnic protest which had begun in the late 1950s was renewed. There have been various attempts by the Ministry of Education to improve this social, economic, and cultural situation through a special program instituted in the 1980s named the "Education Welfare Program." It was intended to intervene at all levels of education, including family and community as well as a neighborhood renovation project (as discussed in Iram & Schmida, 1998, chapter 9). More recent waves of immigration in the late 1980s and 1990s from Ethiopia and the former Soviet Union have added to the complexity of the social fabric of Israeli society and as a result, a greater awareness of the need for a pluralistic, multicultural policy in the Israeli school system has emerged, with more emphasis on the diversity of cultures and traditions in Israeli schools. This relatively new multicultural policy addresses, at least in theory, the three major dilemmas in Israeli society: the division between Oriental and Western Jewry, the division between religious and nonreligious Jewry, and the division between Israeli Arabs and Jews (Masemann & Iram, 1987). Our focus here is on the third issue.

As discussed earlier, this particular Israeli hegemony is rather unusual and difficult to resolve because of the traumatic psychohistorical burden of genocide that lies behind it. In terms of Jewish collective psychology, one can understand the original "melting pot" policy that was initiated in the early days of statehood. Shoshana Keiny (1999, p. 513) explains this national ideology within the context of the modern notion of human rights: "Israel is both a young country, struggling with her existence, as well as an old traditional culture, carrying wounded memories of torture and genocide, a rather complex case to deal with in respect to the modern concept of human rights first declared by the UN at the end of World War II." Within the educational system, it is noteworthy that Israel's national ideology has varied over time, moving from universalist, civil values to somewhat more particularist, ethnic (Jewish) values (Resnik, 1999). Indeed, the division between the Jewish religious and nonreligious populations is not only unresolved but rather is intensifying as the religious groups gain increased political power.

The Israeli Arabs are left out of the picture altogether. Where do they fit in the overall construct of Israeli national identity and ideology? In spite of such complex social-psychological conundra, the state must focus more fully on comprehensive reforms given the increased violence in the West Bank and vicissitudes of the Israeli-Arab peace process. As Yaacov Iram and Miriyam Schmida point out (1998, p. 93–94), "an impressive change in learning standards at Arab high schools occurred in the middle of the 1970s . . . nevertheless a wide discrepancy still existed between the achievement levels of Arab and Jewish students, based on ethnic and religious factors. . . . Although Arab schools are maintained in reasonable physical conditions, the gap between them and Jewish schools has grown larger in other areas. Many services that naturally exist in Jewish schools cannot be found in Arab schools." They write that "psychological counseling, and lessons in music, art, or sports are lacking in the majority of Arab schools" and that "one of the basic problems of Arab education from the beginning was the lack of teachers with adequate training. In the last twenty years there has been a considerable improvement in the educational level of Arab teachers. . . . Another aspect of criticism is related to the quality of training given to Arab students in teachers' seminaries" (p. 95). Fortunately, in recent years more opportunities are beginning to open up for Arab teachers as a result of collaborative efforts with well-established teacher training institutes around the country.

Finally, the asymmetry of the Jewish and Arab school curricula is still prevalent. Iram and Schmida (1998, p. 99) claim that "the critique of the Arab curricula began in the 1950s. It was asked why students in Arab schools were learning the Bible and not the Koran, and why the teaching of Arabic, Arab literature, and history did not receive proper attention. A comparison between history teaching objectives in Jewish and Arab high schools reveals that while Jewish schools stress national contents, the Arab curriculum overlooks them. Values of Arab-Jewish coexistence, together with Jewish majority status, are planted in the Arab student by repeatedly stressing the role that Arabs and Jews shared during history and the common fate of both peoples. However, values of coexistence are not passed down to Jewish students. Moreover, an Arab student is expected to know the importance of the State of Israel to the Jewish people, not to both Jews and Arabs" (p. 94). There have been some salient changes in the curriculum in the early 1970s, mainly the mention of the Arab nation as a central objective, but it remained ambiguous and did not relate to the Palestinian people. In the past few years, far more profound reforms began to take shape in light of the peace process, but there is still a long way to go in order to undo the asymmetry that exists.

The Language of Peace: A Reflective Look at the Teachers and Learners in the Village School

What is hopeful about the Neve Shalom/Wahat Al-Salam model is the radical psychological shift in the village in its attempt to reconstruct ideology for the next generation. There is an existential recognition of the need for a reconceptualization of society—which is open to restructuring and therefore unsettling, but creates the basis for an alternative space. For example, in the summer of 1999 one of the villagers offered an intensive Arabic course for the Hebrew-speaking teachers; it was attended by almost all of them. These are not easy moments for the participants, even those with the best of intentions. I tried to locate myself in this compelling human landscape in order to be able to pay respect to the efforts of these individuals pushing against all odds. I entered a space of personal, social, and moral reflection, of anxious and hopeful narratives, of social and political polemic, and of ambiguity. There was a story to tell about the choices being created by the teachers and I wanted to be worthy of the task of teller. Sara Lawrence-Lightfoot (1997, p. 9) suggests that the researcher as portraitist can search for what is good and healthy; she believes that there are "myriad ways in which goodness can be expressed" and the researcher must try "to identify and document the actors' perspectives." I was interested in observing what was indeed going on in the classrooms of the village school that were expressions of "goodness" within a context of language awareness and peacemaking. Were the children in fact crossing linguistic, literary, historical, and national borders, and in what ways? As ethnographer (and portraitist, in Lawrence-Lightfoot's terms), I stood "on the edge of the scene—a boundary sitter—scanning the action, systematically gathering the details of behavior, expression, and talk, remaining open and receptive to all stimuli" (1997, p. 87).

Effective schools should be sites of linguistic, political, and cultural negotiation which encourage teachers to situate and scrutinize the borders of their own ideological discourses. "Borders elicit a recognition of those epistemological, political, cultural, and social margins that define 'the places that are safe and unsafe, [that] distinguish *us* from *them*'"(Anzaldua, 1987, p. 3, as cited in Giroux, 1991). "Teachers need to be reflective practitioners who first examine themselves—their knowledge base, their attitudes, beliefs, values, and practices—and then develop approaches to teaching and learning which challenge and empower" (Jackson, p. 41, in Larkin & Sleeter, 1995). Teachers also need to become cognizant of what I call the "unconscious myths" that have shaped the mental and physical landscape of their lives and which now motivate them in the planning of curriculum and in their choice of interpersonal classroom strategies. The Neve Shalom/Wahat Al-Salam school experience certainly affirms Henry Giroux's claim (1991, p. 516) that teachers become "border crossers" by being able to listen critically to the voices of their students. How are these shared narratives being played out in the village school? One of the main questions I asked was, "How do teachers and students in this school negotiate knowledge of Arab and Jewish values through their language interaction; for example, in history, geography, current events, and literature classes?"

In order to explore the discourses of peace and conflict resolution within curriculum development, pedagogical strategies, and interpersonal communication at Neve Shalom/Wahat Al-Salam, we now turn to excerpts of in-depth interviews I conducted with students and teachers both formally and informally as well as reflections of my classroom observations in the school. These data were tape-recorded and later transcribed. The methodological tools of field-note gathering and journaling were always central to this inquiry and were used on a daily basis.

I begin with a Palestinian teacher in the school, who explained how language awareness has offered a new pedagogical and social paradigm for the Jewish and Arab children:

> In this school Arabic and Hebrew both hold prominent positions and the children are fully aware of that in all classroom activities. Because each class has an Arab and a Jewish teacher, the children are exposed to two points of view. For example, I teach actualia (current events) with a Jewish teacher and we are able to discuss difficult, controversial issues immediately with our pupils. Language is such a key point here. Let's face it, learning the history of Israel in Hebrew is totally different from learning it in Arabic! Learning its history in both languages is the beginning of a whole new future. This is radical stuff! The Israeli War of Independence has a totally different connotation in Arabic and that awareness that we teachers can offer them opens new doors for these young people.

He is in effect agreeing with many researchers who claim that language is the essential means by which teachers shape their experiences and explain the world to themselves and also to their students. This participant went on to explain how he struggled to become not only fluent in Hebrew but also to excel in Hebrew literature at the Hebrew University in Jerusalem. This was quite unusual for an Arab in the early 1970s and still is even today. I asked him about his motivation to pursue this course of study. He replied:

> To become a student in Hebrew literature meant I could conquer my insecurities about being an Arab minority person in Israel. It gave me a sense of confidence that changed my life and eventually brought me to this place in order that I can help other Arab students to overcome their inferiority feelings. It's all about language, identity, and power. Using both languages is a symbol of coexistence and the possibility of friendship, and gives me a sense of equality with Jewish Israelis.

This same teacher discussed at length his frustration about living in the "space between borders," where he had no sense of belonging either to his Israeli self or to his Palestinian self. He, like Palestinian Israeli author Anton Shammas, who writes in Hebrew instead of Arabic, is "in the space of exile at home . . . exile from a homeland that no longer exists except in nostalgia and ideological space" (Shammas, 1991). "By writing in Hebrew, the language of his conquerors," Rena Potok (1998, p. 298) observes, "the Arab Shammas can realize Derrida's ideal of speaking the other's language without renouncing one's own." These words embody those of Maxine Greene (1973): "For a man who no longer has a homeland, writing becomes a place to live." Smadar Lavie (1992) suggests that "these are individuals who must continually remap their border zones so that they can maintain their exilic home in the claimed homeland of the Jews" (quoted in Potok, 1998, p. 305).

The theme of cultural dislocation and fractured identity underlies the ambivalence that so many Palestinian Israelis experience in their everyday lives and is evident in the asymmetry of status between Hebrew and Arabic in Israel. Therefore, the original attempt at Neve Shalom/Wahat Al-Salam to teach both Hebrew and Arabic in the school curriculum in the early 1980s was more than just an interesting pedagogical idea; it was and still is in essence a powerfully subversive act. This community decision mirrors the tremendous force and agency of those Palestinian Israeli authors who write about their own lived experience in new literary forms and specifically in Hebrew, thus creating alternative norms and value systems. The pedagogy in the school at Neve Shalom/Wahat Al-Salam can thus be regarded as a political act of resistance as well as an act of self-empowerment and carries within it the kind of critical language awareness that liberates.

Palestinian author Shammas, on a visit to the village in 1992, used these eloquent words to describe its pedagogy and educational commitment to peace in the village newsletter: "It is always risky to be lured by metaphors, especially in the Middle East, but those who live in this 'Oasis of Peace' have managed to achieve the impossible: by refusing to be lured, they have concretized a metaphor. We, who are still wandering in the desert, envy them." He speaks of his feelings in terms of language awareness: "At the age of eighteen I chose what I had no choice but to choose: namely, to regard Hebrew as my stepmother tongue. Sometimes I feel that this was an act of cultural trespass, and that the day may come when I shall have to account for it" (quoted in Shipler, 1986, p. 455).

Another Palestinian teacher in the school discussed the surprise that his father showed when he first came to visit his son in this village and met some of the children in the school:

> My father grew up in a little Arab village in the north of the country and was at first uncertain about why I should teach in a school where Jewish and Arab kids were together. He just wasn't sure how this would work. Then, on the first afternoon that he was here a little nine-year-old girl came up to him and spoke to him in Arabic. They had a lovely conversation and afterwards I told him this young student of mine was Jewish. He had assumed she was an Arab because her Arabic was so fluent. When he heard she was Jewish, his eyes filled with tears and he said he thought he would never see this. He was amazed at how all the children were getting along, jumping back and forth into Hebrew and Arabic. They were friends, and that was a revelation to him. That is the beauty of this place.

As participant-observer in this school, I came to recognize that knowing the existence of the "foreigner," as Julia Kristeva puts it, is a central aspect of language awareness. I believe this can be defined as a sensitivity and a conscious understanding of the myriad languages and cultures in our world and of their roles for humanity. I began to understand more fully the dialectical relationship between language and thought in practical educational settings (see, for example, Bakhtin, 1981; Dewey, 1938; Vygotsky, 1962). As discussed earlier, I have been involved in multilingual education both personally and professionally as far back as I remember, and I believe that the bilingual (and multilingual) classroom must be a space where dialogue is seen as a necessary way to relate authentically to one another through collaboration, reflection, and expression (Kaiser & Short, 1998).

A Jewish teacher in the school confided in me:

> I never had the opportunity as a child to learn Arabic the way the Jewish children do here. And only now do I truly realize how it changes everything to simply be able to speak to one another in both languages. It really changes things; it's very symbolic. And the children are unconsciously very aware of this, I think. I will give you a concrete example. A new child came into my class from [a nearby Jewish village] and she did not know Arabic and stayed away from the Arab children. As time went on, she of course began to interact with the Arab children and she began to learn Arabic. It was wonderful to see how her attitude changed in such a positive way. The very same is true for the Arab children who come to this school and begin to learn Hebrew and become friends with the Jewish kids.

A grade-six boy from a Jewish village stated why he enjoyed learning both languages at the school:

> I feel very different now that I can speak and read and write Arabic. I didn't have much to do with Arab kids before coming to this school and I was afraid of them because of all the terrorist things. But now I'm making friends with them and I can read stories about their lives and their heroes and their culture and it makes me understand them more and feel closer to them.

This kind of thoughtful teaching and learning is a transformative process which appreciates the complexities of bilingual, bicultural, and binational education within a landscape of conflict and war (see Figure 3–1). It embodies Freire's (1970, p. 75) revolutionary perspective of social liberation in his assertion: "There is no true word that is not at the same time a praxis (action-reflection). Thus to speak of a true word is to transform the world." Indeed, I had the opportunity to observe the dynamics of meaning making through language and cultural awareness, which was grounded in reflective practice. This is what shapes the pedagogical landscape of Neve Shalom/Wahat Al-Salam. Knowing that one must learn to coexist with "the other" is already a form of action, and naming the challenge is a way of overcoming it. The signature discourses of conflict resolution in each classroom underscore the school's fundamental commitment to peacemaking.

Figure 3–1   Young students on their way into school, passing through the rainbow of peace arch. (Courtesy of NS/WAS.)

In Chapter 1, I mentioned that in the weeks that I spent in the school during my first sojourn, one bulletin board was dedicated to a project about the city of Jerusalem from the different religious and cultural perspectives. Linguistically, the symbols of peace were evident in the textual material that accompanied the various drawings. The Al-Aqsa Mosque was described in Arabic; the Western Wall had a text in Hebrew explaining its significance; and the Church of the Holy Sepulchre was discussed in Arabic. In the center of the wall display was a large story narrating the long and tumultuous history of Jerusalem in both languages. It seemed to me, as an observer, that the use of both languages in the story was a salient symbol of peace and it clearly explained that each child is taught to understand his or her culture and also learn about the culture of the others. The drawings, with their individual language texts, indicate that the goal is coexistence, respect, and friendship, but not assimilation. Religion is taught separately, but there are also joint discussions. What is essential, I was told, is that no one is appropriating anyone else's history or religion or culture. When possible, however, shared narrative accounts are created.

During my many classroom visits, I watched a constant effort at moral negotiation and dialogue for curriculum development within the differential sociohistoric and geopolitical narratives of that particular moment in history. Meron Benvenisti (1995) quoted the famous Israeli author A. B. Yehoshua to indicate the difficulties therein: "History is potent, it has direction, and it has meaning" (p. 154). The tension arising from these issues was authentically and sensitively dealt with in classrooms, in the staff room, and on the playground.

One Hebrew literature teacher discusses the difficulties in creating curriculum that honors the perspectives of both peoples in its textual material:

> When the children learn Hebrew and Arabic it is crucial that they are exposed to narrative texts that open their eyes to the realities of the conflicts between their cultural groups. They need accurate, authentic accounts in their language classes as well as all across the curriculum. In fact, each teacher teaches his or her subjects in his or her own language. The children are exposed to both languages right from the beginning of their schooling. For each subject matter, time is set aside for vocabulary and grammar. It is a great challenge for the Hebrew- and Arabic-speaking teachers to provide pedagogy and materials that are linguistically and conceptually appropriate in meaningful contexts. We have had very tough moments of discord and loud debate in this work, because we do not sweep things under the carpet, and therefore we touch very painful and often unresolvable issues. But we go on, knowing that it is better to acknowledge the problems than to avoid them. And I think in the end only that kind of honesty makes learning possible.

I observed a great deal of peer tutoring between older and younger students, with both Arab and Jewish students helping each other with subject matter on the common ground of each other's language and culture. I was impressed by the power created in their collaborative learning and sharing of knowledge; this is encouraged by the school's emphasis on acknowledging the children as experts in their own literacy development. There are various writing activities: writing on personal subjects (for example, journal writing) as well as general class writing, and small-group cooperative writing ventures that are often presented to the class as a whole.

This kind of pedagogy creates a place where identities are constructed and is based on the belief that language learning takes place within a setting of authentic learning contexts that comes directly from the experiences of the children. For example, I recall the activities in a grade-one class where the children, guided by their teacher, a vivacious young Arab woman from a nearby village, were crafting themes revolving around war and loss and a hope for peace and normalcy. Hebrew and Arabic were being used simultaneously and students' discussions reflected the actual experiences of their everyday lives. The students' "ownership" of the curriculum was evident in this class, as it was in all the classes I visited. This approach is in keeping with Michael Byram's (1993) proposal for a model of language teaching for cultural awareness that combines both experiential and reflective learning, allowing for a greater degree of abstraction and critical analysis. (See also Feuerverger, 1994; Gumperz, 1977; Heath, 1983; Michaels, 1981; Nieto, 1992; Tabachnick & Zeichner, 1993.)

What I continually witnessed in the classrooms was the contextualization and integration of language activities through the encouragement of real dialogue, inclusion, and fairness, and the sharing of stories as a means for better understanding "otherness" and "difference." The asymmetry of the position of Hebrew and Arabic in Israeli society remains a huge issue. Below is a short interchange between myself and a Palestinian teacher of an upper elementary grade. She discussed how the school attempts to respond to this problematic reality with various innovative pedagogical approaches. She also shared with me her personal story of how she learned Hebrew in a [regular Arab] school when she was a young girl, which was so different from what goes on at Neve Shalom/Wahat Al-Salam:

Q: Can you tell me how you learned Hebrew and what it means to you?

A: I mean I know Hebrew. I had to learn it in order to succeed. But I hated what it represents to me as a Palestinian. Hebrew was powerful, and Arabic had no power. And the way the Ministry of Education designs the curriculum for learning Hebrew is ridiculous for Arabs. It's all about the Jewish identity and Hebrew Bible and literature. That is no way for an Arab child to want to learn Hebrew.

Q: And you had no place in it. I mean, there was no talk about Arab literature or history?

A: No.

Q: Not about your identity?

A: No, not at all. Now it is changing with the peace process. There is a lot more material about Arabic and Palestinian issues in the Hebrew classes in Israel. But then I needed it for university and so I learned it in spite of how bad I felt about Hebrew.

Q: It's good to know it's changing.

A: It is, but slowly. And still Arabic is seen as a foreign language rather than a second language. Those are two very different things.

Q: And it's not compulsory; it's not compulsory, huh?

A: Finally, many [Jewish] schools are changing that into a compulsory course. But they still don't see it as equal.

Q: I think it's a very important distinction that you just made. Because it's very different, learning a language as a second language as opposed to a foreign language. And what about on the other side, in Arab schools?

A: In the Arab schools, they start to learn Hebrew from the fourth grade.

Q: Of course the Arab kids need it more; it's not the same thing.

A: Yes, they really can't survive without it.

Q: But they must learn it with, as you say, with ambivalence, because, as you say, if they're learning that language in school without using symbols from their own culture in the texts, it's a problem.

A: Right. I see how the staff here at Neve Shalom/Wahat Al-Salam uses books from the beginning that teach Hebrew but are sensitive to the Arabs' needs. The kids accept each other and each other's language and culture. The schools in other parts of Israel need to do this very much.

Q: It makes complete sense.

A: Yeah, the child feels a sense of belonging. . . .

Another Palestinian teacher shared some information regarding an increased awareness about the teaching of Arabic in the school, a new ad hoc pedagogical strategy using the Hebrew alphabet in order to overcome the barrier to Arabic conversational skills. (Conversational Arabic is completely different from literary Arabic, and as such poses enormous problems for Hebrew speakers, whose first language does not include such a complicated dichotomy.)

Q: [Could you] give me a sense of what you've been doing the last few months? [Describe h]ow things are changing or interesting things happening in the school, especially in terms of language, of course, that's my major interest. . . .

A: You know, change takes a lot of time, so you understand that not everything that we want can be done in only one year, but at least we can start. So during the summer, we usually open a lot of questions about the educational system here, then we'll have decisions.

Q: With the parents do you mean, or with the teachers?

A: With the whole staff.

Q: With all the staff, yeah.

A: The big change that has happened is for the Arabic language. We now know how difficult it is to really make it as dominant as the Hebrew language. So, this year, the Jewish kids are learning more how to communicate the slang language, the daily language, much more than to read and write in Arabic. In the past, usually, they knew more to read and write than to speak, but we want them to communicate [colloquially].

Q: Yes, conversational.

A: They can't communicate in the literature of the language; they need the spoken language. So there are some books and some exercises that we can give them in Hebrew because they know to read Hebrew. From the second grade onward, we can give them these exercises in

Hebrew letters, Hebrew letters instead of Arabic letters so they can read easily but they can learn how to speak, how to communicate. So we say that instead of taking up such [a] huge [amount of] time sitting and learning the [Arabic] letters and how to read (which is much more complicated than Hebrew) we want them to speak; and we know that they do not speak enough. There's less emphasis and there are some hours where they can still learn how to read and write but most of the hour, they do speak, and are finally learning to communicate and which kind of words to use daily at school, in the street, and so on.

Q: I see.

A: Hopefully that will help; and, of course, a lot of music with songs because the kids really like songs, so if I want them to know those words, I can put them in songs so they can really remember them.

Q: That sounds really wonderful.

A: You know, the Hebrew language, for the Palestinian Arab children, is not a problem. They feel that they need it and they can have it.

Q: That's true.

A: So this [approach] is for teaching the Arabic language to the Jewish children.

The Sociolinguistic Background

The teachers whom I interviewed suggest that the intersection among education, language, and society cannot be ignored. As discussed in chapter 2, teaching and learning are dialogic in nature. Freire talks about dialogic action as an awareness of oneself as "knower," an attitude which he named *conscientizacao*. This critical consciousness is informed by his philosophy of language and inspired by his respect for humanity. The villagers at Neve Shalom/Wahat Al-Salam embody Freire's focus on the discursive power of language, which brings them to the heart of Freire's pedagogy of knowing: that "naming the world becomes a model for changing the world" (Freire & Macedo, 1987, p. xv). They are practicing an emancipatory theory of bilingual literacy by developing an alternative educational discourse and reclaiming authorship of their own national identities.

Indeed, Freire (1987) suggests that "schools should never impose absolute certainties on students. They should stimulate the certainty of never being too certain—a method vital to critical pedagogy. Educators should also stimulate the possibilities of expression, the possibilities of subjectivity. They should challenge students to 'discourse about the world'" (p. 57). My participants also reinforce Giroux's (1987) assertion that ". . . the pedagogical should be made more political and the political more pedagogical. In other words, there is a dire need to develop pedagogical practices, in the first instance, that bring teachers, parents, and students together around new and more emancipatory visions of community . . . that the present is always a time of possibility" (p. 6). This chapter investigates how this Jewish-Arab elementary school distinguishes itself in the way in which emancipatory theory is used and encourages the subordinate status of Arab students to be liberated within the structures and discourses of the school. In order to reflect on these issues more deeply, the next section presents a discussion on second language learning in the wider Israeli society based on recent scholarly work in this area. From the macrosociolinguistic context of Israel we then will return to the microsociolinguistic one of Neve Shalom/Wahat Al-Salam in order to see how it represents a radical departure from the hegemonic approach.

Language Awareness and Second Language Learning in Israel

Learning a second language is a social phenomenon and is therefore influenced by social practice and context. Lev Vygotsky (1962, 1978) argued that learning begins in social interaction and continues on an individual basis, "first between people . . . and then inside the child (1978, p. 57). Learning becomes socially meaningful, however, within particular social contexts: "through culture humans share learned systems for defining meaning" (Erickson, 1986, p. 32–33). The society in which the learner lives may either be supportive or nonsupportive to the second language learning process (Cummins & Danesi, 1990). Indeed, personal knowledge of the world has an overarching influence on how the written word is perceived by students. "Reading does not consist merely of decoding the written word of language; rather it is preceded by and intertwined with knowledge of the world. Language and reality are dynamically interconnected. The understanding attained by critical reading of a text implies perceiving the relationship between text and context" (Freire & Macedo, 1987). Therefore, the discussion in this chapter is contextualized within a framework of socialization in two different cultural and linguistic "worlds."

Just as students' educational experiences inform their learning, so do their personal life experiences. What is exciting about Neve Shalom/Wahat Al-Salam is that these two separate worlds intersect in an unprecedented way and create an alternative interactional process. In this special case, language awareness is closely tied to a method of negotiating identities and inventing a new place to "be." It might be helpful to provide a context for this discussion by sharing findings from a research study carried out by a colleague from Haifa University, one component of which focused on the issues of Arab students learning Hebrew as a second language within the Israeli school system (Abu-Rabia & Feuerverger, 1996). The findings indicate that, in the Israeli-Arab social context, the learning of the second language (for example, Hebrew, by Arab students) is impaired to some degree due to the almost exclusive Jewish content of the texts. The Israeli-Palestinian conflict, which affects all aspects of society in Israel, is a major contributor to this problem; therefore, under these delicate circumstances it is imperative not to impose Jewish cultural content, but rather have Arabic content in the learning of Hebrew, the dominant language. The issue is a complex one. As many of my participants told me, the fact that Hebrew represents the "oppressor" for Arabs in the Israeli context results in their consciously or subconsciously developing negative or ambivalent attitudes toward learning the language.

Furthermore, the Arab community comprises 17 percent of the total population of Israel. The members of the Arab minority learn the language of the majority group and spend more hours learning the Hebrew language and Jewish culture than they spend learning their own Arabic culture and language (Abu Saad, 1991; Al-Haj, 1995). Suffice to say that the learning of Hebrew as a second language is a very problematic activity for Arab Israelis on both a personal and institutional level. Embedded within this intergroup conflict is the competition between the learning of Arabic and Hebrew within the school system (for details about difficulties within the Arab educational system in Israel see Abu Saad, 1991). As the interviews indicate, the Palestinians, in the midst of their deep cultural ambivalence, are well aware that in order to succeed in Israeli society, their Hebrew language skills must be excellent. This second language success, however, interacts on a psychological level with a sense of betrayal toward their Arab national identity. The Arabs in Israel feel threatened by learning the Hebrew language and consequently show their motivation toward the Hebrew language only as an instrumental one, rather than one of identification with it, which is an integrative orientation (see, for example, Gardner, et al., 1979, a classic work on this topic). These observations corroborate the research work on various Arab minority educational situations in Israel which clearly indicates this sense of cultural ambivalence and feelings of deprivation on the part of students (as discussed in Al-Haj, 1987, 1995; Falah, 1989; Mari, 1985). Indeed, in most cases Arab and Jewish students are schooled separately; this makes the learning of Hebrew seem even more forced.

When minority students feel mistreated by the dominant group they often tend to reject second language learning and show loyalty to their own language and culture (Cummins, 1984; Cummins & Danesi, 1990). In this case, the pervasive tension between Arabs and Jews invades the school environment and hinders second language learning, thus exacerbating the Arab students' negative feelings as a deprived and discriminated-against minority group (Abu Saad, 1991). Furthermore, these findings are congruent with Jim Cummins (1994), who focuses on "the relations of power" in schools and suggests that the traditional teacher-centered transmission model can hinder the potential for critical thinking on the part of both teachers and students. He stresses that students from socially dominated communities are most at risk. Corson (1993) describes this learning problem in terms of cultural mismatch and misunderstanding. "The conceptual world of a culture includes many classificatory systems and most of them are expressed or supported in the language of the culture. When the classificatory systems of two cultures come into contact, there is often a mismatch" (p. 49). He states that teachers need to be able to make the content of their lessons relevant to minority group children by "interweaving the known experiences of the children themselves with the content of the curriculum" but he also argues that the most important challenge is in "establishing a context for learning that is genuinely congruent with the culture of . . . minority children" (p. 51).

I concur with Cummins and Corson that schooling is mediated through discourse in some form or another, and therefore priority in establishing congruency depends on the appropriateness of the discourse. Corson goes on to cite John Gumperz (1977), who explains that through their interactions with others, individuals develop "co-occurrence expectations" and "contextualization expectations" as part of their communicative competence and that these expectations are often culturally specific. These concepts are very relevant to my interviews as I discuss with my participants the cultural content and cultural values of specific texts used in the second language learning classrooms of the Neve Shalom/Wahat Al-Salam elementary school—the only school in Israel where bilingualism, biculturalism, and binationalism are at the core of all learning and teaching. It is not surprising, then, that Neve Shalom/Wahat Al-Salam stands as a potential role model for change.

The New Language Center in Neve Shalom/Wahat Al-Salam: Implications for Language Pedagogy

A greater awareness and imagination on the part of policy makers and educators are crucial in order to respond to the needs of minority language children struggling to balance their lives in more than one cultural world. Furthermore, in a social context in which there is overt intergroup conflict, a second language curriculum which reflects the cultural content of the learners could provide a very effective strategy to create feelings of self-esteem and equality and to narrow the psychological distance between the minority and majority groups, thus enhancing academic achievement. A critical language awareness is therefore required in order to encourage students, teachers, and policymakers to approach the social imbalance in the dominant-subordinate educational paradigm which Corson terms as "a site of human struggle" (1993, p. 191). Accordingly, second language educational reform must include a restructuring of language curriculum that will take into account the motivational orientations of students in relation to their group status within differential sociopolitical contexts; for example, social settings where intergroup conflict exists, as opposed to more neutral settings where a problematic historical legacy is not part of the cultural and national ethos.

We as teacher-educators and researchers need to further explore these issues with a view to the construction and reconstruction of the meaning of language teaching and learning within a landscape of social change and transformation. A concrete example of this ideological stance is embodied in the recently created Language Center at the Neve Shalom/Wahat Al-Salam elementary school. At the end of the 1997–1998 school year, the co-director of the school wrote a short description of the status of the school at that moment, and then discussed the new Language Center as an innovative response to the asymmetry between Hebrew and Arabic as well as a supplement to the English language classes. An excerpt from his report follows.

> *As a Hebrew-Arabic educational framework, the Neve Shalom/Wahat Al-Salam school must still work in a society in which one of the languages—Hebrew—is dominant. Even here the Arab children find it easier than the Jews to acquire the second language. One of the school's objectives is to find innovative ways to strengthen language skills in general and to raise the level and use of Arabic among the Jews in particular. Professor Elite Olshtein [is] from the Hebrew University's Research Institute for Innovation in Education. Professor Olshtein created the idea of a language learning center used for Hebrew-English language training in a few other schools in Israel. Professor Olshstein sent Judy Yaron to work with the Neve Shalom/Wahat Al-Salam teaching staff, which invested a great deal of energy in creating the first trilingual language center including Hebrew, English, and Arabic. Opened in December 1996, sessions in the Language Center have become an integral part of the school curriculum.*
>
> *The center is a large room, comfortable and attractively designed, in which pupils independently choose language learning tasks that are well defined and explained so that students can work with a minimum of guidance. The center supplements the regular language courses by providing an enjoyable, unpressured learning atmosphere, which raises the pupils' motivation to take initiative in language learning. The room is furnished to provide "corners" for audiovisual equipment, games, reading, computers, drama, worksheet activities, [and so on]. The children look forward to sessions in the Language Center and this is in itself a sign of success. The center serves the school's broader goal of developing teaching techniques and materials that can be utilized by other schools. In this regard, the Language Center enjoys two particular advantages over other projects in the school. First, similar projects can be developed in conventional schools that do not necessarily have a Jewish-Arab enrollment. Second, the cooperation with the Center for Innovation in Education ensures that the experience accumulated in this project will in fact be used to enrich other schools in the country. The center has already become a place of pilgrimage for teachers and academics from Israel and abroad. (See Figure 3–2.)*

In one of several more excerpts from interviews with participants, one of the teachers in the school said:

> And now we have the Language Center—which is beautiful and has made a big difference and the kids love it. It really gives Arabic an equal status and shows the children that it needs to be learned just like Hebrew and, of course, English—which everybody wants to learn because of its international importance. And I do think other schools in Israel will start to use the model of the Language Center. It could revolutionize the

Figure 3–2   A teacher in the elementary school, with some of his students in the Language Center. (Courtesy of the author.)

attitude toward Arabic in the society from what is in effect taught as a "foreign language" to a "second language."

Another teacher who teaches Arabic and English explained it this way:

> It is great to see the children really enjoying learning Arabic and Hebrew in a very "hands-on" way. They feel like it's a real treat with all the lovely activity centers and the language games that they play. It's a very egalitarian atmosphere.

A grade six boy discusses his view:

> I always look forward to the Language Center. I can feel like I'm a merchant in a store, or buying a dog in a pet shop, or going on a trip, and I have all sorts of conversations about these things with my friends in class. We make up skits and stories and then present them in class to everybody. We do it in Hebrew, in Arabic, and in English. It's a lot of fun and everybody gets involved. (See Figure 3–3).

The co-director continues in his report:

> *Only a few years ago our hopes were raised that a new era was about to open between Jews and Arabs in which problems would be solved by*

Figure 3–3   Students involved in role play at one of the activity centers in the Language Center. (Courtesy of the author.)

negotiation. Unfortunately, four years after the beginning of talks, peace still appears to be a distant dream. We are afraid of our past, of returning to the all too horrible and familiar periods of war. Yet our present offers little hope as the negotiations between Israel and Palestinians reach stalemate after stalemate and hostile and hateful acts continue to claim victims on both sides. This complex reality provides the seedbed for the Neve Shalom/Wahat Al-Salam Primary School, with its goal of educating a rising generation for peace and understanding between the two peoples. Ultimately, we feel sure that we will succeed. Despite the setbacks, dialogue is now accepted as the most appropriate means to reach a solution to the national conflict in our area. Perhaps a reflection of this is found in the growing interest in our program from many different directions: the government, the academic community, the media, and Jewish [and] Arab families from a wide radius of the village. We can now point to other initiatives in the field that have been inspired and helped by our work and today we are more confident than ever that our educational model will become a growing influence in the field of Jewish-Arab education.

The school year ended with the tremendous news that our school has been accepted officially as an "experimental school." Hundreds of schools applied for this status and the the Neve Shalom/Wahat Al-Salam Primary School was one of the only two primary schools to be accepted. When the school was finally recognized in 1993, we celebrated the fact that the Ministry of Education had given legitimacy to the existence of a Jewish-Arab bilingual school. The acceptance of our school as an experimental school means much more. It means that the Ministry is prepared to explore our methods to see what can be learned from them and what can be applied elsewhere in the country. This has been our dream from the outset. The extra funding that comes with this status (three to five years) will be primarily for curriculum development[.] By the end of the experimental period the school is expected to serve as a center that produces material and offers in-service teacher training in the field of bilingual Jewish-Arab education. Such recognition from the state is certainly a milestone in our development.

Implications for Multilingual Education

One of the significant implications of the Language Center to the field of second language learning and multicultural education, in general, is that language curriculum becomes meaningful to students only when it is relevant to their personal lives and cultural backgrounds. In the case of many minority students in the North America, many researchers claim, as Henry Trueba did, that "the curriculum is not appealing to children because it escapes children's experience, and thus their interest and grasp of concepts" (1989, p. 143). Within the context of Jewish-Palestinian intergroup conflict, the need for establishing balance in the curriculum content is all the more urgent. The interviews with my participants certainly support this view. In this regard, teacher-educators and curriculum planners in Israel, for example, must provide an explicit framework of the expectations and needs of Arab students according to their minority/subordinate status. Michael Apple (1990) argues that the question for teacher educators and students is not *what* knowledge is most worthwhile in terms of curriculum, but *whose* (p. vii). For Arab students in Israel and, as mentioned earlier, for all students who perceive themselves to be in a subordinate position in their societies, it is important that their values and cultures be represented within the textual material of their second language curriculum, especially when that language represents the dominant group. It is therefore essential for language educators to listen to the students' own perspectives on the choice of texts and other materials as well as on teacher-student interaction, and even more generally, on the discourse of the second language classroom. We need to listen to the voices of the learners themselves concerning strategies for dealing with issues of reform in second language programs. The curriculum has the potential to either enable or handicap the student within the sociopolitical contexts that can encourage or hinder second language reading comprehension. These issues must be made more explicit at the teacher education level through the Ministry of Education in order for teacher-educators to gain a deeper understanding of how the dominant culture impacts on the realities of learning in the second language classroom.

The Allure of English: A Language of Dominion

Concerning language awareness, it is interesting to note that the necessity to master English—the *lingua franca* or perhaps more appropriately, the *lingua dominatrix*—is perceived by all as essential. On this point there is no dissension between Jew and Palestinian anywhere in Israel. Its cultural imperialism is accepted by both sides, like it or not. Israelis are pragmatists; there is wholehearted agreement in this vision: English is neither yours nor mine; it is what we all need to succeed. English transcends the conflict, the cultural borders, the animosity. English is the world. English is freedom. English is power. English opens the door for all of us.

This is what one male Palestinian teacher says in regard to personal and professional reaction to the dominance of English in the world:

> If you don't know English, then you're not in the game. Today, for an Arab, it's very hard to keep up with what's happening in the world without English. For example, the works of Edward Said are in English. Only now are some being translated into Arabic. In the Arab world, they have books at universities and some are not updated; if they don't have the scientific books in English, then they don't have the latest books. English has the power; that's just the reality. We want to make sure we don't fall behind.

This female Jewish teacher explained it this way:

> Nobody will complain about learning English in schools anywhere in Israel. When it comes to English it's never enough. Without a good knowledge of English, we would become a country without any power in the world. Let's face it, Hebrew is certainly not very important; and even Arabic, which is spoken by many, many millions in the world, still doesn't have much international importance. Like I say, without English you might as well disappear. Who can change that? So everybody is interested in learning English.

Here is what a little eight-year-old Palestinian boy said:

> I know you want to practice your Hebrew and Arabic; but honestly, I want to talk with you in English because I want to learn it so bad. What does English mean to me? It means being able to travel when I get bigger.

A six-year-old Jewish child confided:

> English doesn't have any problems the way Arabic and Hebrew [do], which are always fighting with each other. I always feel excited about learning English.

A female Palestinian teacher describes below her childhood love affair with the English language, which continues to this day. She grew up in a town in the Galilee, a famous pilgrimage destination and therefore always full of tourists. As a young child she was fascinated by them and by the possibility of the different lifestyles that they embodied. Many of them spoke English, and she practiced using this language (which she was beginning to learn at school) whenever she could. English always represented for her a passport to freedom, opportunity, success, adventure, and joy.

> I would hang around the Church of the Annunciation and wait until the tour was over and then start to talk with the tourists. Maybe they humored me or maybe they thought it was exotic to be speaking with this little Arab girl in English.
>
> I first started learning it in school in grade four. I couldn't believe when I could start speaking in full sentences and they [the tourists] didn't mind. Also, I loved my English teacher in grade four. And the others also. Later in junior high school, I had a very bad teacher and I almost lost my English with that teacher.
>
> But in the last year of junior high, we had a wonderful, marvelous teacher and he had an American accent. That's where I got my accent. It's amazing how one teacher can make such a huge difference. He said, "I will not let you go on until I see you progressing properly in English."
>
> Arabic is my first language, so it didn't have adventure. Hebrew wasn't exciting because of what it meant for us Arabs in Israel. I wasn't attracted to it and tried to rebel against it by not learning it well. But I realized pretty early on that if I wanted to be accepted to university then what kind of bullshit am I doing—I needed Hebrew. And to communicate in the country where I live. . . .
>
> But English was the dream! You know, it was like the dessert of life. It's the topping on the cake—you don't have to put it on top, but it makes everything so beautiful and sparkling. I know it sounds silly but you have to believe in love. So that's how the whole story began with English. I just love it.
>
> And so I would just say what I could to the pilgrims. It was such a good feeling and they always seemed so relaxed (maybe because they were on holiday). If I didn't understand something, I would ask them. I would throw what I could in English. I encourage my own students to do that. Not to feel ashamed about what you know or the mistakes you make. I always say that language is like the sea. You throw into it what you can and you hold onto to what you have; you touch anything that will save you. It may be right, it may be wrong, but you're grasping onto it. Someone will correct you anyhow. But at least you're keeping the conversation afloat.
>
> Oh, I was crazy. I looked everything up in the dictionary. I just enjoyed looking at the words. Now I try to give my students that feeling.

Who can explain this *coup de foudre,* this falling in love with a language? I certainly understand it because it happened to me also, although in another context. I was able to relate to much of what this teacher shared with me. We grew up in very different places, yet we both recognized the learning of a second/foreign language for the magic carpet ride that it can be—given the right circumstances. To be seduced by a language is a profound experience. It can be as special as icing on a cake, or it can have the power to save your life. This is language awareness in its finest hour. The following section offers the reader my personal narrative about the meaning of languages and cultures both in my early years and to the present day.

Insider-Outsiderness along the Sociolinguistic Border: A Personal Narrative

The shaping of my interpretations and the construction of this story about Neve Shalom/Wahat Al-Salam are necessarily filtered through the multiple lenses of my own life story: as an immigrant/minority language child in Canada trying to find dignity in my school experiences a couple of decades ago; as a former elementary school teacher; and as a university professor and educational researcher devoted to giving voice to teachers and students within the educational enterprise in a multicultural world. I am heartened by Lawrence-Lightfoot's (1997, p. 96) assertion that "the portraitist's reference to her own life story does not reduce the reader's trust—it enhances it. It does not distort the responsibility of the researcher and the authenticity of the work; it gives them clarity." Furthermore, we cannot forget Clifford Geertz (1973, 1988, 1995) who implores us again and again to ask, "What is the meaning of this to me?" This bilingual, binational, bicultural educational enterprise at Neve Shalom/Wahat Al-Salam resonates for me, on a personal as well as professional level. Personally, I identified with this school in an "if only" sense: "If only my childhood schooling as a minority language student could have been more inclusive—like this one!" Certainly the context is totally different, but the quest for equality in education remains the same. As a reflexive ethnographer and sociolinguist, my cultural baggage necessarily gives shape to the presentation of my findings and allows, as Robert Coles (1997, p. 25) suggests, for more discursive freedom and aesthetic sensibility in my research work. "Once again the issue is that of *location*—how a particular writer or researcher decides to commit himself or herself with respect to those being studied, watched, heard, made the subject of a writing initiative" (ibid., p. 32). I agree with his notion that who we are, especially in terms of our personal lives, has a great deal to do with how we interpret the stories of our participants.

This section focuses on autobiographical aspects of ethnography because it is all about "our willingness to put ourselves on the line in this way, our willingness to indicate that the documentarian, the listener, and the one who sees, the witness, can be both a vehicle and an obstacle on a journey . . . the need in fieldwork to take into account the person (ourselves) who is offering an account of others" (ibid., p. 44). In many cases, ethnographic interviews and observations mark the first contact that the researcher has with the social world that she or he intends to describe. These are social processes of mutual accommodation during which information is transferred; indeed, they are phenomenological encounters of subjectivities (Marcus, 1998). Like all techniques in qualitative research, in-depth interviewing and participant observation have their limitations. Sandra Acker and I (1999) suggest that "at the heart of the situation is the fact that there are humans involved, with all of their emotional investments and interactions. The growing professional discourse . . . honors the researcher in qualitative research as an integral part of both the research process and research results, rather than simply being a conduit through which findings flow." This notion has informed my ethnography about Neve Shalom/Wahat Al-Salam and has breathed life into it.

My professional intention here is to share, within the telling of my participants' stories, pieces of my own life history. This has emerged out of a profound need to explore my reasons for researching this particular site. As Stephen Crites (1971, p. 295) puts it, "consciousness awakes to a culture's sacred story." That is what all stories aim to do—to transform. I therefore draw on the notions of reflexivity and intersubjectivity as a positive feature—"not only the personal history of ethnographers but also the disciplinary and broader sociocultural circumstances under which they work have a profound effect on which topics and peoples are selected for study" (Davies, 1999, p. 5). Ruth Behar (1996, p. 13) tells us that it is essential to "locate oneself in one's own [ethnographic] text. Writing vulnerably takes as much skill, nuance, and willingness to follow through on all the ramifications of a complicated idea as does writing invulnerably and distantly." In the following excerpt from my personal narrative, I try to confront "the matter of the specific location of oneself as documentarian amidst one's struggle to locate oneself as an observer and writer, as someone who saw and now wants to represent, in the sense of conveying or picturing, so that others will say or feel 'I got it,' or, better, 'I'm really getting it'" (Coles, p. 48). It is also a matter of confronting the question of how the ethnographer documents his or her own struggle to make sense of the research within the lives of the participants and his or her own life—it is the struggle with our subjectivity and the "actuality of the work" in James Agee's terms (in Coles, p. 88). What a messy business it is, but that is the stuff of reality. I also follow Lawrence-Lightfoot in claiming that "goodness" does exist outside of our moral imagination, and that it is a good thing to look for that site where it resides: "to see the world we are looking for" (1997, p. 224). We search for good role models; is this not how we improve the world?

The immigrant/refugee landscape—specifically, my being a child of Holocaust survivors—has informed every aspect of my life story and forced me to enter the multicultural and multilingual educational discourse as far back as I can remember, long before it became a fashionable topic of research inquiry. In fact, this legacy continues to provide a significant guiding motif in my professional life. In terms of my own childhood education in the schools of the

Protestant School Board of Greater Montreal (PSBGM) in the 1950s and 1960s (a city which was, and still is, a large culturally and linguistically cosmopolitan center), I was well aware that I was not part of the majority cultures (neither English nor French). I can still feel the humiliation as I sat in my kindergarten class witnessing (as did all the other students) the displeasure in my teacher's voice as she mumbled my family name. I wanted to disappear into thin air when she imperiously asked why my parents hadn't considered shortening that unwieldy immigrant name in order to make life easier for everyone! What saved me was that I was not the only immigrant child in school. In fact, more than half of the students in my school were children of displaced persons from World War II. Playing in the streets of my childhood meant being immersed in a cacophony of languages and cultures from Eastern and Central Europe. Multiculturalism was as natural as breathing the air around me. My own home was linguistically and culturally diverse. My teachers, however well meaning most of them were, did not recognize the value of our backgrounds. They made us feel that we had an unfortunate burden to carry and that the quicker we rid ourselves of it the better. Not surprisingly, I hated the Yiddish classes that I was forced to endure after school hours. They seemed like a great interference and waste of time. It wasn't hard for us to figure out that what really counted was what happened in the "regular" school day.[2]

Below is a brief excerpt from my personal journal on minority language education, which demonstrates a particular minority child's vivid awareness of the devaluing of her home language:

> *My minority language educational experiences in childhood were a very dismal affair. I was sent to a Yiddish language program after regular school hours (twice a week from 4 to 6 p.m.) which took place in the basement of a dilapidated community center. The teacher didn't know how to engage her pupils and so our main activity in class was to gaze out the window at the other children who were playing in the street. There might as well have been bars on those windows. It was clear that nobody wanted to be in that classroom. The books were old, torn and gray. That is what I remember. No pretty pictures. The stories held no meaning and certainly no excitement. The only fun in class was when the more "creative" boys would "slingshot" erasers through the air. Suddenly the room would be transformed into a carnival of rubber snowballs. At least then we could imagine that we were outside. Once an eraser hit the teacher in the face. Dead silence. She sat down at her desk and began to cry out of sheer desperation. Poor woman. I felt sorry for her and disgusted. I compared her to the exciting French teacher at (regular) school. And I remember saying adamantly to myself that I would not be a party to such a sham. Indeed, I had more respect for language learning than that. I knew it didn't have to be that way. I had seen the dregs of "minority language education" and I wanted out of there. I raised such a tantrum at home that my parents finally took me out. But at night I*

*secretly felt guilty for having abandoned my Yiddish schooling. I would
try to hold on to the spelling of the words in my mind. As the months
went by, the letters became fainter and fainter. It was a slow miserable
death. I felt like a criminal.* (Feuerverger, 1995)

Again I draw from Behar (1996, p. 19), who contends that ". . . in much contemporary writing ethnography [was] becoming more autobiographical while
autobiography had become more ethnographic." And so I write the following
section "vulnerably," to use Behar's terms, about the need to be "able to draw
deeper connections between one's personal experience and the subject under
study" (p. 13). As a child, I had to figure out a way to escape the bleakness of
my emotionally devastated family life, and I first found it in the loving embrace of the French language. The following personal narrative was written
after my participant observation in classrooms at the village school during my
first visit to Neve Shalom/Wahat Al-Salam in 1991–1992. As I sat in those
classes witnessing the sharing of languages and cultures between the Jewish
and Palestinian students, my bittersweet memories of how language awareness
(or, should I say, the awareness of *other* languages and cultures) offered me a
means of survival: the keys to a new kingdom which promised nourishment—
indeed, life itself. I became a "border crosser" at a very early age.

Ma Chère Langue Française: Escape from Despair

*I will never forget the excitement—the "rush"—I experienced the first time I
heard those French sounds coming out of the radio. Different. More
interesting. New. Foreign. Enticing. Unknown. Glamorous. Their songs
seemed full of life and their life seemed full of songs. I ran into the arms of
French like an orphan child seeking warmth and shelter. There she was—"la
langue française"—so lovely and so accessible to me. I was in heaven.
Transfixed. I was about four years old and I knew I had found my foster
home. I believed in French as a devout Roman Catholic believes in salvation.
French classes at school really were a blessing. I loved them in such a
profound way as only a child can. Like when you get your first really fancy
toy. I never had any fancy toys or dresses. French became my fancy dress, my
escape from the bleak world in which I found myself.*

*My French teacher in elementary school was Madame Lazare. They didn't
hire French Canadians in the Protestant School Board of Montreal in those
years. And the mirror image was also true. There were no non-Catholics in
the Catholic system. A great way to keep the "two solitudes" apart! Anyway,
Mme. Lazare was originally from Morocco but had lived in Paris before
emigrating to Canada. I admired her from a distance. She was slim, elegant,
and well-groomed, and her voice was so soft. Even today I can hear the
pleasant clicking sound of her high heels as she walked. I felt at peace in my
seat as she would read out the words and phrases that we copied during
"Dictée." My ears delighted in her Parisian accent. So chic! That, I vowed, is*

how I was going to speak French! I felt that if I could speak French like that then I would become as elegant as Mme. Lazare. She wore stunning outfits every day. It was like participating in a fashion show. Blue was definitely her best color. It accentuated the cobalt of her eyes and contrasted with her silky jet-black hair. The scent of her perfume wafted in the air. And I thought, "So this is what a French teacher looks like!" I tucked that knowledge away in the back of my mind for future reference.

Mme. Lazare could not help but notice my fervor in class. I always had my hand up and I was always answering questions. I jumped at every opportunity to be able to let those French words pour out of me. They poured from pencil to paper as well. I wrote stories about an imaginary family with a kind, gentle mother and a cheerful, robust father and children with names like Chantal and Lisette and Marie-Thérèse who went to ballet class and wore pretty dresses and had lots of relatives who brought them gifts and laughed with them. Life in my French imagination was wonderful. It was a great escape and I hung onto those stories as if they were a life raft. I kept embellishing the characters with more and more detail, using my continually expanding vocabulary. I also figured out a neat trick. I realized that certain television programs (for example, Father Knows Best) would appear on the French channel with the current episode dubbed in French. And so I began a self-taught, personalized course in contrastive analysis. I would diligently watch the English language version first and then the French one, figuring out the new words. When I ran into difficulty I would transliterate the words and then ask Mme. Lazare about their meaning the next day in class.

Mme. Lazare was thoroughly amazed at my motivation. So were my classmates, who were mainly immigrant children (like me) and were satisfied with their English language curriculum. They didn't see the value of French in their everyday lives. For them even the one lesson of French each day seemed superfluous. In all fairness to them, it is they who were "normal." I was the atypical one. In those days, the English and French Canadians definitely lived within their "two solitudes" and the immigrant communities struggled to learn English in order to survive economically. The English definitely had the power and controlled the purse strings; there was no question about that. Even the immigrant (non-French) kids who were Catholic would attend English-speaking Catholic schools. The Jewish kids went to the Protestant schools. The educational system was a confessional (Christian religion–based) one[3] and in order for Jews to have a place, a bylaw was created in the early 1900s that allowed Jews to be Protestants for educational purposes. Interesting logic. For others it made sense. For me, it became the bane of my existence. I so desperately wanted to go to the Catholic school around the corner from my home. It was there where I would have learned French in an authentic French-Canadian atmosphere. But that option was closed to me. I would have to find other ways to create authentic ties to that community.

Throughout my years in Montreal, I created personal and professional relationships in the French-Canadian community. My first best friend was a sweet little girl named Françoise who introduced me not only to the French-Canadian culture but also to the Roman Catholic religion and to the Virgin Mary, who continues to hold a very special, if unorthodox, place in my life. Françoise and I enjoyed each other's company so much. She was really a part of that world about which I wrote my little essays. Here fantasy and reality merged. I studied her life like a devoted anthropologist. Oh, how I wanted to "go native," but I could not overstep that boundary. I could, however, speak French with Françoise all the time—any time. French was definitely my magic carpet. Languages are more than the sums of their parts. They are the world; they are the reshaping and restructuring of our perceptions and of the very meaning of our lives. Languages and cultures became the bread and wine of my life.

I became immersed in French and Italian literature at McGill University. I entered McGill at the age of seventeen and felt the breath of fresh air float through my brain. It was going to be different from here on in. And, by golly, it was. I cavorted with authors like Jean-Paul Sartre, Paul Claudel, François Mauriac, Gustave Flaubert, Marie-Claire Blais, Gabrielle Roy, Anne Hébert, and so on, and one of my classmates and I had a crush on our French professor. We used to visit him in his office after class and discuss in French the existential woes of "la condition humaine" and "le péché originel." Professor Lapointe recognized a certain quality in me and said that he thought I "ran the risk of being too intelligent for my own good"! I have been trying to figure out those words ever since. I took courses in sociology, Latin, Russian, and English as well as French. I won highest marks in German that first year. It was a heady beginning to a new world.

Then a new chapter opened up in my life when I decided to study Italian literature in my second year. The choice for me had been between Spanish and Italian. My mind floated back to the Sunday mornings of my childhood when I would watch local Italian-Canadian singers performing on television. Those songs were pure magic for me. They opened up sunny new horizons. Their raw energy seduced me. Italian has always had that effect on me. When I am in the midst of Italians, the sun always breaks through the clouds and life is suddenly breezy. All my personal angst just disappears and I am somehow miraculously set free. Many people have commented on the fact that when I speak Italian, my voice, my mannerisms, and my spirit seem transformed. This is the magic of languages and cultures for me. There was no contest. I did not only choose Italian; it chose me. The following year, as a result of a McGill competition that I entered and won, I was awarded a scholarship to study at the Università per Stranieri in Perugia, Italy. I was never the same again. (Winter, 1992)

Is it any wonder that my professional life of teaching, researching, and writing is devoted to issues of language, culture, and identity within contexts of inter-group relations, both locally and in international educational settings such as Neve Shalom/Wahat Al-Salam?

Concluding Remarks

The innovations at the Neve Shalom/Wahat Al-Salam school have opened a space for reshaping the pedagogical processes in its classrooms and in its school policies, and have made it possible for the participants at the school to become free to be "border crossers" and thus challenge and redefine the limitations created by hegemonic domination. I have included in this chapter excerpts of my own personal narrative which shows how I became a "border crosser" very early in my childhood in order to connect with other cultures and languages as a vehicle to escape my own specific family life history. For the participants in this village, language and cultural awareness is also connected with "border crossing," and has become a metaphor for the realization of the need to create a fully egalitarian Hebrew-Arabic curriculum for all students, thereby inviting them to cross over into uncharted territory in order to become familiar with the "other." Stated another way, "border crossing" becomes the enterprise of reconciliation with "otherness" (Kristeva, 1991; Shabatay, 1991)—which is, at bottom, the enterprise of peacemaking.

In this chapter, I explored the imagination and courage of all those involved with the organization of Neve Shalom/Wahat Al-Salam and have attempted to document how they have succeeded in creating a whole new way of looking at the world in terms of the pedagogical relationship among teacher, student, and textual material in the midst of conflict and war. Neve Shalom/Wahat Al-Salam can thus be envisioned as a new "borderland" where emancipatory discourses of cultural and linguistic equality are being created. This community's little school offers the hope that the biblical Tower of Babel does not necessarily have to be regarded as a punishment for humankind. Perhaps we can reconfigure the Tower's meaning that it places before us—that is, to learn to live in peace with ourselves and with our neighbors in a multilingual, multicultural, multiracial, multifaith global society.

Endnotes

1. As discussed in chapter 1, each class has one Jewish and one Arab teacher who work in a team-teaching mode. Since 1991, children from neighboring Arab and Jewish villages have begun to attend the school.
2. It is finally in adulthood that I am reconnecting with my first language, Yiddish, and reclaiming my heritage through cultural and linguistic activities that are now entering mainstream society. There are, for example, very successful cultural activities in mainstream venues in Toronto focusing on Yiddish klezmer music and theater. These performances draw very large crowds, both Jewish and non-Jewish.
3. In fact, there was no (secular) Ministry of Education in Quebec until the early 1960s.

Chapter Four

Witnessing Trauma:
The "School for Peace"

Is there a relationship between crisis and the very enterprise of education? To put the question even more audaciously and sharply: Is there a relation between trauma and pedagogy? In a post-traumatic century, a century that has survived unthinkable historical catastrophes, is there anything that we have learned or that we should learn about education, that we did not know before? Can trauma instruct pedagogy, and can pedagogy shed light on the mystery of trauma?

—S. Felman and D. Laub, 1992

Introduction to an Interpretive Inquiry

This chapter[1] provides an interpretive inquiry into the traumatic relationship among Jewish and Arab high school students and their facilitators within an outreach educational program sponsored by the "School for Peace" (SFP). I focus on the lived experiences of Jewish and Arab high school students and their facilitators at a three-day intensive "School for Peace" workshop encounter, which I observed for the first time in December, 1991. This chapter explores the complex and multiple feelings of strangerhood, victim identities, and the longing for legitimacy that both Jews and Palestinians possess in the Middle East. As a participant-observer[2], I discuss the sites of struggle and negotiation in the "border dialogues" the students and facilitators gradually created for themselves in their search to give equal expression to their national identities. In so doing, I offer a reflective analysis of what conflict resolution means for these participants within the specific context of the trauma of the Jewish-Palestinian conflict, which may have international implications for teaching conflict resolution and for peace education.

The target populations for the SFP workshops are adolescents, teachers, educators, psychologists, social workers, and activists in peace organizations who are interested in specific training for facilitating group processes within the context of the conflict. Each of the programs at the "School for Peace" takes place over a period of three to six months and includes one very intensive three-day workshop encounter in which the participants from high schools all over the country are divided into a small mixed group of twelve to fourteen Jews and an equal number of Palestinians. Numerical equality between Jews and Palestinians is always maintained, and each group's needs are given equal priority. The facilitators are a permanent, professional staff of Jews and Arabs (in equal numbers) trained at Neve Shalom/Wahat Al-Salam. Before the participants come together for the three-day intensive encounter, they attend a number of monthly meetings that are conducted in a "uninational" group setting (either all Jewish or all Palestinian) at the SFP in order to respond to each group's separate learning needs. All the meetings, including the three-day encounter, take place in the village in a plain one-story building and its adjacent courtyard. During the three-day encounter at the SFP, the students live in the youth hostel and guest rooms nearby, four to six in a room—strictly separated by gender. This intensive encounter is conducted in Hebrew and Arabic and is headed by two facilitators, one Jewish and the other Palestinian.

Ahmed, a Palestinian facilitator, discussed the purpose of the three-day encounter in a personal interview:

> The structure of the "School for Peace," and of its workshops, is guided by principles of equality. The three-day workshops are all conducted in both Hebrew and Arabic, and each working group is small and is headed by two facilitators, one Jewish and the other Palestinian. This framework provides support and assures the legitimacy of every participants' position. . . . The encounter has a power that no other activity related to this subject has. It is an experience that opens a variety of both possibilities and risks, but there is no substitute for it. The realities of Israel do not give the young people of both groups a chance to meet on equal terms. So the encounters that take place are usually accompanied by feelings of fear, humiliation, disappointment, and distrust. What we try to do is to provide a way to process and understand these feelings, helping our young people to be better able to cope with the Jewish-Palestinian conflict.

Conflict resolution and peacemaking are inexorably intertwined. In fact, peace comes not from the absence of conflict in life, but from the ability to cope with it. Peacemaking therefore can be regarded as a long, arduous process toward conflict resolution, which is ongoing and is never to be taken for granted (Apple, 1979; Lasch, 1995; Reardon, 1988). For example, many schools in North America are now becoming committed to the principles of peace education (Adalbjarnadottir, 1992; Banks, 1990; Brock-Utne, 1989; Delpit, 1995; Graff, 1992; Hanson & McAuliffe, 1994; Merelman, 1990; Posner, 1994; Stevahn et al., 1996; Wallis, 1994). Peacemaking becomes possible only if we are able to confront human differences and to acknowledge their legitimacy. One of the most widely accepted notions of peace education reform in the United

States and Canada is the school conflict education strategy of peer mediation training. This program teaches students how to manage conflicts constructively using negotiation procedures and peacemaking skills. The Community Board Program and Anti-Violence Program in the United States are examples of how students can take responsibility for changing the level of violence within the landscape of racial and ethnic diversity in their schools and communities (Kreidler, 1989; Larson, 1991; Mathews, 1994; Sadalla et al., 1987). Developing models of nonviolent leadership, conflict mediation, and respect for differences are key features of these programs.

Many workshops take place at the SFP every year. For example, it organizes encounter workshops between Jewish and Palestinian adolescents, as well as many other workshops for schoolteachers, graduate students, and peace workers. The philosophy behind such educational initiatives is that relationship building and problem solving are two sides of the same coin. Having taken these American models into consideration, the overall emphasis of the SFP encounter groups is on developing communication and negotiation skills to be used in interpersonal and intergroup situations within the teaching/learning environments of Israeli schools. The aim is to provide a significant, "hands-on" opportunity for teachers and students to gain an understanding of and share knowledge about the social and psychological dilemmas that plague both Palestinians and Jews in this war-torn region. These workshops encourage the process of sensitive listening, essential to all forms of professional development both for the learner and the teacher. The sessions stress the importance of assuring the legitimacy of every participant's position, empowering participants as storytellers, and opening a space where dialogue becomes possible. These "border zones," which Gloria Anzaldua (1987) describes as "those . . . multicultural spaces, sometimes called 'common ground,' where disparate cultures meet," are intended to provide a nonthreatening, nonevaluative setting and to foster a sense of community and respect for differences in the midst of violent conflict. Through the sharing of pedagogical experiences and personal as well as professional stories, a new paradigm for peacemaking is thereby created. In these workshops, facilitators and students are encouraged to explore pedagogies appropriate for the development of conflict resolution skills as an inductive process (that is, proceeding from observation), and to understand that these initiatives occur in the context of praxis—participation in an action/reflection process.

Since its inception in 1979, the SFP has had funding from private foundations and personal donations. In 1993 the workshops were recommended to public schools by the Israeli Ministry of Education, which now provides partial funding through its "Education for Democracy and Coexistence" program (Shohat, 1993). Moreover, the teachers who now take part in these workshops receive in-service training credits. The "School for Peace" has attracted tens of thousands of participants. They include not only Jews and Palestinians from within Israel but also, more and more, from the West Bank. Briefly, these are the main objectives of the encounters, as expressed in the curriculum guidelines of the SFP prepared by Michal Zak (1992, p. 5), a key person involved in its decision-making processes:

1. To deepen the participants' familiarity with themselves and with the other side.
2. To raise the participants' awareness of the complex reality of relations between the sides, and to enable them to absorb this complexity.
3. To make the participants aware of their ability to select their attitude toward the conflict, to influence their lives and their surroundings and thus, to help mitigate the conflict.
4. To bring the participants to choose nondiscriminatory positions and modes of behavior and to give legitimacy to all peoples' needs, rights, and aspirations.
5. To give the participants an opportunity to experience cooperation between the sides.

The rationale for the SFP is succinctly stated in its position paper:

> *In the reality of the enduring conflict between Jews and Palestinians that has cost many lives and caused irreversible damage, the need for finding a just peace solution is more urgent than ever. One way of bringing about social change is through relationships incurred between groups participating in an intergroup process in the context of the conflict. Facilitating such a delicate, sensitive process requires specific professional skills, and there is a need to develop opportunities for training practitioners in this field in Israel. . . . A natural and suitable place to establish the training project is Neve Shalom/Wahat Al-Salam. . . . [The village] provides a safe and supportive environment for such training. The main outreach program of the community is through the SFP. For the past eleven years the SFP has been developing and conducting unique models for conflict management workshops for Jews and Palestinians.*
> (Sonnenschein & Halaby, 1991, p. 1)

The overriding goal of the SFP therefore is "to enhance the participants' awareness of the complexity of the Jewish-Arab issue, and to develop the ability of the participants to take a multidimensional view of themselves, others, the different identities, and the complexity of the two very different peoples engaged in a difficult conflict" (Sonnenschein & Halaby, 1991, p. 3). The model was developed jointly with faculty members of the psychology department at Tel Aviv University (see Sonnenschein, Halaby, & Friedman, 1992). It derives from classical scholarly work on intergroup conflict and cooperation; group dynamics theory; models of small-group interaction, motivational/cognitive processes, and their effects on intergroup attitudes; stereotyping and the formation of prejudice; and majority/minority group experience of "otherness," within the dynamics of conflict resolution. (See Adorno et al., 1950; Amir, 1976; Bar & Bargal, 1988; Bettman & Moore, 1994; Katz & Cahanov, 1990; Lewin, 1958; Stephan, 1987; Tajfel & Turner, 1985.) The emphasis is on cognitive and emotional processing of the different aspects of the conflict and their influence on each of the participants. Nava Sonnenschein and Rabah Halaby (1991, pp. 3, 4) explain:

> *Psychologically repressed hostility and anxiety and long-lasting frustration in intergroup relations may create aggressiveness on one hand, and hopelessness on the other hand. The intergroup encounter aims to create a possibility to live with the conflict (even while there is no political solution to it) at a minimum of personal, interpersonal, and social cost. Among the ways to "live with the conflict" are:*
>
> 1. *Realizing the conflict has at least two sides and that from each side things are perceived differently.*
> 2. *Understanding that each individual living in the area is influenced by the Israeli-Palestinian conflict in a different way.*
> 3. *Developing self-awareness and feelings of self-worth; working through the fears of the other people; differentiating between fantasies and realities; raising awareness that there is no simple and one-sided solution to the conflict, and working through the feelings of loss that derive from this; strengthening personal and national identity.*
> 4. *Developing a certain mutual trust.*
> 5. *Assessing the relations between the peoples, recognizing the solutions to the conflict as perceived by each of the peoples, and examining the complexity of each solution.*
> 6. *Getting acquainted with the other people and recognizing their full and equal rights in all domains.*
> 7. *Raising awareness of the asymmetry in the situation between the two peoples.*
> 8. *Developing the awareness that each individual has the power to produce change and thus contribute to a reduction in the level of the conflict.*

Due to the sensitive nature of the SFP program, the names of the two facilitators and their students are pseudonyms in the remainder of this chapter. Tirzah, the Jewish facilitator, articulated the *raison d'être* of the SFP in these words:

> We hope these workshops here in Neve Shalom/Wahat Al-Salam will be relevant for peace education workers everywhere. We increasingly believe that what we are doing here in Israel and in this village has direct meaning for situations in other places around the world. We have no solutions, but at least people from both sides are being given a chance to air their feelings. At least, that's a start. It has been an amazing learning experience for me, and working with Palestinian facilitators and students has opened my eyes to a lot of issues that I had simply taken for granted before. Conflict between groups is a global problem and we have to learn

how to break through. Peace has still not been achieved but in these workshops we're trying to address the problems, no matter how messy and scary they are.

According to Ahmed, the Palestinian facilitator:

In spite of the very difficult situation that is filled with violence and extremism which is getting worse on both sides, we have to encourage the young ones to come and meet and break through the impasse. They are so afraid of the encounters; they are afraid that they will lose control of their feelings. So many are full of rage and fear. Our aim is to tell them that those feelings are justified—that they are a part of reality, our reality. The SFP gives them the extraordinary chance to see one another face to face, and to realize the complexity of the conflict that we are all immersed in. Our agenda is not political grandstanding; we want the teenagers to get in touch with their deeply hidden but deeply felt emotions, so that they can be authentic with each other. Of course we can't avoid the politics but we try to show both sides—that each group has economic, social, and family problems. We try to get past only this political and military face of the conflict, and see it in more human terms.

Toward a Pedagogy of Hope: The Mystery of Mediation

As researcher and as a member of the Jewish people, I have attempted to construct a collective story of different but parallel journeys into the nomadic experience of "exile"—which I believe is central to any discussion of peace efforts between Jews and Palestinians in Israel. I tried to examine the epistemologically complex implications of understanding the search for peaceful coexistence as a dialogical relation within the specific context of this Israeli educational setting. Martin Buber's (1958, 1965) theoretical focus on the centrality of dialogical meeting—that is, on an understanding of the self as both personal and social in an ongoing process of construction and reconstruction through encounters with other selves—informs the discussion that follows. I collected and examined data from the adolescent participants and their facilitators through in-depth interviewing and observation in the encounter workshops. My aim was to underscore the power of these peace workshops in terms of transforming the hegemonic discourse into an emancipatory one, thus creating the seeds of a pedagogy of hope. In fact, the participants became reflective practitioners who began to examine themselves in relation to the "other"; they became architects rather than pawns in their own education.

The theoretical framework of this study and of the SFP encounters is situated in the critical need to scrutinize and analyze the historical and ideological conditions that have prevented these Jewish and Arab students from openly communicating with one another. According to Pierre Bourdieu (1996), "to write an educational program is a philosophical act in favor of reason. Forms of collaboration across boundaries have an urgency in this time of restoration. . . . We must defend open-minded and democratic educational endeavors in a time when dark forces in society are trying to eradicate reason." Indeed, the workshops for peace can be seen as "borderlands . . . where the interrelationships of different cultures and identities . . . [are] sites of crossing, negotiation, translation, and dialogue. . . . Within such a pedagogical cartography, teachers [and students] must be given the opportunity to cross ideological and political borders as a way of clarifying their own moral vision, as a way of enabling counterdiscourses . . . to expand the possibilities for different groups to enter into dialogue to understand further the richness of their differences and the value of what they share in common" (Giroux, 1994, p. 340).

This interpretive or qualitative approach already discussed in Chapter 2, is congruent with many postmodern theorists interested in issues of intersubjectivity and reflexivity in research activities. I focus on the cultural narratives of my participants and their ancestral longings—and how their lived experiences were revealed in their fundamental values, their beliefs, their perceptions, and in fact, in the worldview that they carried (consciously and unconsciously) with them into the workshops. For example, bell hooks (1994) discusses the need for rethinking ways of using life history to focus on issues of identity and to challenge the notion of identity as static. In the case of these SFP workshops, the meaning of identity—especially national identity—is of paramount importance. Thus, the centrality of emotion in this pedagogical journey suggested that issues of identity and nationhood cannot be explained solely through an intellectual and cognitive process, but rather through a different focus on affect, interaction, and interpretation. In other words, the lived experience needs to be seen as an interpretive rather than a causal story. In terms of the "biographies of vulnerability" that permeated the discourse of the workshops, I as researcher was mindful of Valerie Olesen's (1992, p. 218) claim that "body and self are intertwined. We need to attend to cognition and emotion, using both phenomenal and interactive approaches." Indeed, I observed how emotionally powerful these educational encounters were both for myself as researcher, and for the participants in their struggle to reenvision and reshape a meta-text for Jewish-Palestinian relations in Israel.

The Three-Day Encounter

This section offers some excerpts from the in-depth interviews that I carried out with many students and with the facilitators during my research stay at the "School for Peace" in Neve Shalom/Wahat Al-Salam in order to further conceptualize the discussion. I used field notes and journaling as a tool to try to make meaning out of the stories my participants shared with me in and out of the lived experiences of the workshop encounter. The interviews were tape-recorded and later transcribed. (My knowledge of Hebrew is passable, but my knowledge of Arabic is very poor; a number of Israeli colleagues (Jewish and Arab) helped me to translate the transcriptions from Hebrew and Arabic into English.)

In order to convey a sense of the scene and mood of the SFP and its participants, I tried to create the story through personal narrative. Elliot Eisner (1991, p. 30) argues that "schools . . . have moods, and they . . . display scenes of high drama that those who make policy and who seek to improve practice should know. The means through which such knowledge is made possible are the enlightened eye—the scene is seen—and the ability to craft text so that what the observer has experienced can be shared by those who were not there." The story of the school, its "high drama," can be read as a "natural psychological unit" (Rayfield, 1972, p. 1085). Through an account of the participants' "lived experiences" in the three-day encounter, I present a picture of the "border dialogues" of these individuals, who are paradoxically located at the margins and at the center of history and ideology. These dialogues are as fragmented as the splinters of glass that continually explode in the terrorist acts that have become, tragically, a common occurrence in Israeli life; they dwell together in an immense psychological separation created by this vicious circle of violence, and they lie in the shadows of deep mourning, loss, anger—but also cautious hope.

The reflective analysis that follows is intended to show how the SFP offers an innovative conception of Israeli life by exploring the risky business of bringing forth diverse voices for the purpose of inquiring more effectively into the hopes, fears, and dreams of the participant selves from both sides of the Jewish-Palestinian conflict. I was witness to the unconscious and conscious attempts of those involved in these peace education initiatives to break down personal, cultural, and political barriers, permitting teachers and students to rethink the spaces where dominant and subordinate groups are situated, and thus to transform their own relationships. The sections that follow contain a summary of the many interviews and participant observations that took place over the course of this research in order to provide further context for the discussion.

First Glimpse: Personal Musings

The following is an excerpt of a journal entry I wrote the night I arrived in the village after having had dinner with Bob Mark, a teacher at the school, his wife Michal Zak, and their two daughters:

> *There is no way that I'll be able to fall asleep tonight! I'm just too excited. I just had a delicious dinner (of fried eggplant and corn on the cob and hot, fresh bread) with Bob and his family. There is a certain honest innocence about him. He is originally from North America and made "aliyah" [immigration to Israel] about twenty years ago. He has a great sense of humor. We laughed all during dinner. Michal is a "sabra" [born in Israel] and much more "hard nosed" and reality based but also an idealist at heart. I feel so comfortable with them both. And their two children, Naomi and Niriya, were chattering away in Hebrew and trying to speak to me in English. They are also learning Arabic in an immersion setting: a genuine attempt at respect for one another. Is it really possible?*

They look strong and happy and are growing up in such a special environment. The future is in their hands and maybe—just maybe—they will have the tools to create peace in this troubled land. The stars are twinkling in the sky and I feel very snug here in my room. I have finally escaped the big-city atmosphere that has been a part of my life always. This is the village I have always dreamed of. In fact, I feel as if I really belong! I can't wait to see this place in the daylight. (December, 1991)

Michal and Bob had tried to explain how the village operated, but most of all they wanted to know why I had come. This was not an easy question to answer. I offered my "surface" response, which was to document the peace initiatives of the villagers by collecting data from the elementary school and the "School for Peace." In order to explore the educational stories in Neve Shalom/Wahat Al-Salam, however, I had to revisit my own reasons for traveling halfway around the globe to a place engulfed by conflict. On the intellectual level, I came as an educational researcher to document a bilingual, bicultural, binational learning environment which could potentially provide a new and global dimension for exploring moral issues within the context of cultural and linguistic diversity and intergroup conflict. As mentioned earlier, though, issues of conflict resolution and peacemaking do not operate solely on a cognitive dimension. Consistent with William Pinar's (1988) view that identification with marginalized social groups is a key educational, autobiographical, and curricular issue, I came in order to confront my own "authentic voice" of sorrow by witnessing the ideological and moral distress of both peoples—the Jews and the Palestinians—who are enmeshed in this primordial struggle for survival while competing for the same physical space. Each group, in its own way, longs for legitimacy in the Middle East.

Edward Said (1990) claims that the loneliness of exile is "compelling to think about but terrible to experience" (p. 159). He goes on to say, "Exiles are cut off from their roots, their land, their past. . . . [They feel] an urgent need to reconstitute their broken lives, usually by choosing to see themselves as part of a triumphant ideology or a restored people" (p. 163). As mentioned earlier, being Jewish, for me, has always been a painful journey from the center into the margins; that is, it represents, in part, an experience of mass expulsions and genocide, a nomadic wandering throughout the centuries in order to find a sense of home and of legitimacy in the world. This "strangerhood" or "otherness" in the Diaspora[3] is a disturbing way to live. The Palestinians now also inhabit a diaspora of their own, remarkably enough as a result of the Jewish attempt to end theirs. The wounds are deep and the rift unhealable. The challenge is to learn how to accommodate the "stranger" and his or her language and culture in Israeli society, as well as in other societies (Shabatay, 1991).

Border Dialogues: Language, "Otherness," and Exile

Both Jews and Palestinians deeply feel their "otherness" as a result of very different historical realities. For example, the resurrection of Israel after the

Holocaust of World War II, and of Hebrew as a communicative language (Fellman, 1973) may be looked on as acts of Jewish redemption and of hope. "In language we inhabit, construct, and extend realities. . . . Language is what permits our being to be, to occur, to be explored, carried out and carried on. . . . It is where what we refer to as our historical, cultural, and personal identities are not simply formed, but, more significantly, performed. Language calls out for a voice, a body. Such a summons propels us beyond the limited refrain of instrumental speech and writing into song, dance, and dream" (Chambers, 1994, pp. 132–33). In the case of the Jewish people, the dream is to reshape historical space through the modern revival of the Jewish nation and thus to reenvision the place of Jews in the secular world. Hebrew has become the linguistic vessel for this dream. Being Israeli (and Jewish) can thus be looked upon as a metaphorical journey through cultural, historical, and personal borders (Derrida, 1979; Giroux, 1991).

But what of the journey of the Palestinians? What of their language and culture? As discussed in chapter 3, language is not solely a means of communication; it is also a way of constructing our cultural selves and creating a sense of belonging in the world within the context of the historical narratives of one's particular group (Chambers, 1994; Fishman, 1991; Garcia, 1994; Lambert, 1982; Spolsky, 1989; Adams & Tulasiewicz, 1994). In these SFP encounters, language plays a major role in shaping the experiences of the participants and in the construction and negotiation of knowledge within the workshops. I agree with the theoretical position of Robert Donmoyer (1985), which asserts that questions of meaning are questions about what language should be used to frame propostions about the world. "Languages are not true or false; they are appropriate or inappropriate or more or less adequate." A great obstacle to meaningful contact continues to be the asymmetrical relationship between Hebrew and Arabic in Israel. Although both are considered to be official languages, Hebrew is, in fact, the dominant language in the country. Most Palestinians are bilingual, but many feel an emotional ambivalence toward Hebrew language competence because this may represent a sense of betrayal regarding their Arab national identity (Abu-Rabia & Feuerverger, 1996). Furthermore, most Jews in Israel do not have a strong command of Arabic.

Here are two perspectives, one from a Palestinian and the other from a Jewish participant in the SFP workshop:

> To us [the Palestinians] Hebrew is the language of the oppressor. We are always approaching the Jews from a position of weakness because our Hebrew is obviously not as good as theirs. We always feel in a second-class position because of this. It's right there in the language choice. And yet if we would speak Hebrew as well as they do, we would be assimilated and lose our Arabic identity. We can't do that. It's out of the question. It's not even possible. So it's a real problem, which will not be solved until the Israelis give our identity full equality. (Palestinian male participant)

For Israeli Jews there is so much invested in Hebrew. It represents a deep victory for Jewish survival. So Hebrew is dominant. Many Jews are more hesitant to speak Arabic because, being the majority, they can get away with not knowing Arabic well and also they are afraid to have contact with Arabs because the media present them as menacing, as all being terrorists. So there's a great impasse and these workshops are trying to undo this sad state of affairs. There is suspicion on both sides. If the Palestinians choose to speak Hebrew in these discussions, there has to be a supportive atmosphere because obviously most don't speak Hebrew as well as the Jews. And if the Jewish students speak too quickly or use too much slang, then the Palestinians have lots of trouble following. I've seen it happen and it's important for the facilitators to not allow it and keep things in balance. (Jewish female participant)

Nava Sonnenschein, the codirector of the program, explained to me that one of the main goals of these SFP encounters is to overcome the obstacles of language and cultural inequality and to engage the participants in meaningful communication by personal interaction with their own lived texts. The workshops, in effect, give them the permission to embark on that journey. Some of the workshops are conducted in a "uninational" group setting (all Jewish or all Arab) in order to meet each group's emotional needs. The majority of the sessions, however, take place in a "binational" format where numerical equality between Jews and Palestinians is maintained and each group's needs are given equal priority. The SFP workshops strive to create an atmosphere in which Hebrew and Arabic hold equal balance in the workshops, and the meaning that is created is one of inclusiveness, mutual respect, and a commitment to peacemaking.

As participant-observer in a number of workshop sessions, I explored the multiplicity of tensions situated in the systemic lack of recognition in some parts of Israeli society for the legitimacy of a Palestinian national identity. On the other side, the Arab minority group is unwilling to recognize the legitimate fears that reside deep within the psyche of the Jewish group as a result of the genocide of the Holocaust, and also as a result of the hostility that most Arab nations display toward Israel's existence in the Middle East (Ajami, 1998; Benvenisti, 1995; Darwich, 1997; Friedman, 1995; Shipler, 1986). The advantages of the SFP program reside in its grassroots attempt to give Arab and Jewish young people a chance to meet on equal terms in order to begin to manage this delicate and complex conflict constructively, by using negotiation procedures and peacemaking skills. The stark reality is that without a program such as the SFP these teenagers would never have the opportunity to express their feelings toward one another. On the other hand, one disadvantage of the program lies in the fact that three intensive days in a neutral environment are not enough to come to terms with the enormity of the issues that must be faced. In fact, one difficulty that may arise is that the participants might treat what happens in this special place as unreal or as "just a dream." This, in fact, is a good argument to place more emphasis on the follow-up aspects of the program. The courage to bring together these two groups in their formative teenage years, however, stands as a profoundly significant step in the right direction toward peace.

The First Day: Narratives of Vulnerability

I remember vividly the icy silence that descended on the room as we began the first meeting of the workshop. I sat quietly in the back, as nervous as everybody else that morning. We could all hear the deafening sound of chairs creaking in the cold and damp. It was a moment heavy with waiting, but open with infinite possibilities. There was so much meaning in this silence of brooding and pain. The only movements were coming from outside the door, where the village dogs had congregated as if they knew something special and difficult was happening. I sensed that they wanted to help us through this terrible impasse. I wonder if any of the participants felt this. They were all so self-absorbed in their mutual fears. Many sat stooped as if they were carrying the weight of all the Israeli-Arab wars on their backs. I thought of Atlas, the Greek god with the globe on his shoulders. It was a sublime moment of perfect symmetry—a moment at which everything stood before us, where we could make or break anything. It was a moment of awe.

Finally, Ahmed, the Arab facilitator, calmly outlined the schedule for the morning and allayed fears by clearly stating that this was not going to be easy and that there were no expectations. There was a reassuring quality to his voice and warm sighs filled the air with relief. Ahmed was very firm on the following point: differences between the two groups must be acknowledged at the outset; these included differences in nationality and culture and religion, majority or minority affiliation within Israel, and the varying ways in which political and cultural and linguistic realities affect each side. He pointed out that one significant feature of the workshop was, in fact, to supply students with information on the conflict relevant to the encounter, and which would prepare them for a constructive dialogue. For example, Ahmed explained to me in private later that morning that in Palestinian schools in the West Bank in particular, students are exposed very selectively to their own history and culture. They have little or no exposure to Jewish history. Similarly, the Jewish teenagers arrive at the workshops with many preconceived notions and stereotypes about the Palestinians. There was a half-hour break and we all shuffled out into the courtyard. The dogs, wanting to play, were eagerly waiting for us. The air felt a little less heavy as I watched some participants mingling together, drinking soda and chatting about the dogs. Others stayed in their respective corners. Then it was time to return to the room.

At the beginning of the discussions, many Jewish participants opted for a blurring of the differences between the two groups in order to avoid painful and threatening divisive issues. When the facilitators asked the group whether the focus should be on interpersonal issues or on political ones, the majority of the Jewish group chose the former; most of the Palestinian group chose the latter. Interestingly, the Jewish option won out. Rachel, a Jewish participant, explained, "It's better we get to know each other, before we go to the controversial issues." An unrealistic fantasy of "togetherness" began to take hold. But after a while Yasir, an Arab participant, quietly protested by saying, "It's very frightening to look at the real issues, but if we don't, nothing will change. And this whole meeting will be a waste of time." Many of the Jewish participants glared belligerently at him. What he did was invaluable, however. He opened a window onto an agenda for real dialogue about living in a state of war and terror. In fact, it was critical to get past the niceties of good manners and empty words as quickly as possible. Evidently, it was difficult to overcome the fear and mutual suspicion that lay underneath the sanitized surface of fragile smiles.

Ahmed remarked later in a personal interview:

> While the starting point of the work is based on recognizing our similarities, from our standpoint, it is equally as important to stress the differences in order to recognize and cope with the conflict. Every attempt to remain on the level of "we're all human" mitigates the opportunity to touch upon the painful issues that divide the two peoples. It is not easy but there is no other way. As time passes and the participants become more familiar with one another, through discussion and through sharing meals, and [through] "breaking the ice" sorts of activities as well as leisure activities, they begin to loosen up and start to skirt around the real issues of the conflict. Then we know there is a chance for a real dialogue to begin. The question of who is more of a victim, who is more guilty, who is more humane emerges and then unbearable feelings start to come out.

Finally, after many attempts on the part of the Palestinian group to tell the Jewish group to "face the reality of the conflict," a Jewish participant, Ariel, exclaimed, "OK, we'd better get down to business and start talking honestly. I didn't come all this way for nothing! Let's face it, we do have stereotypes that all Arabs are terrorists." It was a pivotal moment—and a painful one. Ariel was then made to feel like a traitor by some of the Jewish participants. A number of the Jewish teenagers jumped in to say that they did not feel that way and that Ariel was being an "idiot." They had entered a danger zone in terms of who was in control of the situation. Ariel had shifted the balance of power and thus placed the Jewish group in a vulnerable postion. I could sense that the Jewish participants on the whole wanted to escape from dealing with the situation. The Arab group was silent. At that moment, Ahmed, the Arab facilitator, stepped in and pointedly asked the Arab participants whether anyone had a response to this impasse. Tirzah, the Jewish facilitator, then spoke softly but with conviction:

> We are here not to be polite and show how well-mannered we are. We are here in order to try and deal with this terrible reality in our lives. Let's try to take advantage of the opportunity. I promise you that I won't point any fingers at people. I know for one thing that I have felt that stereotype very

strongly when I was growing up. Ahmed and I have had some pretty heavy discussions about how Jews and Palestinians perceive each other. What are your feelings on this?

By confessing her own biases, Tirzah was in effect giving permission to the Palestinian group to enter the discussion. A space was created to shape text and to liberate voices. Ahmed continued the process by stating that all topics of discussion should be negotiated among all participants. The facilitators tried to legitimize the anxieties that both Jews and Arabs suffer in Israeli society. It was time for another break, and I noticed how the Jewish and Palestinian students were beginning to mingle more freely with one another. In fact, when they returned to the room, some began to "border cross" by choosing to sit with members of the other group. Ahmed and Tirzah continued to mediate and to prevent some participants from manipulating the discussion. They talked very openly about the processes occurring in the room. They focused on the dynamics of dominant/ subordinate group relations and how the realities inside the room paralleled those outside in the wider society. For example, in reference to the "Ariel" incident, Ahmed pointedly chastised Menachem, one of the Jewish participants who had attempted to silence Ariel by calling him an idiot, and by delegitimizing Ariel's comments about Jewish stereotypes of Arabs:

> Do you not realize that you completely annihilated Ariel's voice because you were so intent on keeping the status quo? I understand that you were threatened and felt anxious by [because of] Ariel's comments but that's why we're here. You have to allow people to speak and you have to listen to their point[s] of view even if [they are] disturbing. It's the only way to begin facing the conflict.

He asked what Menachem thought about this. Menachem responded in this way:

> Maybe Ariel has a point but we come by these images honestly. I am afraid of the terrorist attacks, like the one on the bus in Jerusalem not long ago. I hate the feeling of being the "weak Jew" who can be attacked. It goes back to the Jews in Europe during the war. They had no power and they were slaughtered. And the truth is the Arabs in the neighboring countries here in the Middle East don't really want peace with us. They are enemies to us. They make us feel like we don't belong here. We have to defend ourselves.

Another break. This time the students started to mix even more freely as they walked to the cafeteria. I decided to take a walk to the elementary school to clear my head. On the way, I saw two of the workshop participants: a Jewish girl, Shira, and Assam, a Palestinian boy. They were sitting on a rock, deep in an intense discussion. They saw me and motioned me to join them. Assam looked upset, insecure, and angry but was willing to talk to Shira, who had luminous brown eyes and very pale skin. His eyes were a flashing blue set in a dark, sensitive face. They were both seventeen years old, and voicing for the first time their fears and concerns in this emotionally safe place located on the margins of society. They both spoke with great feeling—trying to cross the abyss that had separated their peoples for so long.

> *Assam:* It is time for Israeli Jews to realize that we have an identity as a nation, the Palestinian people. We want our existence to be accepted.
>
> *Shira:* I came here very afraid and I still am. But I want to do something positive with my fear.

Assam and Shira sat next to each other when they returned to the workshop. I could sense that all of the students were more prepared now to acknowledge the complexity of the conflict. Their actions illustrated the words of bell hooks (1990, p. 150), who writes that "marginality is much more than a site of deprivation. . . . It is also the site of radical possibility, a space of resistance. . . . It offers to one the possibility of radical perspective from which to see and create, to imagine alternatives, new worlds." Clearer lines were drawn in terms of national identity. Stories of desperation and despair emerged from both sides. Power struggles between both groups became apparent. Many of the Arab participants expressed frustration over what they saw as intransigence on the part of their Jewish peers. They struggled to gain recognition for the acts of oppression committed against the Palestinians, particularly those in the Occupied Territories.

An Arab participant:

You never legitimize what happens to the Palestinians. You always put us down. You see us as primitive, cruel, knife wielding. When will that stop?

A Jewish participant:

Maybe we do put you down, but if we stop, you will do the same to us only more cruelly. If power will be in your hands, when they come to stab me—will you defend me?

The session ended in a painful cliffhanger. It was the end of the first day. We all returned to our rooms. I was living with a family in the village and quietly walked into the little guest room. I was thankful that nobody was home; I was too exhausted to speak. I wrote in my journal that night:

Neve Shalom/Wahat Al-Salam. Words with an exotic flavor. An adventure that I want to be a part of. This little village where people have given Life meaning. Here one confronts one's own existence, one's identity, one's "neshama" ["spirit" in Hebrew]. What inspires confidence is the sheer will and energy that these villagers have chosen to give to this place in order that their children may have the possibility of a more peaceful future. But hearing the stories, today, of these young teenagers in the "School for Peace" is heartbreaking. The suffering, the fear, the anxiety is almost too much too bear. You see it in their eyes. I don't know how they handle all the tension. Can this hideous conflict ever be resolved? It seems so unfair that these young people are in a situation of war with one another. I think of young people in other countries whose lives are more carefree and I ask myself, Why does it have to be so harsh here? I think my Holocaust background makes me even more sensitive. I am vascillating between hopeful highs and devastating lows of despair. This place will do it to you. I'm emotionally drained. I want to see a happy ending for a change! My heart is full of pain. What is illusion, what is truth? So full of beauty, and so full of conflict! I feel a bottomless well of sadness for this tragedy here between the Jews and Arabs in this "promised land." It's an emotional hurricane! (December, 1991)

The Second Day: Longing for Legitimacy

Each group had great difficulty recognizing the needs of the other. Various activities were organized to familiarize the participants with the conflicts in each other's lives (for more detail on the specific organization of SFP workshop activities, see Sonnenschein & Halaby, 1991; Zak, 1992). One technique that was very helpful in this regard was a role-playing activity, which lasted most of the day. It was fascinating to watch how the skits unfolded, and how key they were in allowing the students to bring out their voices. It gave them an opportunity to confront real problems and to be critical and empathetic of the processes that occur around them. The group was divided into subgroups of three or four participants. Each participant in the subgroup described a conflict in which he or she was involved within the family, with friends, in class, or elsewhere. Most participants who dramatized the stories played the role of someone else.

After half an hour of preparation for each skit, the subgroups reconvened and presented their dramatizations before the whole group. I watched as a Jewish student played the role of a Palestinian mother in the West Bank who had just been informed that one of her children had been killed by Israeli soldiers in a confrontation. She began to cry and so did most of the participants. It was a pivotal moment. One Jewish boy blurted out in the silence of sorrow, "Why choose that example? It's not very common." Many Arab as well as Jewish peers retorted in disapproval. One Palestinian girl said, "The fact that it happens is horrifying. Don't you understand that?" Another skit involved a bus in Jerusalem which was attacked by Arab terrorists. Many (Jewish) passengers were killed or maimed. It was also a very frightening portrayal. Again, there were many sorrowful tears and much anger.

The following are some of the comments that emerged out of this role-playing:

> You [the Palestinians] always see us in the aggressor role. You never want to acknowledge how afraid we are with all this terrorism. In fact, we're such a small nation engulfed by huge Arab countries all around who want to get rid of us. All the wars show that. (A Jewish male participant)

> But you [the Israelis] have one of the strongest armies in the world. You don't want to give the Palestinians their rights and their nationhood. Violence brings more violence. We deserve to have our homeland too. (A Palestinian male participant)

> When I close my eyes and imagine Palestinians [from the West Bank] I see masses of angry people wanting to take out their revenge on me. And suicide bombers killing my family on a bus or in a shopping square. These are my nightmares. I know it isn't rational but it is happening and there is so much tension everywhere. (A Jewish female participant)

> What do the Israeli Jews have to be afraid of? Their settlers run around with guns and what do the Palestinians respond with? Stones and knives. Do you have any idea what it is like? Permission from the military authorities to do anything, the military roadblocks, the soldiers everywhere . . . (A Palestinian female participant)

> So many of us [Israeli Jews] are in favor of a Palestinian state. It's not like Israel wanted to conquer territory and oppress a million Palestinians. The Arabs threatened to wipe us off the map in 1967 and we protected ourselves. And there have been more wars since then. Of course I sympathize with the Palestinians but there are two sides to it. We're also losing lives and coming out of this with broken bones and a broken spirit. The Hamas is a dangerous, fundamentalist force that is intent on our destruction. (A Jewish female participant)

The complexity of the issues began to crystallize for many. Ouaffa, a Palestinian female student, explained her feelings to me halfway through the workshop:

> At the beginning both groups were very suspicious of each other. We didn't feel safe to express that right away. We just wanted to show that our position was right. We were totally blind to each other's needs. There was lots of politeness, silence, and then as time went on, lots of arguing, and then we finally got to negotiating what we would talk about. Our facilitators were great. They just let things come out. They were supportive of how we felt no matter what. That opened room for discussion and new ways of understanding one another. For example, we the Palestinians have over and over again brought up the issue of discrimination and vulnerability as a minority in Israel, which is of course so true, but for the first time I listened as the Jewish students expressed their fears as a minority in the Middle East. I never really appreciated how afraid they were and that they had a right to that fear. After all, they really are a tiny minority in the Middle Eastern world, and most of the terrorist attacks are against them.

One participant, a Jewish male, expressed the issue very succinctly in one of the group discussions:

> When someone feels that his or her pain is not being recognized—especially about our feelings about the Holocaust—it is difficult for that person to listen and give empathy to someone else in pain.

A Palestinian participant retorted angrily:

> You always bring up the Holocaust. We [the Arabs] are not responsible for that. You may feel very vulnerable in the Middle East but that doesn't give you the right to oppress and humiliate us, the Palestinians. What about the terrible stuff happening in the Occupied Territories? You can't turn your eyes away from it and pretend it isn't happening!

The atmosphere was highly charged. I held my breath and choked back my own painful feelings. The participants were opening up, and the raw divisions were becoming exposed. Conflicts were coming to the fore in the form of pressure that one group exerted on the other—and one voice on the other. Through role-playing, the students were given the opportunity to cross personal and cultural borders as a way of clarifying their own journeys toward a vision of their national identities. These are dialogic works in Mihail Bakhtin's (1981) sense. It is a way, as Roger Simon (1992, p. 17) puts it, "of getting students beyond the world they already know in order to challenge and provoke their existing views of the way things are and the way they should be." There was an overwhelming need for these adolescents to claim their cultural, social, and historical places in the world—to give reality to their vulnerabilities.

The Role of the Facilitators: Teaching Conflict Resolution

At some point during the second day the role of the facilitators emerged more clearly. Their task in this charged environment was a formidable one indeed. They were cognizant of the fact that they had an asymmetrical power relationship with their participants and that an unintentional verbal comment or nonverbal expression could greatly influence the dynamic of the group. Theirs was truly a tightrope walk, the metaphor used by Michal Zak (1992). I continually witnessed their profoundly intricate excursions around the injured lived experiences that the participants began to reveal as a sense of safety and trust was created during the hours that followed. Ahmed, the Palestinian facilitator, told me during one break:

> I am not a politician but I have a real feeling that I am now doing political work, in the good sense of the word. The SFP is an educational institution, which devotes itself to a political goal—but only in the context of bettering human relations. I consider myself therefore to be an educator who works in the political terrain. It's as if this village and this SFP is a daily protest against war and injustice. And our conflict resolution work is full of tension. A friend of mine [who is an Arab living

in a village in the north of Israel] sees this place as a devious means for the Israeli government to justify its actions by saying, "But look, we are doing good things to bring the two peoples together." He's never been here and yet he's making this terrible judgment. He simply doesn't want to see that here the process of peace has begun, that it IS possible if we want it to be. And it isn't as if the Israeli government is so happy about this place. [It's] quite ambivalent. So again, where does he get this information? It's all stereotyping and misinformation. I live here. I know it's real. Faisal Husseini, a Palestinian leader, was here last year and he said very openly that what goes on in this village and in the SFP is the ideal that we are striving for. For me that confirms that what I am doing is valid and has political as well as human significance. Without a political consciousness it is hard to work out our problems here. So that is always in the background as the students come together to the workshops. What excites me is the dynamic that is created during the encounters. Most of the adolescents that come are interested in speaking about the political situation and that's a point of departure. But they quickly begin to realize that it's much deeper than that. I demand from them something more—to sit together, to dare talk about their fears and their mutual distrust, to talk about their personal problems, to reverse the wall of ignorance that separates them. They have to start looking at the issues in a more balanced way, and that's authentic political expression.

According to Sonnenschein and Halaby (1991), the working method for the facilitators is based on intensive experiential knowledge in social and psychological intergroup processes, specifically designed for the Jewish-Palestinian workshop context. They are trained to explore the conflict through the lived experiences of the participants as they unfold in the sessions. In the sessions that I observed, there was a constant linkage between the discussions in the workshop and the reality outside, working from the premise that the SFP group serves as a microcosm of the larger reality. The facilitators continually returned to the central thread that runs through the conflict and the group dynamic of the workshop: the power struggle over who controls the situation and the failure to grant legitimacy to each group as part of that power struggle. Many Jewish students found it difficult to grant legitimacy to the Palestinian national identity, whereas many Arabs were not willing to grant legitimacy to the fears felt by the Jews. At bottom, each group needed to acknowledge its own history, and especially that of the other.

What emerged for me, as I observed the unfolding of the sessions, was the salience of the personal stories. As researcher, I believe now more than ever that without crossing into the land of personal history, there is much territory we cannot begin to walk on within the context of peace education (Felman & Laub, 1992; Bar-Tal, 1995; Geretz, 1995; Gumpel, 1996; Lemish, 1995). With every passing moment of my participant observation, I saw this conflict resolution enterprise as a kind of group psychoanalysis in action. Right from the start, the facilitators carefully deconstructed the masquerade of polite manners that blocked the potential for dialogue. The encounter sessions, too, followed the experiential learning model of Paulo Freire in that he always envisaged the teacher as facilitator, not as a lecturer or transmitter of all knowledge. These sessions focused on pedagogical exercises essential for teaching conflict resolution and peaceful coexistence (Pivovarov, 1994).

Both Tirzah and Ahmed showed me how teaching conflict resolution can be seen as a hall of mirrors, a central symbol of the confusion in society about the urgency of peace education. They were not afraid to unearth the "cosmic silence" (to borrow Matthew Fox's phrase) buried in the failed hopes, humiliation, sorrow, and rage of the primordial struggle that both Jews and Arabs in Israel and in the West Bank find themselves. They were, after all, dealing with participants in their formative stages of development, and these tribal bonds to the land intersect with everything in their spiritual and psychological lives. Refusing to look at the illusions and realities of this attachment to a common homeland is a dangerous game, and this understanding is, in fact, a fundamental issue for the survival of both peoples in this tormented land (Benvenisti, 1996).

I documented the voices of these individuals on the margins in order to explore the epistemologically complex terrain of conflict resolution in the SFP program. Teaching conflict resolution, therefore, has a literal life, but as I watched the sessions unfold, I sensed that it also has a spiritual dimension. This SFP encounter attempted to empower the participants individually and as members of two different national groups—but also as a group of human beings whose purpose it is to examine the thorny issues that bar the road to peace. The facilitators tried to engage their charges in a discourse of deeply rooted existential anxieties because that is the reality of the situation. They did this without pointing fingers at anyone; the goal was to give each individual adequate protection and respect. This is not a simple matter, given the gravity of the conflict and the resulting narrowness of vision and blind constraints that permeate the polarized landscape. What struck me most of all was how the facilitators—each in his or her own way—were able to incorporate aesthetic and moral dimensions in the midst of the distress experienced within this peace education enterprise. "We have to confront the deep feelings of humiliation that Palestinians feel [especially in the West Bank]. That can hurt more than physical violence. We have to take our share of responsibility for this situation," explained Tirzah to the Jewish participants at the end of the afternoon.

A Palestinian participant described the role of the facilitators this way:

Ahmed and Tirzah were like our intellectual leaders. They taught the values of democracy and coexistence. They didn't preach politics. Sometimes they played the devil's advocate, but that was for educational reasons. As a young Palestinian, I felt [as if] they were listening to what I had to say; they made me feel important. Inside that room [where the workshops took place] they made me feel equal and gave me confidence in myself and made me feel like a member of Israeli society where real reforms are necessary. They understood when I showed my anger and hatred. My only regret is that all Arab students don't get a chance to have this opportunity.

The facilitators displayed, in spite of the difficulties, the joys of being fully present within the participatory dynamics of involvement and detachment in their work. They seemed to know when to speak and when to keep silent. And no matter what the tone of each conversation, they never failed to honor the experiences of the individual participants, and in so doing, showed a profound caring which, as Bakhtin (1981, 1986), Carol Gilligan (1982), Nel Noddings (1984, 1991), Mark Tappan (1991), and so many other educators posit, is at the root of all good teaching. These facilitators embodied the notion that there is no difference between teaching conflict resolution which is consciously displayed and teaching conflict resolution which is unconsciously lived. To my mind, therein lies the power of the SFP peace encounter.

The Third Day: Deconstructing the Discourse of Victimhood

Throughout the third day, the participants grappled with their feelings of victimhood. Underneath the surface of the immediate moment lurked the profound woundedness that makes reconciliation between Palestinian and Jew very problematic. Bourdieu (1996) suggests that metaphor can be used as a powerful device that both conceptualizes and illuminates the educational discourse. Indeed, the metaphor of the "suffering victim" stands guard like Cerberus, the three-headed dog of Pluto's underworld in Greek mythology, forbidding entrance through the gate of Jewish-Palestinian relations. My commentary is not meant to minimize the victimization that both Jews and Palestinians have suffered as a result of profound historical and political realities. Their victimhood is the ghost that lies in the shadows of every interaction—the disturbing presence which has caused their estrangement. This sense of deep injury comes from two specific events: the displacement of the Palestinians as a result of the Israeli War of Independence in 1948, and the genocide of the Jews in Europe during World War II. These catastrophes are deep wounds in the hearts and minds of both peoples and have had severe consequences. I do not by any means claim that the two woundings are symmetrical. But they are indeed intertwined within the Jewish-Palestinian conflict. The collective ethos of the state of Israel is based on the affirmation of the nation as a refuge for the Jewish people in the aftermath of the devastation of European Jews during the Holocaust of World War II, as already discussed. Israel, therefore, has become a symbolic representation of the passage from the annihilated soul of the Jewish people to its resurrected personhood, and therein lies the struggle to establish a sense of national identity and to claim a political and cultural place in the Middle East.

The Intifada[4] arose from another kind of wounding. The Israeli Arabs want to be recognized as a legitimate national minority which is linked to the Palestinian's demands for a state in the Occupied Territories (the West Bank and

Gaza). The sad truth is that this yearning for legitimacy is shared by both Jews and Palestinians. The Palestinians long for their own state and the Israeli Jews long to be wholly recognized as a legitimate state within the geopolitical framework of the Middle East. Both hopes are still only dreams. The "border pedagogies" used by the facilitators focus directly on this existential anguish. When the participants in the workshops slowly began to recognize the legitimacy of each other's national liberation movement, that of the Palestinian people and that of the Jewish people, the dialogue became equal. Or, at least, the possibility of equality emerged. Not all problems were solved in the workshops; however, a place of equal dialogue was painfully created, and in that place, progress became possible. Ahmed said to me in private, "The feelings of the participants should not be suppressed; indeed they must be honored and allowed to surface." I witnessed how the facilitators encouraged the students to move beyond the impasse and open a space where each group could attempt to conquer the obstacle of its own pain and express empathy for that of the other group. The intention was for the encounter to become a safe place where trust is built and therefore can become the psychological container for these "bad" feelings and permit the participants to recognize their problematic emotions toward one another. In this site of authentic negotiation participants are encouraged to abandon any pretense to a fixed truth about their views of the others—and the concrete structure of their mistrust and anxieties thus begins to crumble.

The stories that emerged opened up a space for bringing the specificity of needs to a common ground. The disputes, arguments, and anger-filled discussions about injury, loss, and the death of loved ones shaped a territory of the unexpected which the participants on both sides recognized for the first time as their common inheritance of exile, displacement, and diaspora. I was confronted with a vista composed of diametrically opposed subjectivities that had to be restructured into a meaningful present. Mordechai, a Jewish male teenager, confessed in the middle of the day:

> Before this workshop I was embarrassed to show emotions; to speak about love, sympathy—about how afraid I am to go into the army and to have to deal with what is going on in the Territories. The fact that the workshop focused on emotional rather than merely rational elements helped me with this. Today I will not hesitate to say what I feel.

After an arduous discussion about social injustice in the Occupied Territories, Temada, a Palestinian female participant, said:

> It's about time that we Palestinians are able to show our anger about the situation. When I think about what is going on in the Territories, and I have relatives there who are suffering daily—I want to scream.

Ronit, a Jewish female participant, sighed in relief as she explained what she felt was important about these workshops:

> These workshops don't just deal with dry theoretical material, but confront the conflict head-on through a very experiential approach. So

many people feel a sense of powerlessness and anger in our society. That kind of frustration is so deadly. And yet we're all afraid to really talk about it from our hearts. We're discussing the effect that all the terrorism has on each of us personally. I have hardly ever discussed that in my regular classrooms. It's too overwhelming. So we try to bravely go on after every attack. But inside our hearts are being torn up. We still feel like the persecuted Jew deep inside.

Rafiq, a male Israeli Arab, captured the mood of the day:

I always had the feeling that the Jews in Israel were so confident about their place in the world. It comes as quite a revelation to realize that underneath their external bravado, they have terrible feelings of being in exile and feel so worried because of their history of persecution. It's so strange to learn this. I've had some personal discussions with some people here that I will never forget, no matter what happens. It is really quite a strange mess.

In the midst of their dialogues and journal writing, the students became familiar with their unique, personal perceptions of their places in society, their search for justice in this conflictual existence, and ways in which they might contribute to changing the status quo, at least in their own minds. The complexity of identity always pervaded their narrative inquiry. Discussing subjective perceptions of ethnic, national, and linguistic identities involves a great deal of personal reflection, which strikes at the very core of how we define ourselves in the world. The students discovered that this is all tied into their sense of purpose and self-worth in society. Through the sharing of their journals, they heard the voices of the "other" within lived experiences, and as a result of this influence, their own stories become reconstructed and retold from a fresh new perspective.

It seems as if a collective story was being written; from the particular to a general understanding of identity issues. The students inspected their individual, familial, and cultural differences to find that within these differences they actually have something in common. Michael Connelly and Jean Clandinin (1990) discuss the multiple levels at which narrative inquiry can proceed: "As we engage in a reflective research process, our stories are often restoried and changed as we as teacher and/or researcher 'give back' to each other ways of seeing our stories." We become "plurivocal" (Barnieh, 1989) in writing narratively. The "I" can speak as researcher, teacher, woman, commentator, of seeing our stories. One of the "I"s is as a member of one or more ethnolinguistic groups. And yet in living the narrative inquiry process, we are one person. We are also one in the writing. But in the writing of narrative, it becomes important to sort out whose voice is the dominant one when we write "I." The experiences of these participants in the "School for Peace" program concur with recent research in philosophy and psychology which states that narrative structure is fundamental to the formation of the self (for example, Brockelman, 1985; Carr, 1986; Hanson, 1986; Polkinghorne, 1988; Sarbin, 1986).

The facilitators encouraged reflective practice on the part of the students about their life histories. Their narrative inquiry led to startling new insights into their personal and professional lives and to a more compassionate understanding of the complexities of the Israeli-Palestinian impasse.

The Specter of the Holocaust Revisited: Reactions to the Persian Gulf War

The workshop dialogues above represent a vision of reality that inhabits the shadows and lies in the shadings of ambiguity. The memory of the Holocaust was the eternal ghost that haunted the sessions, but it was especially apparent on the third day. Many Jewish participants spoke of the tension that was engendered by the Persian Gulf War in 1991, which began eleven months before this workshop was held (when Saddam Hussein of Iraq invaded Kuwait and, among other actions, sent SCUD missiles into the heart of Israel) and how it created a kind of posttraumatic response to the Holocaust for many people in Israel. Whether they personally were survivors or children of survivors did not matter. The Holocaust festers like an open wound that demands attention in the "here and now" of the Jewish-Palestinian conflict. "We [the Israeli Jews] are once more tasting collective fear . . . that is a very elementary taste drawn from primal depths" (as cited in Benvenisti, p. 131). Most Palestinians, and Arabs generally in the Middle East, find it difficult to understand this phenomenon, according to David Shipler (1986). They see the conflict as localized and the Jews as oppressors. Many are indifferent to this utterly unimaginable trauma that has marked Israeli (and other) Jews irrevocably. Some Arab participants said that they thought the Jews were using the Holocaust as "a ploy to get what they want in the Territories and to justify their oppressive behavior." The Palestinians, too, have suffered greatly (as a result of the Middle East conflict) but they fear that in comparison with the Holocaust, their pain will not be taken seriously. "It is as if we, the Palestinians, have to pay for what the Nazis did to the Jews in Europe. It's not fair," confided a Palestinian participant from the West Bank in private. Indeed, it is not fair, and here, I believe, lies the paradox that stands in the way of reconciliation and healing.

As discussed in Chapter 2, the Gulf War also underscored the differential emotional reaction of Arabs and Jews (those already committed to peaceful coexistence) toward the reckless behavior of Saddam Hussein. At the end of the day, Tirzah described how the events of the Gulf War deeply affected her:

> There was a sick feeling that overcame me in the sealed rooms meant to protect us against the toxic chemicals that Saddam promised to deploy with the missiles. He boasted that he would burn half of Israel! The feeling went straight back to the gas chambers of the concentration camps where many of our relatives were murdered. We Jews shared in a collective fear. It was a totally different experience emotionally for the

Arabs—as if we, both Arabs and Jews, were in the same room but watching two totally different films!

Ahmed added:

> The Holocaust was an event of such horror and magnitude that of course, we Palestinians can't compete with that kind of suffering. But I think that the Jews have to get past that and acknowledge our own pain. Saddam, rightly or wrongly, came across at the beginning of the Gulf War as a leader in the Middle East who could restore our badly broken Arab identity and pride. Many Palestinians were entranced by that. It is important to realize just how low and injured we feel. I hope we can get over this "gulf"—literally. We [the Jews and Palestinians] have to keep talking and listening to one another.

In spite of this existential tragedy of conflict between the two peoples, their language in the SFP workshops traveled from the margins of the web of enmity in which they were entrapped to the center of the discussion—where their discourse created a sense of belonging in their common suffering, rather than in a competition of suffering. A kind of blended story of victimhood began to emerge. In other words, each group began to recognize in the other's narrative its own story, and the interconnected themes of displacement and strangerhood which bring the wandering Jew and Palestinian together from their arid terrain of enmity and despair. The intertwined destinies of Ishmael and Isaac now stared one another in the face. Participants began to name the historical sources of their conflict, and to name is to gain power through language. A Jewish participant's reflections at the end of the third day are relevant.

> Trying to find a route to peaceful coexistence is a very radical political act. You look at this country, where there is so much hatred and fear and a closing of the mind. For the most part, the Arabs live in their villages and we live in ours, side by side. And each one creates their own fantasies and myths about the other, all embroidered with fear. In this workshop, I feel as if some of those myths are being broken down and we are examining one another directly. We have escaped from our "ghettos" and I think that's radical. It's an authentic encounter. There have been some horrible arguments in these workshops but in spite of the fact that we're still far from having solved the problem, I personally feel less despairing. Because nobody forced the other to give up [his or her] identity. There were times when we got past the power games and that was incredible.

One of the most interesting aspects of that third day was not so much who spoke but who listened. In the shadowy spaces, the rage of injustice was given a hearing, thus stretching the boundaries of language and meaning. The listening invited the participants to construct knowledge and to maneuver within the zones of ambiguity, to rethink their sense of time and place within the depths of the conflict. These observations encouraged me as researcher to consider the epistemological value of the images that were woven into the fabric of the discussions. These images became a pedagogical device for conflict resolution and peacemaking residing on the precarious borders of reflection, speculation, and reconsideration.

A Palestinian male participant discussed the Intifada as a struggle toward coexistence:

> The Intifada for me is a struggle for equality, liberty, and the realization of our rights. In this workshop we talked about creating better relations between these two peoples who live on this land. I don't know whether we were successful. But I am persuaded more than ever that we have no choice but coexistence. I feel after this workshop that the conflict isn't just territorial or geographic, but very much more centered on the quality of our relations as two peoples who are bound to one another whether we like it or not—we have to find ways of understanding that. To me it becomes a spiritual issue as well as a political one. I never thought of that until today. For example, the problem of who owns Jerusalem is so important. Neither side wants to give up [its] rights to Jerusalem. Can we find a way to appreciate each other's cultures? Peace. What does that mean? Learning to trust the other? Putting down the weapons? Believing in each other's fears? Is it utopia only, or is it possible? I see that in this village it's possible. So maybe it is.

A Jewish male participant gave his reaction:

> The workshop offered us the framework and the time to confront difficult questions, and to reach a point at which we could listen to each other without feeling a need to compete over who suffers more. We saw that as Jews and Palestinians we shared a mutual need to have our pain recognized, or understood, by the other. Without answering that need I'm not sure that we will succeed in building the trust which is essential to any serious attempt at cooperation.

All during the three-day workshop there was a remarkable oscillation between the frontier perspective of facing the enemy and acknowledging differences on the one hand, and the static wasteland of hatred and fear on the other. Within this passage was the struggle to establish a modus vivendi—to release diverse voices in the wilderness of competing victimhood. The sessions were permeated with the internalized guilt, doubt, fear, sorrow, and hatred that both groups experience within the mental prisons of this bitter conflict.

At the end of the third day, a Palestinian female sadly asked:

> My younger brothers are already terrified of the Israeli soldiers. They see the violent stuff on television and they know it's real. How do I explain it to them?

A Jewish female participant summed it up:

> We're both drowning in quicksand next to each other, but can we stretch out our hands to one another or will we sink in the mud with our raised fists?

That last evening the students enjoyed a social gathering filled with laughter and traditional Arab and Israeli dancing and singing. They exchanged telephone numbers and addresses. The next day, in the morning fog, they slowly bid one another good-bye, tears in many eyes. I asked a Palestinian girl whether she thought this workshop would make a difference. She confided to me as she climbed onto the bus:

> It has already made a difference. Something in me has changed. We may not have solved the problem, but I come away with a real treasure—my heart is now filled with less hatred and instead there's a greater understanding of how complicated this conflict is. I saw what's behind the mask of my enemy. I think the process has to start from there.

Figure 4–1 Some of the School for Peace participants on the last day of the workshop at Neve Shalom/Wahat Al-Salam. (Courtesy of the author.)

Concluding Remarks

The "School for Peace" workshop's purpose is to create a perspective for conflict resolution and an awareness for both Jews and Palestinians of the need to live together in everyday circumstances, albeit holding onto their respective wounds. My intention was to document the experiences of the participants and their facilitators in order to present a multilayered picture of the very complex and arduous process toward coexistence. This workshop encounter represented for me a reframing of social and psychological spaces, a radical shift in understanding and interpretation of events, attentive to the nuanced differences in the Jewish and Palestinian histories. Throughout my observation in these sessions, I was confronted with elements of poetry amidst the fragile relationships that emerged—of misery, fear, ambiguity, and sometimes bliss. Conflict resolution does not operate from a limited menu but rather must be infinitely variable in order to be effective. The salient message that weaves its way through the fabric of the workshops is the continual need among the participants for negotiation, discussion, dialogue, and change in their search to give equal expression to their national identities. They have been too fearful, too angry, and too isolated to recognize the legitimacy of each other's presence.

I attempted to inquire into the social and psychological complexities inherent in this three-day educational odyssey toward peaceful coexistence. Indeed, my researcher self acknowledged that whether in open conflict or not, we are all in search of balance and we seek in our peers or participants the "other" that is missing, or the "self" that is recognizable. Conflict is not a wholly fixed thing; sometimes it is the tiny and seemingly irrelevant comments that can damage or destroy our relationships. Sometimes it is the blatant terrorist attacks. The workshop discussions coalesced with a consistency of themes, images, and poetic voices that could be appreciated as a unified sequence of altercations, confrontations, and negotiations. I have tried to weave together a research story which would walk inside and outside the center of things, acknowledging the illusions, fantasies, and possibilities of peace in this troubled part of the world. Within the layers of each dialogue, the concept of teaching and learning conflict resolution often seemed more fiction than reality. Sometimes it was a magical connection of special intimacy. The search for negotiation and reconciliation was at the core of this dialogical relation. It is not formulaic—what we long for in peace education is a "communion," in Buber's terms, the dialogue between persons which results in mutual validation. It is what Freire calls liberation as a mutual process. To my mind, teaching conflict resolution is an intuitive art. In the end what matters most is how we treat each other—how much respect and care we give each other in and especially out of the peace classroom, in and out of our texts and our curricula.

Jews and Palestinians continue to search for an affirmation of their places in geopolitical terms, and the power of their unresolved history stands as a moral dilemma within the larger framework of the search for global peace. The reentry of the Jewish people into the geopolitical cartography of the world, through the modern state of Israel, has been hard won. Two thousand years of exile, wandering, persecution, and ultimately genocide, lie deep within their psyche, creating a collective story of the quintessential stranger-outsider in the geography of humankind. Their place in the Middle East is still highly contested with great hostility by the Arab nations that surround them. Many Palestinians do not understand this. They see the Israeli Jews as aggressors and oppressors who have come to take away their homes. The Palestinians have their own story of dislocation, and misery, and they are entitled to it. Their story is now also one of diaspora and exile. This is the tragedy of the Jewish-Palestinian conflict that now stands at the crossroads of war and peace, of hope and anguish. This is why I felt privileged to be present at these "School for Peace" education workshops.

The eloquent words of Moroccan French writer Tahar Ben Jelloun seem to encapsulate the dreamlike quality of this three-day encounter for me as I watched the harrowing discussions of these participants in their journey toward the threshold of the possibility of peace:

> *This story has something of the night; it is obscure and yet rich in images; it should end with a feeble, gentle light. . . . This story is also a desert. You will have to walk barefoot on the hot sand, walk and keep silent, believing in the oasis that shimmers on the horizon and never ceases to move toward the sky, walk and not turn around, lest you be taken with vertigo. Our steps invent the path as we proceed; behind us they leave no trace, only the void. So we shall always look ahead and trust our feet. They will take us as far as our minds will believe this story.* (1989, pp. 7–8)

Endnotes

1.   Some of this chapter's material appeared in *Teachers College Record*, Vol. 99, No. 4, 1998, under the title "Neve Shalom/Wahat Al-Salam: A School for Peace."
2.   Due to the very sensitive nature of the encounter, I was not encouraged to participate in the workshop sessions but rather to observe only. I respected the wishes of the facilitators and therefore interacted with the participants solely outside of the sessions.
3.   Diaspora: the dispersion of a people out of their homeland; being in exile.
4.   The Intifada is the uprising of the Palestinians in the West Bank and Gaza which began in 1988.

Chapter Five

Portraits of Peace

When Jews and Arabs get together, work together, live together, they create their own miracle: Neve Shalom/Wahat Al-Salam is such a miracle—it deserves our warmest support, for it justifies our highest hopes.

—Elie Wiesel, Nobel Peace laureate

Bridges of Hope: Reflexive Interviewing

It is, I suspect, an experience every field anthropologist has, and certainly one I have had so repeatedly that I have come to think of it as emblematic of the whole operation, to come upon individuals in the course of research who seem to have been waiting there, at some unlikely place, for someone like you, bright-eyed, ignorant, obliging, credulous, to happen along, so as to have the chance not just to answer your questions but to instruct you as to which ones to ask: people with a story to tell . . . I (the anthropologist) too have stories to tell . . . to describe a culture . . . is to look at things . . . by journeys, books, witnessings, and conversations, to look at them: to take an interest.

These words by Clifford Geertz (1995, p. 61) guide me as I write this chapter about the conversations I have shared with some of the most extraordinary people I will ever meet. They are, to my mind, artisans of mending and builders of bridges of hope. I seek to explore each participant's distinctive story and construct, along with and through my own story, a narrative journey of our desires, dreams, fears, works—past, present, and future. I follow the poet Theodore Roethke (1966) in that "I learn by going where I have to go" (as cited in Geertz, 1995, p. 133). Not so hidden within my participants' imaginings of peace for two national homelands is my own desire for a unified self—the "more inclusive and fundamental aim of building and rebuilding a coherent and rewarding sense of identity" (Giddens, 1991, p. 75). Michel Foucault (1984, pp. 37–38) commented that using your own reason (instead of working according to what others want of you) is essential for becoming conscious of your own inner thoughts and desires and in so doing becoming the person you would like to be. For the poet Charles Pierre Baudelaire, the task of modernity was in fact the challenge of attempting to invent ourselves, all the while understanding that we are very limited by our life experiences. The starkly honest oral texts of my participants demonstrate that their journey of conflict resolution and peacemaking may not reach its goal within the wider Middle East arena in their lifetimes, but it is making a difference in their village and their immediate surroundings, as well as in some other sectors of Israeli society.

Methodological Considerations

In undertaking this study of the pursuit of peaceful coexistence in a Jewish-Palestinian village, one must remind oneself that the investigation brings this particular lived experience into the core of one's own lived experiences. Due to my professional history as a teacher and an educational researcher, I decided to inquire into this study as a social scientist rather than as a storyteller; therefore I struggle with my own subjectivity in interpreting my findings. I am in good company, however, when I say that the two approaches need not be mutually exclusive; in fact, Martyn Hammersly and Paul Atkinson (1995) point out that they are both intrinsic aspects of social research. Indeed, one can (and must be) both storyteller and social scientist at the same time in order to do justice to the complex reality of the human endeavor. In fact, theorists have suggested that even the most objective of social research methods are clearly subjective (Davies, 1999).

The interview process convinced me that my personal relationship with the participants in the village formed the basis of my reflective theorizing. This social interaction as well as my field notes turned out to be central in the construction of my participant observations, which became my data. This methodology corroborates Hortense Powdermaker's (1966, p. 19) classic stance that participant observation requires both involvement and detachment, achieved by developing the ethnographer's "role of stepping in and out of society." Robert Coles (1997, p. 13) suggests that "If we don't somehow settle a score with ourselves, never mind those we 'study' while we are out there, in that elusive, ever-changing entity abstractly called the 'the field,' we are apt to show that ambiguity of feeling to others in our writing." I return again to the eloquence of Geertz (1995) as he describes his professional path, one which speaks deeply to me: "You see what you have been doing (if you see it at all) after you have been doing it. . . . Theory and practice are not, as the idealists suppose, cause and outcome. Nor are they, as materialists do, outcome and cause. They are pursuits in a calling" (pp. 98–99).

Who can know how the educational innovations in this village will reverberate in the lives of its children? The participants' stories show how they are creating a landscape of coexistence and cooperation between Jew and Arab. British writer Lawrence Durrell (1945, 1960) suggests that "landscape holds the key to character." It is "the invisible constant of a place." Canadian author Wade Davis (1998) comments that "just as landscape defines a people, culture springs from a spirit of place." He explains, for example, that "the weight of the North hovers in the imagination of every Canadian child." So too, I believe, landscape is essential to the imagination of the Israeli child, as is vividly evident in the poem by a twelve-year-old girl from Neve Shalom/Wahat Al-Salam in the Introduction of this book. Her poem represents the wisdom of lives lived directly in the eye of the storm and the hunger of those who hope to discover a pathway to liberation of spirit and soul. Every time I spoke with the villagers I was mindful of the spiritual rhythm of their daily lives full of energy, dignity, and morality. They live close to the edge—passionate in their lonely struggle—full of heart and glorious possibilities as well as of human failings and limitations. For example, I recall the words of William Carlos Williams—"a local pride"—when he wrote about the heroism of the ordinary people in his little town in New Jersey. I understand now the universality in those three words; they are so relevant to this little Israeli oasis of peace.

The Reflexive Ethnographic "Gaze": A Story about Others

I cannot help but think that Coles was discussing my own reflexive ethnographic "gaze" when he wrote, "To some extent we see the world we are looking for. We select for ourselves visually what our minds and hearts crave to notice. . . . How differently each of us sees even the same scene, selecting from it what we want to emphasize out of our personal needs and nature" (pp. 224–25). Perhaps I, as border dweller, have been searching for Neve Shalom/Wahat Al-Salam all my life and finally have found it. As a child, I longed to live in a world of harmony and joy and peace. Sometimes in the dark of night, I wrote little stories about the end of war. I tried to hide from the suffering of my parents through the vehicle of my stories, which always featured people of different cultures and religions living happily together. When I was very young and very wounded, I knew I needed to find a way to survive. I chose life because I did not want to drown with the corpses of my relatives in the quicksand of the Holocaust; I was terrified of losing contact with humanity. Nightmares frequented me, in which Hitler's henchmen found me in hiding, an orphaned child, and threw my body crashing against a barbed wire fence like a shrieking piece of garbage. I see other little children with their tattered dolls and teddy bears being marched to the gas chambers. These scenes haunt me still. I know in my soul that for the surviving victims of the Holocaust, "the injury," as Primo Levi (1988, pp. 224–35) stated, "cannot be healed; it extends through time . . . denying peace to the tormented." I, as the child of two such victims, needed to escape from the torment in some way. I found my way out in the texts of the "other"—those living in other languages and other cultures, as is explained at the end of Chapter 3. I especially discovered my escape in my educational experiences, both in public and in higher education.

As I assembled my narrative portraits for this study, I was amazed at the mystery of their power and also at the similarities of this present professional work to my earlier life experiences—the overwhelming need to find a place of refuge, an "oasis of peace" mediated through language, culture, and identity.

My objective here is to share what I heard and saw in the village in order to reflect on how we can make a difference in our personal and professional lives—in spite of our despair, or even perhaps because of it. Maybe this village is only an apparition, but without it we are lost. On this note, let us turn to the stories of the participants. I begin with the man who created it all.

Father of the Dream: An Interview with Bruno Hussar

> *When God comes into our midst, it is to upset the status quo.*
>
> —Father Bruno

> *La sagesse consiste à tenter de voir les signes des temps,*
> *A discerner l'esprit dans ces certitudes qui sont en train d'évoluer,*
> *à nous raccrocher à certains rochers solides qui restent au milieu de cette*
> *nebuleuse.*
> *Le rocher le plus solide, c'est l'amour fraternel.*
> *Là on est sur de ne pas se tromper.*
>
> —Father Bruno, October 1994

I translate those thoughts of Father Bruno:

> *Wisdom is found in trying to see the signs of the times,*
> *To distinguish the spirit in the certainties which are in the*
> *midst of happening,*
> *To attach ourselves to certain solid rocks which are located in*
> *the midst of the void,*
> *The most solid rock of all is fraternal love.*
> *We can never go wrong with love.*

Father Bruno Hussar, a man of faith, had a vision to bring together Israelis from all three monotheistic religions in order to build an "oasis of peace." The term originates from the prophet Isaiah's biblical call in the Old Testament: "My people shall live in an oasis of peace" (Isaiah 32:18). Father Bruno lived those words to the best of his ability. My first encounter with Father Bruno was on a cold, rainy December afternoon in 1991 in the little house where he lived whenever he came to the village from Isaiah House, his residence in Jerusalem. I was immediately impressed by his sharp blue eyes, which twinkled at me as he set the teakettle on his little stove to boil. In spite of his slight stature, there was an omnipresent power surrounding him, like a halo. He was not a young man then—he was in his late seventies—but his voice was full of strength. We spoke in both French and English. I felt grateful that this busy man had made time for me. I felt safe and at ease in this little spot alone with this legendary figure, the man who had created the village (and who had received prizes for it). I asked whether he minded being tape-recorded and he answered, "Not at all; this way you will be able to do your work more efficiently." He may have been a dreamer, but he was also a pragmatist!

The following is an excerpt from Father Bruno's autobiographical account, *Quand la Nuèe se Levait (When the Cloud Lifted)* (Veritas Books, 1989), which was translated into English:

We had in mind a small village composed of inhabitants from different communities in the country. Jews, Christians, and Muslims would live there in peace, each one faithful to his own faith and traditions, while respecting those of the others. Each would find in this diversity a source of personal enrichment. The aim of the village: to be the setting for a school for peace. For years there have been academies in the various countries where the art of war has been taught. Inspired by the prophetic words: "Nation shall not lift up sword against nation, neither shall they learn war anymore," we wanted to found a school for peace, for peace too is an art. It doesn't appear spontaneously; it has to be [learned]. People would come here from all over the country to meet those from whom they were estranged, wanting to break down the barriers of fear, mistrust, ignorance, misunderstanding, preconceived ideas—all things that

Figure 5–1 Father Bruno Hussar, in the village. Courtesy of NS/WAS.

*separate us—and to build bridges of trust, respect, mutual understanding,
and, if possible, friendship. This aim would be achieved with the help of
courses, seminars, group psychology techniques, shared physical work,
and recreational evenings.* (p. 103)

Father Bruno Hussar was a genuinely transnational, transcultural, and multilingual individual. He was born in Egypt in 1911 and had Hungarian citizenship, and then Italian citizenship. His father and mother were nonpracticing
Jews, and his mother tongue was first English and then French. He completed
his secondary education at an Italian *lycée* in Cairo. In 1929 he moved to Paris
and entered the École Centrale des Arts et Manufactures where he received his
diploma in 1936. It is at this time that he chose to be baptized into the Roman
Catholic faith. In his autobiography, Bruno writes:

*I was baptized on 22 December at the age of 24. . . . From that moment
I entered a world where all was holy, unaware then to what extent my
Jewish self was finding expression. I lived only for God, with God, and in
God. Then came the question of my future. I would be a religious, that
was clear, but where?* (p. 15)

From 1936 until 1942 he worked as an engineer; he received French nationality in 1937. During the Nazi occupation he was obliged to flee Paris and enter
the Free Zone where, he says, "I tasted the bitter experience of anti-Semitism.
I became much more conscious of my belonging to the Jewish people as a result." In 1941 he fell ill. "Trois anneés de repos dont deux d'immobilité com-
plète, permirent à beaucoup de choses de murir." ["Three years years of rest,
two of which necessitated complete immobility allowed much within me to
mature."] In 1945 when he recovered his health, he entered the Order of the
Dominicans, Province de Paris. He studied philosophy and theology at Saul-
choir (a religious institution) where he lived in an atmosphere of calm and
peace. Brother Bruno was ordained a priest in 1950.

*Two years earlier, in May 1948, the United Nations had recognized the
state of Israel. After the War of Independence, Jerusalem was cut in two
by the armistice line that marked the frontier with Jordan. Father Avril
[Bruno's mentor] told me of his wish to set up a center for Jewish studies
in the Jewish half of Jerusalem, along the lines of the Dominican Center
for Islamic Studies in Cairo. He had thought that I, as a Jew by birth,
might undertake this foundation and he asked me to think it over.* (p. 30)

Bruno arrived in Israel in 1953. In his autobiography, he wrote:

*With my arrival in Israel came a growing conviction: I was a son of Israel.
These people I was living among were my people; this country I was
living in was my country . . . but in the eyes of the Israeli civil authorities
I was not considered a Jew, although according to Jewish religious law I
was well and truly Jewish, a Jewish transgressor but Jewish nevertheless.
This is one of the many paradoxes about this country. . . . I am a Jew.*

Just as Jesus, Mary, the apostles, and the first Christians were Jews. . . . I
[learned] to accept what, astonishingly as it may seem, I didn't know—the
shameful, infinitely sad, almost incredible series of sufferings endured by
the Jews over the centuries in so-called Christian countries.

I [learned] how young Christians were being taught to despise the Jews at
the same time that they were taught the gospel of love. I also [learned]
what dire consequences this teaching had: for many Christians it was an
excuse to take vengeance on those they called murderers of Christ, even
murderers of God! Put more simply, it provided culprits against whom
public indignation could vent itself in times of national disaster; expelling
Jews and confiscating their property was a cheap way to settle serious
financial problems. (p. 47–48)

From 1953 to 1959 Bruno ministered in Jaffa in French, English, and Italian:

In 1954, under the initiative of a group of priests of which I was one, was
founded the l'Oeuvre St. Jacques in order to establish relations and
reconciliation between Jews and Christians. . . . We created Isaiah
House in Jerusalem at the beginning of 1959.

Bruno became very active in many ecumenical associations during those formative years. From 1964 to 1965 he participated in the Ecumenical Council of
Vatican II and was appointed to the *Secrétariat pour l'Unité des Chrétiens* in
order to edit and present the text *Nostra Aetate* concerning the relationship
between the Church and the Jewish people. In 1966 he received Israeli nationality and right after the Six-Day War in 1967 he participated in the General
Assembly of the United Nations as a consultant with the Israeli delegation.
From 1968 to 1970 he was sent by the Israeli Ministry of Culture on missions
to the United States, Canada, and many European countries to conduct conferences on the Bible and on interfaith dialogues between Jews and Christians.
These were enormously successful and became the blueprint for many future
ecumenical organizations around the world. Then, in 1970, he acted on his
dream and founded Neve Shalom/Wahat Al-Salam.

If Jews and Christians were to be reconciled, wasn't more needed than
study and intellectual exchanges, however profound? . . . Jews and
Christians are so divided by history and prejudice, shouldn't we try to find
a way for them to share life together, a community where they may be
faithful to their own faith and traditions while fully respecting each
others'? This was how I first envisaged the "dream" of Neve Shalom.
After the Six-Day War there were many changes. Jerusalem was unified
and suddenly the Arab world burst into the city's everyday life and into
my dreams for the future. This Arab world already existed in Israel as a
minority of about 12 percent of the population, but I was unaware of this
aspect of Israeli life, which was far less important then than it was to
become later. It was impossible to imagine a communal life shared by

Jews and Christians in Israel without taking into account those other sons of Abraham, the Arabs, both Muslim and Christian, who live in this country. So the idea of Neve Shalom began to take shape. (p. 100)

Father Bruno was personally nominated for the Nobel Peace Prize in 1988. He was awarded the Prix de l'Amitié Judeo-Chrétienne de France in 1994 and the Japanese Niwano Peace Prize in 1995 as well as many other honors from various countries, including Israel. It was an incredible privilege to interview this magnificent man. I remember holding a glass of fresh mint tea and a plate of shortbread cookies as I turned on the tape recorder. I was in a comfortable chair and Father Bruno sat on a couch opposite me. I asked how this village began. "How did you plant the first 'seed' here at Neve Shalom/Wahat Al-Salam?" Father Bruno told me it was too long a story to tell it all in one hour but that he was willing to have an informal conversation with me. We started talking like parent and child. I hadn't planned that mode in advance—suddenly I felt like a little girl in his presence, hungry for knowledge and also spiritual sustenance. The words spilled out of me. I told him how full of emotion I was from the moment I had arrived in the village. I told him that I was a child of Holocaust survivors and that this place of peaceful coexistence had a powerful effect on my sense of Jewishness and my sense of belonging in the world. I poured out my heart to him: the deep wounding in my soul, the haunting nightmares of my parents, the sense of terror in the night, the lack of safety and continuity and hope, the feelings of darkness and despair. Tears streamed down my cheeks unheeded. Father Bruno found a tissue and put his arm around me. "For a Jew," he whispered, "memory is sacrosanct. It connects us back to Abraham and, of course, to God. But what do we do with the memory of the Holocaust, which destroyed the innocent relation between survivors and God? It is a death of the self and is transferred onto the children of survivors like you."

My tears really began to flow. I realized for the first time that this emptiness inside me was a result of the devastation of home and of the love that epitomizes the family and constitutes tradition. This had, in fact, been one of the first steps in the Nazi program of Jewish annihilation. As a child I had always felt "homeless"; I belonged nowhere. I was psychologically orphaned. (See Patterson, 1998, for a reflective analysis of memory and the Holocaust.) In a dart of his gentle eyes, Father Bruno said: "This is why this village of peace is so important to you. It represents the possibility of home and foundation. It is a sanctuary for you. You chose life, in spite of the horrors that your parents experienced. Neve Shalom/Wahat Al-Salam is life affirming for you. Your professional work gives you a wholeness." He had taken the words out of my mouth and I could not speak for a moment. And we both wept. I was supposed to be interviewing Father Bruno and he was healing me instead. It was a precious time together. Elie Wiesel (1973, p. 64) writes, "To dream is to invite a future, if not to justify it, and to deny death, which denies dreams." To me this village is indeed a dream for a better future as it had been for Father Bruno, who dreamed it first. He said, "I knew in my heart that a place where Arab and Jew could really face one another in day-to-day living would transform their fears and hatred." This powerful yet simple thought reminded me of the words of Emmanuel Levinas: "the face is the origin of discourse" (1985, pp. 87–88).

Then Father Bruno talked about the issue of finding a place for the village. As he stated in his book:

> *The question of land was the most utopian aspect of this utopia. How would we find any without money or influence? After making fruitless inquiries and having our hopes dashed on several occasions, forty hectares of land came to us out of the blue in a most surprising way. The Trappist monastery of Latrun offered us a hill. Before the war in June 1967 it had been a demilitarized zone, a no-man's-land between Israel and Jordan. In return for a peppercorn rent of three pence a year and a 100-year lease renewable for forty-nine years, this hill became the place where the dream of Neve Shalom could come true . . .*

> *Only those who lived there knew how difficult it was in every way, and how it wore you down. There were the first meetings between Arabs and Jews (Muslims and Christians) in Rina's home in Jerusalem; then the life of the first "pioneers" on the hill, without water and without a single tree. (Water and shade are what you need most in our region.) There was no electricity and when it rained the road was impassable. The land was stony and covered with brambles and hadn't been cultivated or inhabited since the Byzantine era. . . . The first meetings took place in an atmosphere of simple friendship. They were unaffected and joyful. We were joined by the Bedouin encamped around us, and by Arabs and Jews from the surrounding villages and kibbutzim. We sang and danced and prayed for peace.* (pp. 104, 106, 108)

The following conversation with Father Bruno elaborates on his utter dedication to his calling—to create an oasis of peace against all odds:

Bruno (B):   It is interesting that in the structure of the Hebrew language the "roots" are very important, and the root is formed by three letters of the Hebrew alphabet; for example, the word peace in Hebrew: shin, lamed, mem. And it's got two meanings, shalom—peace, and shelem as whole, entire, one, as an idea of harmony.

Grace (G):   That's interesting . . .

B: And according to biblical logic, the name indicates the very being and the vocation of the one who bears the name. So Jerusalem should be the city and the land of peace, of unity, of harmony. And it has never been that. Even before David made it his capital, it was a city and a land of divisions and conflicts and wars and so on. And if you look at the country today, it's a mosaic of communities, religious communities, national communities, cultural communities, very different from one another, and each one is versus the other ones, either in a state of conflict, more or less violent conflict, or in a state of complete indifference.

And so the idea was that can we do something to break down walls of indifference or prejudice or misunderstanding, and so on, between those communities, and build bridges of respect and understanding. And we started dreaming of peace in this country. And we started dreaming of a village where people from places of conflict would come and make peace. Later on we narrowed down the dream to the two major conflicts between Jews and Arabs. Because before we thought of Jews and Christians, and Christians and Muslims, and Jews and Jews, and Christians and Christians, all in a state of conflict, all of them. And so we thought, we can't tackle them all, the most important is the Jewish-Arab conflict. We're going to have a village where Jews and Arabs from the country will live together in harmony and peace and collaboration. And the name of that village will be Neve Shalom/Wahat Al-Salam, first to prove by its very existence that cooperation is possible, on condition that you believe in it and that you're willing to pay the price of peace and to give your life over to the cause.

And the second condition, the second aim of the village is that it was to be the framework for a school for peace, a place where people come from all over the country with a motivation of just learning to listen to the other one. That seems a very easy thing, but it's one of the most difficult things when you live in this kind of conflict, like in Northern Ireland. And we were very naive, and I think that's the reason for why we succeeded. I think it's very important to see that. When God asks somebody to do something for Him, and he asks everybody to do something for Him, he gives us what I should call a "brace of unconsciousness." That means we don't know the hundredth part of the difficulties we're going to meet.

G: Otherwise we would never enter it.

B: Basically people began to come from all over the world. They heard it through word of mouth. For the first years we had all sorts of people, young people, who were going through the world, looking for a better society than they had.

G: Yes, it would be very tempting and utopian.

B: And they came from everywhere, from Australia, New Zealand, Holland, Germany, America, Canada, and so on. And many young people went to India for help, to find a guru and understand the guru. And here they found a place where they could build a commune if that's what they wanted. But we understood that it'll only work really when there will be people from this country, Israel. And a few from the country came quite often on Saturdays to visit us, but quite often they said to us, "Well, your idea that I could come and live with you and work for peace with you is good, but I've got a family and a job and a house and kids. We can't come, it's too primitive still here. You're not sure to be here next year. We'll see later if you succeed and we might come."

Those who wanted to come were those young people who wanted a better life, or they were adventurers; they weren't at all interested in the situation of the country, the reason for which we were there. But they had the motivation and courage and they enabled us to exist and to get known during those earlier years. Some stayed a week, some stayed a month or six months. . . . There were two who stayed for about five years, but most of them just stayed for a short time and then left. And my friends in Jerusalem were very cross with me because they said I'm a priest, I'm a Dominican, and they said that I was wasting my time on the hill.

G: Really?

B: I hadn't come to Israel, they said, to live with people who speak all the languages of the world except the two languages of Israel. And they needed me as a priest in Jerusalem. I pretended to be strong—I was not strong but I pretended to be—and I said that there was no country, no town in the world, except perhaps Rome, where there are so many priests as in Jerusalem. If they need one they can just go down to the street and catch the first Franciscan that passes, and ask [him] for the help they need. But if Neve Shalom is to develop and to be known, it will only do so if there is presence on the hill and I must remain. But I was not so sure, I pretended to be, but I was not so sure about it.

G: I like the way you say that, I really do.

B: Because I saw that every year I was not getting younger, and indeed, I did not come to live with foreigners; I came to this country in order to be with Arabs and Jews who live in Israel. So I didn't know what to do, because I thought, "Well, if I continue, maybe in ten years there will still only be strangers on the hill, and then I shall probably have wasted my time. If I interrupt—I could have done something else for the cause of peace, but maybe if I interrupt, all that has been done up until now is about to bring some fruit, and I interrupt it—and what would happen? And so I didn't know what to do, and nobody could advise me and nobody knew the situation enough to advise me.

So I did something very rash that I wouldn't advise anybody to do; I thought there is only one who knows what should be done. So I sent an ultimatum to God, and I gave Him one year to give me two signs, saying that if I don't get those two signs within a year, I would consider stopping the experience and do something else. And those two signs were first, that at least one family from Israel—Jewish or Arab— but from this country should come to build a community on the hill, followed later by others, but at least one. And the second sign would be that we get enough money to start building the "School for Peace." And those two signs were given after a few months. I was going to say unfortunately, because I didn't believe in it and I was already making plans to do something else. It's always very uncomfortable . . .

G: . . .when God answers your prayers.

B: When He seems to, yes, to react in that way, to a challenge that you put in front of Him because then you're committed, you can't go back. And so one very wonderful family came from one of the biggest agricultural centers in the country, Beth Shemesh, [from a] village nearby. A Jewish family, and [it] really created the beginning of a community here . . .

G: There have just been some children here at the "School for Peace" from Beth Shemesh last week.

B: Yes, yes. I thought it was them. . . .

And that was a family that stayed, but unfortunately after one year they had to leave; [there were] family problems and [the family] went back to Beth Shemesh. But thanks to [these people], others came; others who knew them, and then the momentum started, and people really started to come—they were the cornerstone of the whole thing that exists today.

And the money came in different ways, very curious ways: First, a family from Switzerland, from Zurich, had heard about Neve Shalom on Swiss television and came to spend a day with us in, I don't know if it was '76 or '77. And they saw that the reason we couldn't start meetings on the "School for Peace" was a very prosaic reason—we had no toilets—that means what Americans call a bathroom. A place where there's no bathroom, they call it the "bathroom of the saints," and we just had a hole in the ground and burlap sacks around it and when the hole was full, we made another hole and transported the sacks [G: Oh my gosh!] around the other hole. And we had the project of, later on, planting orange trees there because it was very fertile. The young people who came later had other priorities and weren't interested in the sense of tradition, and they had other priorities, so we started planting olive trees. And we didn't have a shower, of course; once a week, we took every car on the hill, and we went to Kibbutz Nachshon, ten kilometers away, where they allowed us to take showers.

G: My goodness, you lived here full-time?

B: At that time, I lived here full-time, yes. And Anne [Le Meignen] also. And another man, Alex. And so we couldn't just invite people to the "School for Peace" to come and work and study for a few days, if when they ask for a bathroom, we showed them just a hole—this in a country where you must take a shower at least twice a day—and we weren't yet in the good relationship we are now with Kibbutz Har-El. Anyway, those Swiss people were very stunned by that. And they not only gave us money to build toilets but they also sent a friend who was an architect to help us build them. And so that is how the toilets became the only solid structure on the hill. We all were sleeping either under tents or in very primitive huts, but the toilets were solid buildings. That shows the relative value of things in this world [laughter]. And I remember, when we finished building the toilets in the middle of the night, we drank wine to the health of all those who would use them to the end of time, and we tossed a coin to see who would be the first two to use the toilets. And that's how we started.

G: Ah, that's a riot! That's really amazing!

B: And then a group of Germans formed an association for peace, and came and helped us to get linked to the water supply, the natural water supply, and eventually to get money to put solar heaters on the houses. We were also able to put some special powder on the road. There was a dust track that comes up from the main road, three kilometers of dust track, it was not yet paved, and when it rained not even the jeeps of the police could come up because there was too much mud. So we had to leave the cars at the bottom of the hill or at the monastery, and come up walking under a storm, go down in the tractor to fetch the things we bought.

G: I don't know how you did it. I really don't . . .

B: That wasn't the worst thing; it was worrying at the beginning that we wouldn't attract people from the country. Because as soon as they started coming [that gave us] a feeling that we were becoming civilized and I hope we never become too civilized. It's not a danger today, yet. So that's it.

G: Wow! How do you feel when, for example, yesterday at the [Christmas] party, having the possibility [of seeing] the children perform and the parents, Jews and Arabs, mingling together?

B: There are two things that show us that Neve Shalom/Wahat Al-Salam is something today: the children and the trees. Kids and trees. That's life; life coming up. And it's very wonderful. I very much liked the school party.

G: Yes, it was really very touching. I tell you, at certain points, I felt as if I was going to totally break down, and I thought I better keep myself together because it would look ridiculous.

B: And it was all prepared by the codirectors of the school.

G: They are very special.

B: We've got very good people . . .

G: Very strong people . . .

B: Very strong people and dedicated . . . I believe there is something happening here, and I believe that something stands on moral ground; it's not a question of having the land, it's a question of respecting what it represents. That means seeing the moral value and being faithful to it.

What Father Bruno taught me is priceless: the notion that learning and teaching conflict resolution is a kind of utopia where there is always room for who we are. He explained that both Jews and Palestinians are wanderers in the desert of war, but they can and have invented a place to "be" here in this village—a shared enterprise of peacemaking through community and education. And he said that history has to be remembered and taught, not only intellectually, but also psychologically and emotionally. When he was criticized by members of a young German fundamentalist group who came to visit the village and commented negatively on the secular nature of the place, as opposed to what they felt should be a *religious* mission, he answered that the essential element of this village is indeed the spiritual one: that God is everywhere within the everyday occurrences of this village and its inhabitants; in the everyday things of their lives. "They are doing God's work whether they realize it or not. These are people who have love in their hearts; surely that is pleasing to God. There is moral and spiritual reflection and action that takes place here constantly. What is more religious than that?"

Father Bruno and I also discussed how in the elementary school and in the "School for Peace," the children are encouraged to create narratives that provide context and patterns through which they can read, understand, realize, and transmit their experience. To quote Father Bruno: "These children have the opportunity to discuss where they come from, what they're afraid of, and how they're going to try and solve it together. They learn and play in the same classes. The school play is a beautiful example of this togetherness. Maybe they will have the capacity to change the world in this region."

The lyricism and eloquence of Father Bruno's words still ring in my ears as I retell and rewrite them here. They resonate with the words of French novelist Georges Bernanos's dying curé in *The Diary of the Country Priest* that "grace is everywhere." The symmetry—two priests both witnessing the sanctity of a worldly landscape—is beautiful to me. This "connectedness of life" is what Father Bruno stood for. Wilhelm Dilthey (1977) equated it with the concept of life history. It was Father Bruno's life history to found a place of peace and reconciliation. He died on February 8, 1996, at the age of 85 and was buried in the little village's cemetery on February 11. "Even the elements were in mourning, for the day was stormy with torrential rain, and there were those who said that this correctly reflected the mood of [those in] the large gathering who came to pay their last respects to the man who everybody had loved" (Village newsletter, No. 47, Sept. 1996). Because of the inclement weather, the funeral service was held in the main hall of the elementary school. In accordance with Bruno's wishes, the service was conducted by members from each of the three religions living together in Neve Shalom/Wahat Al-Salam. The schoolchildren sang together, "You and me will change the world," just as they had done on his 80th birthday, five years earlier.

Here are a few more uplifting thoughts from Father Bruno, shared during our interview:

Bruno (B):   What's very important is that there's a sort of invisible communion [among] all human beings in this world. And beyond the curtain of life—the curtain that we all cross one day when we die. And we are as precious to God when we are dead as we are living. But there is a human communion and we can all help each other, or we can harm each other. And there's a Jewish saying that the individual who helps one single human being, helps the whole world. And what you do for one person—what lies in your heart—has its expression in the world. If you listen for it, this sort of telepathy exists. And we can help each other simply by respecting and loving. We put more love in that community by loving, . . . by loving your neighbor, by loving yourself. It is a sort of deep communal love that helps humanity, and it is thanks to them that in spite of a world where evil is so rampant, there are still some positive things going on.

And we go forward because there's the energy of love that fights against the energy of evil. And I believe that all the souls that have preceded us in the world provide us with this shield of love. I believe that prayer helps. It's a prayer when you sing with joy. "Shout aloud, oh Israel" is God's commandment to us. I imply then in this way one may be faithful to God whether one is religious or secular. Those words are so artificial anyway. Work hard, rejoice in your heart, live in truth. He is within you and therefore you need no longer fear evil.

Grace (G): That's beautiful!

B: I think that God reveals himself in different ways, to different people, and so on. Now He reveals himself in a social project like this village, and a social project needs to exist and develop in some spiritual framework. Faith can be carried out within a social context—which to me is religion. And that's why there are different religions—according to the situation and the different ways in which people reach their inner goals . . .

We created here a place of prayer and meditation called the "House of Silence"—the "Doumia" where the villagers can go and listen to their hearts and the still, small voice, as is discussed in the Bible. I think about Elijah, the prophet, who escaped those who wanted to kill him, and how he walked forty days and forty nights in the desert and then when he came to the Mount of Olives, he knew that God was going to appear for him. And there was a thunderstorm and he listened, but God was not in the thunderstorm. And there was a big wind and lightning, and again he listened, but God was not in the lightning. And then there was a transformation, a small, still breeze, or something like that. In Hebrew, it means the voice of a thin silence. The translators probably could not understand that silence could have a voice, and they translated it as a small breeze. But in Hebrew it's the voice of a thin silence. A still, small voice. We need to hear that thin silence in the midst of the din of conflict and pain in our world. That thin voice in the silence guides us. That voice has guided me to this village.

Father Bruno's words were remarkable in how they provided context and patterns through which I could understand my own experience. There was unity and consistency in his references to the Bible; indeed, the thoughts are lovely in their yearning for peace and justice and above all, for the "small, still voice" that entreats us to love the "self" and the "other." I am awed at the generosity of spirit and abundance of his life work, and I admire his humility. I will never forget the delicacy of expression and feelings that he shared with me, the splendid moments. Father Bruno is a member of a "subversive" group of people: those who know no boundaries—a new form of creative resistance. He brought me closer to the spirit and the magic that enveloped those who were involved in the first stages of creating this village.

The story of Father Bruno's village is certainly not finished. It will forever be a journey of "humanity in ruins," to use Samuel Beckett's (1990) words. Father Bruno, truly a visionary, had an exquisitely brilliant imagination, fierce determination, and an unshakable faith. He walked toward an ideal of life, and we have to keep walking for him and for ourselves in order to honor the work of art—this "oasis of peace"—that he has left for us to nurture.

A Tale of Two Identities: My Interview with Rayek Rizek

Rayek Rizek has been living in Neve Shalom/Wahat Al-Salam since 1984. He was the secretary/mayor of the village from 1997 until 2000. He revealed a personal need for a strong identity and a deep understanding of his cultural dislocation and marginality in Israeli society, which evoked in me a sense of familiarity and solidarity. One might wonder what I am talking about—for he is Palestinian and I am Jewish—but his sadness for the fate of many of his relatives and people who were dispersed after the Israeli War of Independence in 1948 touched a chord within me. I understand all too well the sorrows of dispersion. My family's case may have been more extreme, but that does not stop me from being able to relate to Rayek's sense of loss.

Our respective personal suffering created a bond between us. My interview with Rayek opened a meeting place to which we had each personally arrived from seemingly opposite sides of the Israeli-Palestinian conflict. First, our conversations had to do with what writing signifies: finding the words to carry our sorrows and our joys. We discussed the necessity of writing one's own and others' lives; the act of putting the experience on paper which, we agreed, carries redemptive value. I told Rayek how for me writing about Neve Shalom/Wahat Al-Salam is a lifeline—the act of shaping reality into a story that transforms feelings of powerlessness into agency. He was intrigued by my notion that the moment of writing restores a sense of control and—perhaps even more miraculously—that it offers a sense of peace. Reality becomes a potential story; the idea that even a discussion about pain and exile has the potential to be incredibly uplifting. I explained to him how everything is "grist for the mill" which thus infuses a sense of meaning into my work and life, all the while mercifully allowing me to distance myself from the fears and horrors of a traumatic past.

I liked Rayek on sight. He is a good-looking man in his mid-forties with thoughtful dark eyes set in a delicate face. He has a quiet intellectual strength, and a charming personality. I recall with pleasure the early morning conversations I had with Rayek during my sojourn in June and July 1997 while he was manager of the guest house. We chatted over tea in the dining hall before the working day began. He always buoyed my spirits up. As these conversations unfolded, Rayek and I delved deeper and deeper into our vulnerabilities and our woundedness until there were a multiplicity of voices in the interview text—some irreconcilable, others almost mirrors of each other. It was a stimulating and heavy experience full of intense feelings and profound connections.

These informal conversations were just as important to me as the final formal one which I tape-recorded in the garden at his home one evening toward the end of my sojourn. I was really pleased when I realized that Rayek no longer treated me as just another of the many visitors that come to this village either for fund-raising purposes or for media or political reasons. He did, of course, know of my academic research agenda, but we transcended that formality very quickly. What became apparent to him was that the notebook in which I kept my fieldnotes was not just a theoretical or professional artifact—it was my life.

The story about Rayek that follows derives from three sources: (1) our informal dining room conversations, (2) our "formal" interview in his garden, and (3) a paper that he presented in 1998 to the Annual Meeting of the German Friends of Neve Shalom/Wahat Al-Salam, one of the fund-raising groups devoted to the village. Rayek was born in the city of Nazareth in 1955, where he grew up and lived all his life before he entered the university.

Here is an excerpt from his speech to the German Friends of Neve Shalom/Wahat Al-Salam:

Though a Jewish enclave known as Upper Nazareth was established, the lower city remained entirely Arab, unlike the situation of other cities such as Jaffa, Ramle, and Haifa. As such, I had few contacts with Jews as a child, and little cause to think about my identity as a Palestinian. During the 1950s an agreement was reached between Israel and Jordan that allowed Palestinian Christians who had become Israeli citizens to cross the border for a four-day pilgrimage to the Old City of Jerusalem, which had been under Jordanian control since 1948. My parents would go there for Orthodox Christmas the 6th of January every year. In 1965, for the first time, I accompanied them. I remember leaving early in the morning and crossing the border at the Mandelbaum crossing point, a military compound where Israeli and Jordanian police, situated in separate rooms, reviewed the documents and belongings of those attempting to make the crossing . . .

This first experience of a border invoked my first questions about identity. Why should we need a permit? Why were some people refused? Why did we need to be checked by police on each side? My mother especially would talk and show pictures of relatives she had known in Haifa and of how, during the 1948 war, these people had hastily bolted their houses and businesses to depart to safer ground. They left with the belief that in a few days or weeks the fighting would be over, and they could return to their homes. They had no conception that this would prove to be a lifelong exile. Hearing these stories gave me my first understanding of what it meant to be a Palestinian. I came to understand how my reality, my history, and my obligations differed from those of the dominant Jewish society in Israel. Like other Palestinians, my parents were extremely cautious in talking about their identity. Many were afraid to even mention the past to their children. I was constantly warned never to discuss these matters outside of our house, with anyone." (1998, pp. 9, 10)

If there is one metaphor that most accurately describes my encounter with Rayek, it is the one that has been weaving its way throughout this book—that of "border crossing." Our discourse was a way of speaking about our perceived and desired location in the world as a response to specific social and historical situations, of which we both were pawns. Rayek told me that one of his reasons for living in Neve Shalom/Wahat Al-Salam (he credits his wife, Diana, for this idea) was a desire to transcend the entire problem of marginality by participating in the establishment of this unique village. He spoke vividly to me about how this enterprise held out a promise of peaceful coexistence between Jews and Palestinians, the ultimate dream of a binational space that incorporates the needs of both groups, a future for which Rayek has always longed.

The following dialogue comes from our interview:

Rayek (R):   You know, I remember comparing myself to many kids in my [Arab] neighborhood and in my class in school, and even at that time I kind of realized that I was the most aware child in terms of identity issues . . . I went to a private Greek Orthodox school but, of course, the curriculum was the Israeli one and so we had to raise the flags during Independence Day which for us Arabs was not independence at all; it was called by us in secret Al Naqba—the Catastrophe. The Ministry of Education tried to turn us into Israelis who would be loyal to the state and to therefore disconnect us from our roots. Nobody dared to oppose the government. All during those years, though, we would listen to Jamal Abdul Nasser of Egypt who would give a speech on the Egyptian radio every month. And we would listen to [these speeches]. I remember when he died in 1970 everybody [the Palestinians] was crying and it was a sad day for all. It was the beginning of a sense of my Arab identity. And then later I read books and more books about the Arabs, and the Palestinian conflict with the Israelis. These books in the 1950s and 1960s and into the '70s weren't allowed to be published, but we talked about them.

Grace (G):   Yes, like Mahmoud Darwich and his *La Palestine Comme Métaphore* which is so beautiful. He's inspiring. What a poet. I found his book in a bookstore while I was at a conference in Brussels a few weeks ago.

R: Yes, he's a very special person. He lived under house arrest in Haifa because he was politically active. There were many leaders in that position. The Israeli military rule ended in 1966 but the psychological effects are still there . . .

Rayek and I also spoke about Anton Shammas, the Palestinian-Israeli poet and novelist who writes almost exclusively in Hebrew—which, as mentioned in chapter 3, must be seen as a political act of resistance and rebellion. I recalled an article by Shammas entitled "Amerka Amerka" that appeared in *Harper's* magazine (282, Feb. 1989, pp. 55–61), in which he explains this linguistic choice as a "literary reinterpretation." He described Palestinians as a people who "travel light, empty-pocketed, with the vanity of those who think home is a portable idea, something that dwells mainly in the mind or within a text. Celebrating modern powers of imagination and of fiction, we have lost faith in our old idols—memory, storytelling. We are not even sure anymore whether there ever was a home out there, a territory, a homeland" (ibid., 1989, p. 56). How eerily congruent such a statement is with those that were uttered by Theodore Herzl in the 1800s when he discussed the Zionist dream of return by a people in exile to a Jewish homeland in Israel. Rayek and I were both struck by the sad truth that the diaspora of the Palestinians emerged out of the desperate need of the Jews to end theirs.

In the following excerpt from his paper, Rayek writes about being confronted with the meaning of diaspora for him:

> *In 1975, at the age of twenty, I had a second awakening. This was when I traveled to the United States to continue my studies. There I met other Palestinian students of my generation from the West Bank, Gaza, Jordan, Lebanon, and Kuwait. This was the first time that I had spent much time with Palestinians outside of Nazareth. The encounter shocked me. I saw how much alike we were despite being born and raised in different parts of the Middle East. I learned that we all went through similar experiences of feeling unwelcome and were subject to harassment wherever we lived. I learned that we were similarly ignorant of each other's reality and fate. I learned that we all had relatives scattered around the Middle East and that it was difficult to meet with them due to bad relations between the nations of the region and because we were Palestinians. Every time we wished to cross a border we were suspected and subjected to interrogation. I learned that none of the Palestinians I met felt at home in the country where they had lived their lives, especially those who lived outside of Palestine. . . ."* (1998, p. 10)

Rayek's commentary reminds me of that of Clark Blaise (1993) as he discusses his French-Canadian/American identity: "From a lifetime of crossing borders, I have developed a border consciousness. Borders mean metamorphosis, personal transformation. Borders demand decision, definition, but border crossers are *identity smugglers* [emphasis added]. Borders offer the opportunity to be opposing things without deception" (p. 59). "Crossing the border is like ripping the continent, an act of defiance, tearing its invisible casing. Borders are zones of grace" (p. 50). This is what Rayek and I have in common: living in the space between borders, trying to reclaim a territory both physical and metaphysical. He has never tasted the wholeness of a majority group identity. And neither have I.

Rayek's presentation to the German Friends of Neve Shalom/Wahat Al-Salam continues:

The third experience I would like to discuss is my mo[t]
Arab village of Neve Shalom/Wahat Al-Salam in 1984
return from the United States. Neve Shalom/Wahat A
remains) the only village where a group of Arabs an[d]
live together, rather than having been thrust there b[y]
circumstances. The radical idea of moving to the village wa[s] ...
wife's. In Neve Shalom/Wahat Al-Salam, for the first time, I came into
close contact and interacted with Jews. I mean not only those who lived
in the village but the thousands more who came as parents of
schoolchildren, participants in binational workshops, or simply as hotel
guests and visitors. Though today the village has grown to some 30
families, half Jewish and half Palestinian, it was then still very small.
Before our arrival there were only six families, only one or two of these
Palestinian. The village was still finding its way, and there were many
conflicts over the kind of community we would like to be. Very quickly I
found myself in confrontation with some of the Jewish members over the
question of my identity as a Palestinian. In Israel the standard term for us
is Israeli Arabs. The meaning is that ethnically we belong to the Arab
nations outside of Israel, while we owe our citizenship and allegiance to
Israel. There is no place in this definition for our Palestinian nationality
and culture.

Another question was the significance and role of the village. Was it
defined simply by the issues of coexistence between Arabs and Jews
within Israel, or should we be more vocal in addressing the issue of
Israel's relations with the Palestinians as a whole? I could not accept
anything less since as a Palestinian I felt that I had a duty to struggle for
the cause of the Palestinian people as a whole. I could not accept simply
being defined as an Israeli citizen. I was unable to celebrate with my
neighbors on Israel's Independence Day, and it became clear to all of us
that it would not be possible to commemorate this occasion together as a
community, on any level. In talking about the struggles of the
Palestinians, I was unable to avoid referring to the PLO and its leaders as
the legitimate representative of my people, though the organization was
still seen as a rabble of terrorists by the Israelis. Later when the Intifada
came, I saw this as a legitimate and natural extension of the struggle. On
all of these issues I often found that I had to defend my positions, and
that though everyone in the community wanted peace and reconciliation,
my identity and perspective as a Palestinian was often little understood by
my Jewish neighbors.

In general, Palestinians know more about Jewish Israeli society than Jews
know about Palestinian society. This is partly because the majoriy Jewish
culture is so dominant, but especially because Arabs are more fluent in
Hebrew than Jews in Arabic. Jews are unable to independently
understand the statements of Arab leaders, read Arab periodicals, [and so

ıJ. So the situation is hardly symmetrical. As a child, I had not been taught to hate the Jews, but I had also not learned to respect them, since they were the direct cause of my tragedy. Now, in spite of this, I learned to understand their human needs, which were very similar to my own. I was no longer able to judge them collectively, since I discovered that I could find many partners on their side who sought a humane solution to the conflict.

Yet it has always seemed to me that the negative feelings of the Jews towards the Palestinians, acquired through their education, go much deeper than do ours toward them. Even those in favor of concessions to the Palestinians find it difficult to let go of the deep conditioning in regard to us, and take for granted their superiority in almost every aspect of life. Whereas we had acquired all the traits of a colonized, defeated people, and the educational curriculum had sought to eliminate any remaining national pride or identity, the Jews had come to accept unquestioningly the superiority of their culture, their values, and their society. They have greater self-confidence, national consciousness, and group cohesion, but little tolerance for opinions, behaviors, and traits that diverged from their own. In many ways, I envied them. I wished that I and my people could gain a little of their confidence, sense of security, and group solidarity, not to mention a national home of their own where they could develop, produce, think, and educate their children without the influences of distortion, fear, or intervention . . .

Yet there has been a development in national consciousness among Palestinians in Israel all the same. After the revoking of military rule, it became possible to publish newspapers again, and though these were carefully monitored by the authorities, there was more opportunity of self-expression. The period after the 1967 war brought the opportunity for increased contact between Palestinians in Israel and those living in the West Bank and Gaza. There developed a greater solidarity with the (usually much worse) plight of their compatriots there. The struggle of the Palestinians on the outside became a source of inspiration. The Intifada boosted self-confidence . . .

These excerpts touch on many of the issues that Rayek and I discussed in our interview, but more eloquently. What is missing from this formal text, however, and what was significant in the personal interview, was how we each reflected on the fact that our perspectives are laden with cultural baggage that we have inherited. In the interview process we learned to live out the existence of both our identity stories at once and to discuss the morass of the Jewish and Palestinian conflict in Israel not only within a larger geohistorical context but also within our particular life histories.

During the course of our interview, I had the opportunity to tell Rayek what was deep in my heart. I began to tell him about the death of Jewish selfhood through the genocide of the Jews in Nazi Europe; it was a personal story that he had never heard before. It wasn't a list outlining historical facts nor was it the rhetoric of those so angry that they end up shouting across an abyss at one another. The Holocaust is an evil that has spread its taint on all of humanity in the twentieth century, and it is a story unresolved—a "past that refuses to go away," as Saul Friedlander puts it (1988, p. 44). When I explained to Rayek that the re-creation of Israel after 2000 years of exile was an urgent attempt to "re-create" Jewish selfhood in the face of this disaster, he listened very quietly:

Grace (G):   No other countries were even willing to take in the survivors. Before, during, and even after the war, nobody wanted them. My parents languished in a DP camp for two long years even though they had a blood relative—my father's sister, who had moved to Montreal in 1929—ready to sponsor them. This was because the Canadian immigration department at that time had a certain high-ranking official named [Frederic Charles] Blair who did his utmost to keep Jews out. I can send you a book written by two Canadian historians documenting this shameful period in Canadian history. And anti-Semitism was not restricted to Canada. Not by any means. What were all the other refugees—who had no one to sponsor them—to do?

      The necessity to take action for a return to the Jewish homeland was never greater. This 1948 war was not like some sort of imperialistic power coming in to take over a foreign place. This was a last resort, drowning in the blood of the millions of Jews who were murdered. Where else were they supposed to go? This was, after all, their homeland. The Zionist dream of return had to become a reality—there was no other choice. What would your people have done in the same circumstances?

      You say that Arabs know more about Jews than Jews about Arabs. Did your teachers ever take you to Yad Vashem [the museum dedicated to the Holocaust] in Jerusalem? This deep trauma is still very powerful in the collective consciousness of Jews everywhere in the world and the Jewish Israelis are no exception. Look how it surfaced here during the Gulf War when Saddam boasted that he would gas Tel Aviv with chemical weapons! You saw the reaction of your Jewish neighbors. They were much more upset than you and all the Arab neighbors here were. I think you have to understand the depth of the trauma.

Rayek (R):   I agree with you. But what about the Palestinian problem? Why do we have to pay for what the Nazis did to the Jews in

Europe? Is that fair? We have lost our homeland. It may not be as catastrophic in terms of millions murdered; we can't compete with that. But does that mean that our loss can be ignored? How do we get past such a horrible impasse?

G: Of course it isn't fair. There is no justice in all this mess. I see it is as a sick twist of fate that the Palestinians became indirect victims of the Nazis too. We're both victims, but how do both Jews and Palestinians begin to discuss this in open dialogue [in which] they can both acknowledge one another's pain and loss and fear? To me that's the real impasse. It takes compassion and real courage to do that. I don't know what else to say.

I remember when I was in a "School for Peace" workshop and witnessed firsthand the tensions coming from the lack of recognition by some of Israeli Jewish kids for the legitimacy of a Palestinian national identity. On the other side, many of the Palestinian kids didn't want to recognize the fears of the Jewish group that lie deep within their psyches because of the genocide during the Holocaust, and also because of the hostility that most Arab nations have toward Israel's existence in the Middle East. I wrote about it in an academic article that was published in the U.S. What I saw clearly was what I called a "competition of victimhoods" because both sides are terribly wounded psychologically, whether they look it or not. Each group has been victimized in very different ways, and they have great difficulty accepting that the other group has also suffered. One of the facilitators said to me privately, "The role of the victim carries moral capital and therefore the implication is that the victim is in the right and more humane, so it comes down to who is more of a victim." Those workshops opened up their emotions from a very deep place in their souls and made them realize that [these feelings] were totally legitimate. It was incredible to see how much more empathy most of them had for one another at the end of those few days. It's a real beginning.

R: Yes, it's true, we have to break down those terrible barriers. There is so much hatred, fear, and ambivalence. We have a long way to go in order to eradicate that. But what I like about what you say that they stress in the workshops is that it's OK to have those feelings. It's not our fault; the situation has forced us into these hard lines. For so many years I grew up feeling like the Jews are our enemy—they took away the homes of so many of my relatives; forced them out. It's a feeling of awful humiliation. As I said, I saw the Jews as strong and proud and dominant and my group as afraid, weak, and without a psychological home. And now you're telling me that you as a Jew outside of Israel and coming from parents who suffered the Holocaust, that you always felt the same way. I never really spoke about that before or understood it so deeply. Because here in Israel the Jews are the majority. You might have felt different if you had grown up in Israel.

G: It might have been different; I always felt deep inside that it would have been better for my parents to have come to Israel after the war. But my father had one surviving sister in Montreal who sponsored [my parents and brother] to come to Canada. Yes, it was a lonely existence for survivors and their children. We were on the fringes. I always felt deviant, never quite fitting in. Oh well, I'll never be able to change that.

R: So that's why Israel is so important for you.

G: Yes, one of the reasons—and as a way of feeling proud of my Jewishness.

R: We want that for us [the Palestinians].

G: I understand. It's pretty heavy stuff.

I don't know what I had expected from this interview, but I was moved deeply by the feelings that emerged from it. Rayek and I came from diametrically opposed places in this Middle East conflict but we found common ground in the border zones of our personal stories, drawing new meaning from the deep wells of our respective distress and suffering. Rayek told me that he had never before talked so openly about the misery of the Palestinian "exile" to a Jew, and had never before truly heard a personal account of the emotional woundedness of the Holocaust from a child of survivors. Our psychological vulnerabilities intersected in unexpected ways and in our discussions we moved dialectically back and forth between hope and despair. We were each fiercely holding onto our respective pasts, but we had taken a leap forward to the future. The barriers of anger and mistrust were transcended in this special interview and its complex tensions. We had, in a way, liberated each other, knowing full well that there were no simplistic solutions. Our conversations brought us up against the limits of our experience and opened a fragile door. I would like to give Rayek the last word by quoting from the ending of his presentation to the German Friends:

Living in Wahat Al-Salam/Neve Shalom has shown me that, given a solid framework, where the two sides agree to work together without demanding of each other to relinquish parts of their identity or aspirations, even the most serious difficulties can be addressed and eventually overcome. I am not implying by this that the community presents a model that can be applied wholesale in the Middle East. The majority of Jews and Palestinians will always prefer to live separately, for cultural and social reasons, rather than live in a framework that forces them to live and work together so closely. Yet the success of any attempt to find a solution to the conflict depends upon absorbing much the same lessons learned here by our experience of close cooperation. It will be necessary to work together with the other side, and to become intimate with [its] needs and positions, rather than to pretend that it is possible to dictate a solution based only upon the perspective of one's own side. Just as in building a community, success will depend upon the solid persistence in one's efforts over the long term, despite opposition. Many of the obstacles on the road to coexistence can be traced to negative conditioning we received through the prejudices and distortions instilled in us by parents and teachers. The only hope to overcome these obstacles is to establish an educational system that will strengthen our understanding of our own cultural and national background[s], without denigrating the national identity of the other. Our educational system must lay the foundation for true equality, regardless of our nationalit[ies], religion[s], culture[s] or gender. It must impart humane rather than dehumanizing values, since as human beings we all share the role of parents and children, with similar dreams, wishes, worries, and ambitions. It must teach a more balanced and objective history of the relations between the two peoples, since this is not a conflict between sheep and wolves or good and evil-minded people.

Our educational system must break down the walls of ignorance by creating a truly bilingual society, since if one group is deprived of access to the linguistic resources of the other, there is an undervaluing of its culture. Hearing the other language produces frustration or deep suspicion. Palestinians routinely learn Hebrew as the majority language in Israel. It is time for Jews to learn Arabic in the same way. Our educational system, finally, must impart mutual respect instead of hatred, and a mutual acceptance of our rights, history, and pain, instead of denial. Our dehumanizing educational system must be transformed, or we will pass on to our children a worse reality than the one we have known ourselves.

Fifty years have passed since an event occurred which one side celebrates with fireworks and festivities as the birth of a nation, and the other side remembers darkly as the Naqba, the Catastrophe. Over the intervening half-century, both sides have known a rich variety of experience that has formed their national consciousness and character. Much of this experience has centered on a conflict between each other as two groups that lay claim to the same land. As in real life, the lessons derived from similar experiences can produce different results. One man may turn his acquired anger into hatred, the other may be motivated to seek a solution that offers peace. In my life I have tried to draw the right lessons from my experience. The success of the two peoples in resolving the conflict depends also upon drawing the right lessons from the experience of the past fifty years. (October 1998, pp. 10–11)

I have attempted to paint a portrait here of the former mayor of Neve Shalom/Wahat Al-Salam—of his dedication and his exploration into how both sides might, through this village, do justice to the complexity of life for Jews and Palestinians in Israel, and to the moral responsibilities and dangers that confront the people in this village as they try to create a world that did not exist before. In May 1999 the election results indicating the success of Ehud Barak and the Labor Party had just come in. In an e-mail, Rayek wrote,

> *I feel that the election results show that the majority of Israelis now believe that territorial compromise is necessary for peace. This can only lead me to feel more optimistic over the chances for restoring the peace process to its track.*

In June 2000, Rayek stopped in Toronto while on a trip to the United States and we had a brief chat. In spite of the precarious state of the peace process, he remained as positive as ever: "The important thing is to keep going," he said. "It's about psychology—how do you build trust? I don't have problems with a Jew who is a Zionist, as long as he doesn't cancel off the needs of the Palestinian for a homeland. The problem in Israel is that Jews and Palestinians don't know one another. The Neve Shalom/Wahat Al-Salam experience *humanizes* the conflict. It is called an oasis, but only as compared to other areas in the country. The village has many difficulties but at least we are not being broken. We do have personal squabbles as in any village, but we are living the conflict instead of fighting it. Most people are stuck in a position where they can't trust."

Believing in a Place of Peace: An Interview with Père Abbé Paul Sauma

The Latrun Monastery, adjacent to the village, played a crucial role in its creation by leasing 100 acres of land to Father Bruno in 1972. As mentioned previously, the Latrun Monastery is comprised of French Trappist monks. They are, in fact, of the Cistercian branch of the Benedictine Order founded by Saint Benoît on the principle of working for peace in God's name. I was invited to visit Father Paul, the abbott of the monastery, on the last day of my November/December 1999 sojourn. Rayek confided to me that Père Abbé Paul doesn't usually give interviews but when he heard that I have been doing research in the village since 1991 (and that I speak French), he agreed to see me. I was elated. I began the interview with Père Paul by sharing with him my feelings about the Christmas party that I had witnessed on my first sojourn. Father Paul had also seen this celebration a few years ago and had a lot to say about its symbolic significance. The following excerpts are concerned directly with the peace activities of the village:

Father Paul (FP):   I attended the Christmas party two years ago and I was struck by the seriousness of the children, the authenticity.

The little girl who played Mary was wonderful. I have read the Gospel, of course, and I can tell you that there wasn't one error. And all of them had such respect and dignity.

Grace (G): They were like angels!

FP: From that time on I have [had] a great sympathy for the villagers. I know their defects, all their lapses, their deviations from the path; but the village wants to create peace. It may not take hold in the whole country, it's not guaranteed; but they have placed this little seed in the ground, this grain of hope—which may bear fruit in the country at some point. One can already see certain changes. At this moment we are very engaged with them. We are encouraging them, pushing them, protecting them. They are threatened, always threatened by those who do not want peace. But our interests are in common with theirs, even though they are on a more secular route than we are. In the past, the monastery was upset about that. But I see that what is important to them is important to us. What hurts them hurts us. We are hoping to work together with them for the same goal. You may have noticed that in front of our entrance there is a mosaic with the Latin word PAX on it. This is our symbol. The Benedictine Order. PEACE.

G: Yes, I noticed it. It's a lovely mosaic.

FP: So we are very much at ease with Neve Shalom's program, to live together in diversity. Here at Latrun we live this life very deeply as a community of difference united in the work for peace. Our monks come from eleven different nationalities and we welcome visitors from everywhere. Geographically, we are interestingly placed by Providence as well. So near to the Territories. At Christmas, our Church is full of people from all religions—Jews, Muslims, Christians of all rites. You yourself have seen that.

G: Yes.

FP: Our goal, which I think is the goal of the villagers as well, whether they know it or not, is that the more we approach God, the more we come closer to one another. We appreciate your interest in the village. We're so very happy to see that you are writing about it, Bruno's dream.

G: You know, I will never forget my chat with Father Bruno . . .

FP: Ah, Father Bruno. I always say that Neve Shalom/Wahat Al-Salam was born out of the meeting of two saints. That gives it its strength and its weakness. The two saints are Father Bruno, of course, and Father Elie Cordézy, the abbott at Latrun at the time. He sensitized the (religious) community. Bruno had the magnificent idea but without land it would have come to naught. It was a serendipitous meeting—at the perfect moment. Yes, there were doubts about the faith of the villagers [because they were mainly secular], hesitations on both sides, but they worked it out. I think because of us [at Latrun] they stayed the course. And I hope they will continue on the right route . . .

Father Paul discussed with me the fact that the monastery had decided (through negotiations with Rayek Rizek) to give the land of Neve Shalom/Wahat Al-Salam as an outright gift to the villagers in honor of the new millennium.

Figure 5–2 The PAX mosaic—the symbol of Peace—on the grounds of the Latrun Monastery. (Courtesy of the author.)

FP: We are now giving them the land as a gift of goodwill. To show them that the entente between the two peoples is a wonderful ideal and that we have faith in them. The supreme good in this world is peace. We want to favour that endeavor . . . so we are signing the contract with them on January 1, 2000, for the new millennium. There have been very difficult moments, and we weren't sure if it would work out but now it has reached the satisfaction of everyone. The hand of God is in it. The number of children in the school from all over this area is such a good sign. The fact that parents from outside the village are sending their children to the school—that's important.

G: It is a symbol; it gives hope, it nourishes the soul.

FP: Indeed, it gives off a shining light of hope in spite of all the evil around. Two things go together—peace and joy. You are working for peace and you feel joy. It's powerful; those who work for peace are close to God. The existence of the village is the will of God.

I discussed with Père Paul my anxieties about finding the right publisher for my book:

G: When I return home I will start looking for a publisher for my manuscript. That's a whole new experience for me.

FP: Don't worry! It will be accepted with open arms, because it is important for others to know about what is going on in this village. There is justice, charity, and love behind it. I'm not saying there aren't any problems there. But [the villagers] are trying hard to find peace. It gives meaning to their lives and to all of us. The hand of God is guiding them and all of us who work for peace . . .

G: Is there anything else you would like to say?

FP: My one request is that if you can put any photos in your book, could you please take a picture of the PAX mosaic outside and make sure that it goes into the book. I see that you have a camera with you.

G: May I take a picture of you?

FP: No, not me. Just the mosaic.

Father Paul then brought in two bottles of the wine the monks make from the grapes of the Latrun vineyards: a Chardonnay and a Muscat. They were a gift for me to take back to Canada. He also had two full wineglasses and we shared a toast to the village and to my future book. I hugged him and he escorted me outside and stood watch while I took a number of pictures of the PAX mosaic. I promised that if I were allowed photos, this one would be in the book for sure. Rayek came to pick me up and I waved good-bye to Father Paul as we drove back to the village, his kindly face and white and black robe receding into the background. The two bottles of wine were clinking next to me—telling of celebrations to come.

Concluding Remarks

This chapter belongs to the interview work that is central to this research endeavor—a mix of the subjective and objective—which has brought me closer to why I came to this village in the first place: to collect these stories, and to put myself on the line as listener, witness, researcher, and fellow human on this journey to make sense of our struggles, of our lives, and of our work. On reflection, I am humbled by the stories of these people who offered me their dreams. I shared the bread of hope with them in the telling of their tales and was grateful that they were interested in fitting my story in with theirs. In the interviews with participants and in the pedagogical spaces that were observed, I walked through a land of moral reflection, of pedagogical reveries, of social and political tensions, of painful narratives as well as healing ones. In the creation of their oral texts, the participants' selves intermingled with my own. I know that there is so much of great significance in their stories and so much that will not be resolved in this writing. It seems to me that this research journey is only a small step toward a never-ending search for the "promised land" of our fantasies. Is this what Franz Kafka meant when he said, "No man's life is long enough to enter Canaan, even if he has been on the track of Canaan all of his life." This existential angst seems related to the woundedness that surrounds the historical reality of these two peoples. Certainly the work of the villagers is a dialogic attempt at exploration and reconciliation within a desert of conflict. Their enterprise is remarkable and in keeping with the writing of the philosopher Edmond Jabès (1990), who uses the desert as a metaphor for the wound. The voices that I heard—mixed with joy, faith, vulnerability, despair, and tragedy—are magical because they come from the heart. They enchanted me in their forthrightness and especially in the anxiety of their reckless optimism, desperation, and hope.

Chapter Six

Teaching Peace: The Power of Love, Art, and Imagination

I have come to believe that a great teacher is a great artist and that there are as few as there are any other great artists. Teaching might even be the greatest of the arts since the medium is the human mind and spirit.

—John Steinbeck

Teachers' Stories as Invitations to Understanding

This chapter is based on the conversations that I shared with several "great artists"—the teachers of Neve Shalom/Wahat Al-Salam both in and out of their classrooms. What they taught me is that peace is not the absence of conflict; it is the way in which one learns to deal with conflict. These educators, I believe, would have commanded the respect of Paulo Freire, who wrote about his ideal of education in 1997: "What I have been proposing from my political convictions, my philosophical convictions, is a profound respect for the total autonomy of the educator. What I have been proposing is a profound respect for the cultural identity of students—a cultural identity that implies respect for the language of the other, the color of the other, the sexual orientation of the other, the intellectual capacity of the other; that implies the ability to stimulate the creativity of the other. But these things take place in a social and historical context and not in pure air. These things take place in history and I, Paulo Freire, am not the owner of history." (McLaren, 1999, p. 307–308)

The teachers in the Neve Shalom/Wahat Al-Salam elementary school as well as in the "School for Peace" are creating history in their classrooms. They embody the words "Peace is every step" of Thich Nhat Hanh, the Vietnamese Buddhist monk who drew young people to his school in the 1960s to teach how to act in a spirit of compassion in response to the needs of peasants caught up in the turmoil of the war in Vietnam. This chapter describes my interviews with the school's educators as well as my classroom observations both in the "School for Peace" and the elementary school in search of liberation in

147

education. Through the dialectic between interviewer and interviewee, a cultural, pedagogical, ideological, and familial relationship of intertwined voices was negotiated, nurtured, and interpreted in each conversation. It is in the critical encounter with the "other" that we construct our own self-understanding, which motivates us to deep inquiry and the construction of knowledge. Sandra Jackson (1989) explains the ethnographic pursuit as follows: "Knowledge of the other is not just a product of our theoretical thought and research activity; it is a consequence of critical experiences, relationships, choices, and events both in the field and in the quotidian world of our professional and family lives. . . . Ethnography then becomes a form of *verstehen* (understanding), a project of empathic and vicarious understanding in that the other is seen in the light of one's own experiences and the activity of trying to fathom the other in turn illuminates and alters one's sense of self . . ." (in Lawrence-Lightfoot, p. 136). James Carse (1986, p. 125) tells us: "Narratives raise issues, showing us that matters do not end as they must but as they do . . . narrative invites us to rethink what we thought we knew."

The study of teachers' narratives—that is, teachers' stories of their own experiences—is increasingly being seen as crucial to the study of teachers' thinking, culture, and behavior (Goodson, 1991, 1992). Indeed, a growing number of scholars argue that since teachers are key players in education, their voices should be heard; they have a right to speak for and about the teaching learning experience. Furthermore, narrative research is becoming accepted as a means of understanding teachers' culture from within (see, for example, Carter, 1993; Cole & Knowles, 2000; Clandinin & Connelly, 2000; Eisner, 1991; Goodson, 1991; Schon, 1991; Tabachnick & Zeichner, 1993). Educational investigators, however, have generally paid too little attention to teachers' voices, especially those on the margins of the system. William Pinar (1998) suggests that identification with marginalized social groups is of utmost educational importance. Henry Giroux (1994) claims that "multiculturalism has become a central discourse in the struggle over issues regarding national identity, the construction of historical memory, the purpose of schooling, and the meaning of democracy." Such theoretical notions are very significant in terms of the asymmetrical relations between Jews and Palestinians in Israel and extremely relevant to teaching peaceful and egalitarian relations in this village school.

The Intersection among Teaching, Learning, and Meaning: A Personal Deconstruction

In order to help me explore the educational stories of these teachers, I began to revisit my own reasons for becoming interested in peace education, and to observe the experiences of my participants through different lenses. I wanted "to recount the past in order to reclaim it," as Andra Makler (1991, p. 45) puts it: "in this way we reevaluate ourselves in relation to others." This image of teaching as an interpretive and reflective activity informs the notion put forth by William Ayers (1993) that good teaching requires "a serious encounter with autobiography" and we must consider that a critical knowledge of teaching involves an exploration of one's self. Accepting David Hunt's (1991) claim that "beginning with ourselves" is necessary in order to validate the educational research endeavor, I have attempted in this ethnography to allow the voices of these teacher/educators (including my own voice) to explore the epistemologically complex terrain of peacemaking within the educational context of Jewish-Palestinian relations in Israel. Deborah Britzman (1995, p. 232) suggests that "while [traditional] educational ethnography promises the narrative cohesiveness of experience and identity and the researcher's skill of representing the subject, poststructural theories disrupt any desire for a seamless narrative, a cohesive identity, or a mimetic representation . . . 'being there' does not guarantee access to truth." Thus, the tradition of ethnographic authority derived from participant observation paradoxically becomes a site of doubt as well as confirmation of what exists prior to representation.

I agree with Britzman that my own telling is fragmented and dominated by the "discourses of my time and place" and especially by my sense of being a border dweller, someone still searching for "home." I confess openly to this guilty desire. Perhaps we must indeed acknowledge ethnography as a "regulating fiction, as a particular narrative practice that produces textual identities and regimes of truth" (ibid., p. 236). Moreover, Renato Rosaldo (1989) contends that there are no "innocent" ethnographers. There is always an interior voice crying to be heard, to be acknowledged, to be recognized within the exterior professional world. We are all moved by deep unconscious forces, and that is nothing if not human. The multiple layerings that become the foundation on which we do our "formal" ethnographic work emerge from personal, private experiences and "ways of knowing" (Belenky, et al., 1986) which are not incongruent with theoretical, epistemological frames of reference. In fact, the fragments have in themselves a certain coherence, a raw clarity of purpose: they represent the emotional chaos—the landscapes of loss, pain, fear, and trauma that create the underpinnings of this struggle toward peace with which I became intimately involved. The stuff of ethnography, indeed perhaps of all human endeavor, is in the endless retellings and thus in illuminating the enormous questions located in the vicissitudes, contradictions, and ambiguities of human relationships, in the "us" versus "them" dichotomies.

I did not have the good fortune to grow up in a family that belonged to the dominant society, and never had the confidence to even dream of understanding the difference between "self" and "other." My soul was trying desperately to survive against the annihilation of "self," all the while terrified that there was no place for me in the land of the "other." The "other" had a sharper, more vibrant image: people of color, people who spoke languages different from mine, people who came from countries where their home languages corresponded to their homelands—places and extended families which still existed for them. Where did I belong, a "deviant" child of the Holocaust who was and felt invisible, lost? Craig Kridel (1998, p. 122) underscores the "power of autobiography and biography—the construction of landscapes and the act of making history personal." Indeed, Norman Denzin and Yvonna

Lincoln (1994) suggest that "the means for interpretive, ethnographic practices are still not clear, but it is certain that things will never be the same. We are in a new age where messy, uncertain, multivoiced texts, cultural criticism, and new experimental works will become more common, as will more reflexive forms of fieldwork, analysis, and intertextual representation" (as cited in Kridel, 1998, p. 15).

When I first arrived at the Neve Shalom/Wahat Al-Salam elementary school in 1991, I began to reflect on my own reasons for becoming a bilingual education (French immersion) teacher in Canada almost two decades earlier and then later, a university professor focusing on immigrant/refugee/peace education. What were the unconscious myths or metaphors that motivated me? Carol Witherell and Nel Noddings (1991, p. 5) believe that "to take seriously the quest for life's meaning and the meaning of individual lives, is to understand the primacy of the caring relation and of dialogue in educational practice." So I asked myself in the calmer moments of my journal writing, "Why did I go into education in the frst place?" The following excerpt from my journal, written after I returned home from my first sojourn, clarified for me why I had chosen Neve Shalom/Wahat Al-Salam for my fieldwork. Or had it chosen me?

I knew early on in my life that I had a vision of myself connecting with others, all kinds of other beings, from all kinds of backgrounds. I saw teaching as an opportunity to share knowledge and feelings and different ways of looking at the world. To communicate with people of many cultures and languages. To offer and to receive ideas. To be involved in the teaching/learning enterprise meant entering into a dialogue. It was a yearning for the kind of dialogue that was not possible in my family life. It was a yearning for "inclusion" and understanding and belonging. I hoped subconsciously that in the classroom created by me, there would be justice and tolerance and admiration of talent. I would nurture my students and they would nurture me. We would enter into each other's worlds; we would break down barriers. We would free each other from all sorts of tyrannies. I would rescue my students from their prisons.

I have always seen education as a genuine dialogue, the kind of dialogue that allows, as Witherell and Noddings suggest, "the negotiation of meanings through which the self in relation to other selves and to one's cultural communities is constituted." I wanted to create the kind of dialogue described as "open, that is, conclusions are not held to be absolute by any party at the outset. The search for enlightenment, responsible choice, perspective, or means to solve a problem is mutual and marked by appropriate signs of reciprocity." And most of all I wanted to create an environment of safety and trust. All things that had been so sadly denied me in my own childhood. I wanted to "make it better" and I saw the classroom as a means in that direction. It would give me the power to empower my students and finally myself. And in my classrooms, I did make a difference. I chose elementary school because it was childhood—my own childhood—that I so desperately needed to repair. But my childhood was gone, destroyed before it ever had a chance to flourish. Perhaps I could make a difference in the childhood of my students. I felt like it was a mission . . . (Winter, 1992)

As my journal entry points out, teachers' lives are influenced by what happens to them outside of the classroom as well (Clandinin & Connelly, 1995). Their personal and cultural stories influence their professional lives, and the perceptions of the world that they bring to the classroom interact with those of their students. Peter McLaren (1999, p. 53) paraphrases Freire eloquently: "It is a lifetime struggle that requires counterintuitive insight, honesty, compassion, and a willingness to brush one's personal history against the grain of 'naive consciousness' or commonsense understanding."

One of the pivotal questions that fueled my conversations with the participants was, "How can we make peace education even more meaningful in this village? And how can we make others in Israeli society and even in other parts of the world more aware of what we are trying to accomplish?" For what is peace education if not a strong voice that makes itself heard above the cacophony of conflict and war?

Teaching as Life Experience in Neve Shalom/Wahat Al-Salam

Teaching is certainly a highly personal enterprise. William Ayers (1996, p. 18) goes so far as to say that "teaching is primarily an act of love." It is not merely a question of mastering certain technical skills. It is relational and interactive. As in any profession where there develops over time an intimate relationship between practitioner and client, teaching is more of an art than a science. There is a well-known saying that even the best curriculum materials will fail if the teacher's heart is not in it. Canadian poet and writer Anne Michaels (1996, p. 121) says that "the best teacher lodges an intent not in the mind but in the heart." This notion is consonant with Freire's idea that pedagogy has "as much to do with the teachable heart as the teachable mind, and as much to do with efforts to change the world as it does with rethinking the categories that we use to analyze our current condition within history" (McLaren, 1999, p. 50). Ivor Goodson (1991) argues that in understanding something so intensely personal as teaching, it is critical to know about the teacher as a person. Educational researchers are beginning to focus intensively on the interaction between life histories and the broad social and political context of the schools in which teachers find themselves. Indeed, teachers' perceptions of themselves in terms of their role in the educational enterprise, and their attitudes toward their students, may have the greatest impact on the success of the teaching and learning that takes place within their classrooms (Paré, 1994).

At Neve Shalom/Wahat Al-Salam, the educational enterprise is an exchange, a relationship that involves giving and receiving; it is the dream of a more just society and the promise of hope. I interviewed the teacher-participants individually on as many as three separate occasions in the privacy of their classrooms after lessons were over. In some cases, I collected more of their stories in their homes, and they listened to mine. What emerged was a shared narrative, a collaborative story about the teaching/learning experience within the context of this Jewish-Palestinian bilingual, binational, bicultural school. I focused on the collaborative relationships among the teachers that were promoted by the philosophy of the village and described the interconnected settings among teachers, students, and parents. In this quest for meaning and authenticity in minority language education, I concur with John Dewey's (1938, p. 111) concept of "teaching and learning as a continuous process of reconstruction of experience." Through a process of sharing personal and professional stories, I hoped to locate this enterprise within the complex landscapes inhabited by the participants and their struggle for egalitarian coexistence. The experience of sharing their stories not only empowered my participants, but provided me, in the role of educational researcher, a fresh understanding of their quest for peaceful coexistence amidst the conflict in the wider society. The following section revisits the two extraordinary teachers who facilitated the "School for Peace" (SFP) workshop I observed during my first sojourn in the village in 1991.

Tirzah and Ahmed, the SFP Facilitators

The "School for Peace" (SFP) was discussed in chapter 4. This section includes further discussion about my observations in order to focus specifically on the "teachable moments" that occurred in the workshop classroom.[1] I had witnessed students facing the "enemy" in that small, drafty room on a cold, rainy December day in 1991. It was a shocking moment; I shall never forget it. First, utter silence . . . Then Tirzah, the Jewish facilitator, calmly stood up and said that it was not necessary for anyone to become friends, that this encounter was simply a means to air out any issues, problems, or questions that needed to be explored. That was all. I sensed a collective sigh of relief. I also felt my own body relax in the chair. There were no expectations. Such a declaration helped to overcome the intense pressures that had stifled the room. There was something soothing and yet strong about Tirzah's manner and this comforted the participants. Ahmed, the Arab facilitator, basically reiterated Tirzah's words in Arabic and explained that when he and Tirzah had first come to train together as facilitators, they also had "a lot of heavy ground to cover. And even to this day, five years later, we still have whopper arguments, but we're talking together and we sort of understand where we're coming from. But it takes time and nobody can rush that process . . . And," he said, "your feelings, no matter how full of hate or fear or doubt, are legitimate and they will be honored in this encounter."

I felt I was truly witnessing the so-called teachable moment. Ahmed explained to me during one of our private conversations that his words had represented a call for a shared consciousness, a call toward building a sense of moral development and responsibility in the midst of violent conflict and enmity. He was promising the student participants a commitment to caring and authenticity. The solid bond between him and Tirzah was very reassuring as well.

The following comments are those of an Arab male participant of the "School for Peace" workshop session:

> Here I was, having been taught all my life that the Jews were inflexible, intolerant, and the oppressors and here I see Ahmed [the Palestinian facilitator] really getting along with Tirzah [the Jewish facilitator] and Tirzah respecting his point of view that a Palestinian national identity is crucial. I mean, I didn't expect that. I was stunned for a minute. I didn't know that frame of thinking existed in Israeli Jews. We Arab kids don't get to know the Jewish kids, and the Jewish kids don't know us—so of course we're all confused and we're all stuck with the worst stereotypes. If nothing else comes out of these sessions, at least now I feel I have met Jewish kids in a real way. And I feel less scared.

The collaborative approach of the two facilitators was certainly essential for the encounter's success. Narratives saturated with moral dilemma constantly infiltrated the pedagogical discourse of the workshops. The facilitators showed leadership as they maneuvered delicately through the minefields of the many stories that emerged—stories filled with rage, despair, loss, and death. This is emotionally intensive work; it must be conducted with a sensitivity that can only come from a deep compassion. In fact, during the hours and days of the worksop sessions I was overwhelmed by the craft and artistry in the facilitators' ways of leading their students through the gradual process of social and psychological transformation. Shoshana Felman (1992, p. 54) asserts that "it is the teacher's task to reconceptualize the crisis and to put it back into perspective, to relate the present to the past and to the future and to thus reintegrate the crisis in a transformed frame of meaning." Indeed, Tirzah and Ahmed created a space in which the participants began to speak to each other from a very deep and injured part of their selves.

Emmanuel, a Jewish male participant, told me in a personal conversation during one of the breaks:

> I don't know how Ahmed did it, but when he said that I had a right to my feelings, my belligerent attitude started to change. He made me feel like he was really willing to listen to me. So I became ready to talk.

Ouaffa, an Arab female participant, expressed pleasure because she did not feel marginalized; she explained how the facilitators gave her a sense of having agency in the world:

> I liked Ahmed's calm but strong manner. And he made it clear that he was interested in hearing from the girls, not just the boys. I could tell that right away because of the way he listened to Tirzah, and he acknowledged what she was saying even when he disagreed. It made me feel validated as

a woman and, as you know, in Arab society, that is not always the case, to put it mildly. So I think I began to enjoy the sessions even with all the arguments because you could feel like you were a part of it and things were happening and you were making them happen.

It seemed to me, as I watched the sessions unfolding, that the facilitators' dedication to the personal and professional development of the participants arose out of a profound motivation to act morally in spite of all the underlying ambiguity. Tirzah and Ahmed created a community of learners that encouraged real dialogue, inclusion, and fairness, and instilled a sense of moral responsibility in the participants toward constructing the knowledge and building relationships needed for peacemaking. They shared their own stories of pain and conflict and cautious hope, and journeyed on a process of uncovering and reconstructing the meaning of their professional lives as conflict mediators from the perspectives of their own national identities. I remember being mindful of Tirzah's honesty when she said matter-of-factly to the participants in one session:

> During our first year of working together, I was very suspicious of everything Ahmed said or did. It was as if nothing would be good enough because he was an Arab and the cause of all the problems. It wasn't until I began to accept him as a human being and tell him how I felt that we could begin to know each other.

Even in the midst of very troubled or excruciating moments when there seemed to be no possibility of reconciliation, the facilitators were always accessible to their students and to each other. For example, many of the activities in the workshops revolved around the issue of the legitimacy of national identities—both Jewish and Palestinian—within Israel. These activities focused on ethical and existential dimensions of affirming and living out each identity without negating those of the other. The changing nature of truth was also a theme of the discussions. The participants kept seeking their own perceptions and understanding of the conflict. In one session the facilitators placed photographs of violence, war, and grieving on a dark cloth on the floor. They asked each participant to choose a photo that best expressed his or her feelings that day about the conflict between the two peoples. Both despair and anger were released and the room became charged with emotion.

I watched quietly at the back of the room while a number of Palestinian participants voiced their outrage at the situation of their relatives in the West Bank. Moustafa, a fragile-looking young man with burning dark eyes, held up a photograph that showed a boy crouched near a barred window. "This is what is happening every day in the Territories," he shouted. "Young children are being thrown into prison. There's no hope for a future for them."

From another part of the room, I heard a voice in deep despair. "I feel very sad for the conditions in the West Bank but this image is just as sickening to me and it terrifies me." Nourit, a Jewish teenager, was pointing to a picture showing a train wreck:

This picture reminds me of a terrorist bomb that blew up a bus in my neighborhood, and many people were killed and even more were injured. I was supposed to be on that bus to go visit a friend but changed my plans at the last minute. I still dream of that nightmare. That bomb was planted by someone in the Territories. How can we possibly trust the Arabs?

Ahmed and Tirzah were able to bring more participants into the discussion and to set it into a larger perspective: "Don't you see what you're doing?" yelled out Ahmed. "Each of you [is] hanging onto your own pain and you refuse to see the other group's pain. Don't you realize that both groups are suffering? What are we going to do about that?"

At that moment I wrote in my journal: "These kids just looked at Ahmed as if they were seeing him and each other for the first time. It's quite remarkable. I feel like a charge of electricity just went through my body." (December 1991)

There emerged a heightened awareness of the complexity of the issues, even in terms of curriculum development in schools. In a subsequent discussion, Yonatan, a Jewish participant, reflected with considerable anxiety on his "regular school" study of *Moledet* (a Hebrew word meaning "birthplace") this is an important part of the Jewish Israeli curriculum. The subject is also called *yediat ha'aretz* or "knowledge of the land" and covers geography, geology, history, ethnology, and botany. His words were full of questions:

I realize now that the intention [of Moledet] is not only to increase knowledge but to nurture a deep attachment to the country and instill young people with a love of their land. There is nothing negative about that, but it presents a history that leaves the Israeli Arabs out of the picture altogether. Now I see how that leaves them hanging on the edge. Where do they belong?

Another Jewish participant, Zahavah, disagreed:

I think that Israeli Jewish students have a right to their history and to learn about the early pioneers and the early kibbutzim. After all, it is ours and it is important. We have our history and our Zionism and our legacy in terms of the persecution of the Jewish people for thousands of years. It's important to learn this. So I don't think we can create a cooperative history with the Palestinians because this is not a fairy tale. This is reality and reality is very painful. But we do have to learn to coexist. That goes for their side as well as for ours. I am very upset at how little the Palestinians understand about the traumas that Jews have suffered throughout history and especially during the Holocaust. But at least Tirzah and Ahmed are listening and allowing me to feel my feelings of hurt.

Underneath the surface of the immediate moment lurks the profound woundedness that makes reconciliation between Palestinians and Jews very

problematic. As mentioned in Chapter 4, references to the Holocaust and terrorism against Jews, as well as to the treatment of Palestinians in the Occupied
Territories, dominated the discussions. Tempers often ran high and words
were edged with hate and frustration. This was the first time both groups
could express themselves this freely to each other. An Arab participant,
Ibrahim, explained the process to me in a personal interview:

> We were all ready to jump at each other's throats about our grievances. I
> couldn't believe how cavalier some of the Jewish participants were with
> regard to the terrrible treatment of the Palestinians in the Occupied
> Territiories. It just made me feel sick. I have relatives who were badly
> injured in certain fights. I do see Israelis, therefore, as aggressors. I can't
> help it. But I never thought of the mass murders of their people in Eastern
> Europe. They are more traumatized than I had ever imagined. We have to
> learn about each other's pain and acknowledge it. It's the first time I've
> ever considered that.

Along with their students, the facilitators struggled to achieve a sense of
balance and meaning in the precarious juggling act of conflict resolution. It
was hardly an easy process. For example, after an especially bitter outburst by
Abdul, a male Palestinian participant, about the terrible conditions in the West
Bank, Ahmed finally stepped in:

> Enough already. We heard you the first time. After five times it loses its
> power. It's time you let others express themselves.

Many of the Arab participants sided with Ahmed as Abdul sulked in his
seat. In another session Tirzah cut short Hannah, a Jewish participant, who
commented, "An Arab will remain an Arab. I don't think they deserve ALL the
rights."

Tirzah responded, very annoyed: "What do you mean by that? Do you realize that your behavior and your words are totally different? First, you said
that there should be equality for both peoples. Now when it comes to specifics,
you are controlling what should be given or taken away." These comments
sparked a noisy debate in which many disagreements between Jew and Jew
and Arab and Arab occurred. This turned out to have a constructive effect because it broke the exclusively Jewish-Palestinian division and instead created a
discussion in which the participants argued from more fluid individual perspectives, rather than from rigid group perspectives.

The sad refrains of victimhood echoed throughout the narratives that
emerged within the safety of these workshops. Sarit, a Jewish female participant commented emotionally in one session about her reaction to the terrorist
acts that happen in Israel:

> To tell the truth, I feel very ambivalent about being here. How can I trust
> people who want to destroy me and my people? I am terrified of Arab
> terrorists. And these attacks keep happening. I feel like a betrayer to be

discussing coexistence with Arabs who have wreaked so much violence on us. But I guess I was enticed by these workshops because I wanted to see my enemy close up. I feel, like everybody else in this country, battle fatigued. Can there be a way out of this awful mess? But to say that I can become friends with Arabs, I don't know. But I'm willing to listen and to see what they have to say. I was told these workshops are no-nonsense and that they don't pretend to solve everything. I am learning to question if we Jews have any responsibility in this conflict. I know now that not every Arab wants to blow up innocent people. And it is true that the situation in the West Bank is desperate.

Mahmoud, a male Arab participant, added quietly but forcefully:

My mind races with such anger when I hear how some Israeli soldiers are treating some of the Palestinians in the territories. It scares me to think that if I were there I could be humiliated badly and also could end up in prison. What hope do these people have for the future? And how does their situation relate to my own identity? And so I want to discuss it with some Jews who are willing to listen. Does that make me a traitor?

Concerning such "border dialogues," I noted that what was crucial to the Jewish and Arab participants in the context of these conflict resolution workshops was that as "border crossers," they were being offered the opportunity to negotiate while maintaining and strengthening their own identities. Furthermore, through the vehicle of narrative, the students were enabled to go beyond their culturally specific lived experiences "in order to come to an understanding of the deeper meaning or significance of [this] aspect of human experience, in the context of the whole of human experience" (Van Manen, 1990).

Recent literature shows how narrative can be a therapeutic endeavor and an emancipatory act (Witherell & Noddings, 1991). Throughout the workshops I observed, the facilitators constantly attempted to empower participants to become storytellers and to guide them as they gradually began a process of uncovering and reconstructing the meaning of their cultural and national identities in the shadowy spaces of trauma and fear. Indeed, there seems to be no possibility of achieving peace without facing the ravages of war. At Neve Shalom/Wahat Al-Salam, the participants' stories of the students opened up a broader perspective on their emotional location within their lived experience of conflict and war. The stories also became an excellent vehicle to discuss issues of social injustice and human rights on a personal basis. The feelings of dislocation and exile, and the quest for rootedness insinuated themselves into every discussion in the workshop encounters. Learning is social—it is something that happens when we interact with one another.

The facilitators created social situations in which meaningful communication was achieved by the participants as a result of personal interaction with their lived texts. The sharing of their stories was intended as a vehicle for "border crossing" but also turned out to be an exercise in risk taking. For many of the participants at the beginning of the encounter, the notion of "border crossing" was considered a betrayal to their group and thus fraught with feelings of hostility and vulnerability. Therefore, critical and reflective frontiers needed to be established *a priori* before any real sharing could take place.

The honest manner in which the facilitators communicated their ideas, trying hard not to impose them; their appreciation of the unique qualities in each of the participants; their empathy toward the moral dilemmas and experiences of injustice that have crippled so many on both sides; and their intellectual capacity for supplying knowledge about the historical realities of the Jewish-Palestinian conflict from both points of view offered a pedagogical model that was entirely remarkable. This is not to say that the facilitators did not engage in any difficult arguments with each other or even with some of the participants; indeed, the workshops would not have been authentic excursions toward conflict resolution without such displays of tension and frustration. The secret of their extraordinary skills, however, lay in their overriding desire to allow the students to uncover their voices so as to construct meaning for their own texts. I saw the facilitators relate to their students with knowledge, wisdom, and humanity; they took obvious satisfaction in the progress of the participants as individuals and as members of their national groups. Tirzah and Ahmed were able to bring abstract concepts such as cultural, political, and national identities to bear on practical issues in the conflict. In so doing, they contributed greatly to the search for meaningful curriculum development in conflict resolution and peace education. This section concludes with the words of one of the facilitators:

> How do you teach conflict resolution in a situation [in which] both peoples are right? You have to make them understand that they are both entitled to their pain but that nevertheless they must acknowledge this pain in one another. Somehow they must learn to coexist. They don't have to love each other. They just have to live and let live.

In Their Own Voices: Interviews as Resistance to Hegemony

> *We live our lives through texts. They may be read, or chanted, or . . .*
> *come to us, like the murmurings of our mothers, telling us what*
> *conventions demand. Whatever their form or medium, these stories have*
> *formed us all; they are what we must use to make new fictions, new*
> *narratives.*
>
> —Heilbrun, 1988, p. 37

The following sections contain interviews with three outstanding educators in the village who also touch the territory of conflict resolution and peace education by transforming the social, pedagogical, and political into very personal territory.

An Interview with Diana Shalufi-Rizek

A teacher in search of his/her freedom may be the only kind of teacher who can arouse young persons to go in search of their own.

—Maxine Greene, 1988, p. 14

I was invited for tea to Diana Shalufi-Rizek's home after school one very hot June afternoon in 1997 for our interview. At the time, Diana was the art teacher in the school. She is Rayek's wife and the person he credits for the original idea to move to this village. She certainly echoed this opinion and went on to discuss how involved she has become professionally in the pedagogical innovations of the elementary school. A good part of the interview centers around the personal transformation that took place both for her and her husband as they witnessed their two children learning in a bilingual, bicultural, binational educational environment. The interview below documents and illuminates the complex dimensions of the personal and professional relationships Diana has developed within the village. Throughout this conversation she emphasizes the ongoing tension between the majority status of the Hebrew language and the minority status of Arabic in the school and in the village. For Diana, language and power are synonymous, and although she acknowledged that much has been done to alleviate the disparity between the two language positions, she expressed her desire for Arabic to be used more freely in everyday communication between Jewish and Palestinian teachers in the school as well as in the village as a whole.

In this encounter I felt very much as if I was standing "at the edge of the scene . . . systematically gathering the details of behavior, expression, and talk, remaining open and receptive to all stimuli" (Lawrence-Lightfoot, 1997, p. 87). In some cases I expressed my own views alongside Diana's and together we heard each other's voices. I sought to explore Diana's distinctive narrative and her ongoing desire for a unified self. The interview displays my questions, my interpretations, my interventions, and my evolving relationship with Diana through the dialogue. She is quite a circumspect person; therefore, I was flattered that she was willing to share with me her intimate thoughts and desires about the village school and about her own children's education at Neve Shalom/Wahat Al-Salam.

Diana as teacher:

Grace (G):   I was in two of [your] classes this morning and now we're talking about the elementary school in the village. I do want to say, as I said to you this morning, that I saw Rayek just now in the dining room and I told him what I thought about you as a teacher and he said yes, sometimes you give too much. I could sense that you give everything to them; you're very dedicated.

Diana (D):   Yes, I suppose so.

G: It's interesting; did you always want to be a teacher?

D: No, not at all.

G: Really?

D: This is really something very new for me.

G: You're kidding.

D: No.

G: I say that because you're a born teacher! I really enjoyed being in your classroom and seeing how the students enjoy your teaching and your care.

D: I worked in the past as a counselor working with students in a school, so that helped me a lot to understand the needs of children.

G: Because there's a real sensitivity; just the way you really listen to the children, it was very interesting to watch you.

D: Well, thank you. But you know I have a small group of students in my classes, which is usually the case here at the school—and that makes an enormous difference. Sometimes we separate them for their level or class or whatever. Some children are at a higher or lower level, so we discussed this issue and the solution was that the kids who are in the higher level would come to me and work with me in the arts, and the others would go to Bob for English and in the afternoon we would switch. Good for them and for me, because we maintain the small-group atmosphere. In this way I can read to everyone and individually work with them.

G: You have been teaching at the school for how long?

D: Only four years.

G: I guess it would just be interesting to have a sense of the difference between this school and other schools that you worked in. Could you tell me a bit about that?

D: Actually I was involved in a special art project in particular schools where I worked for two years with the teachers on special projects in artwork.

G: Where were these schools?

D: In Ramle [a town with a mixed Jewish-Arab population not too far from the village]. I've only been in this primary school four years. But right from the beginning I was really very involved because this place is something special, this is a project that I really admire! This is our future with the kids. And we develop more new methods and new things in the school itself, because we are trying our best to give them this opportunity to be somehow much more "normal," if you know what I mean [in terms of the conflict], than we were allowed to be.

G: Yes, I understand. Because they're together, both Jewish and Palestinian kids, and they're learning together and they're becoming friends. It's so hopeful to see that.

Diana as parent:

D: Right. Let me tell you about my own kids, for example. I have two children. One of them, my older son—you just met his grade-four class. And my other one is in grade one. My older son, for example, was really lucky to have all his education here. They are both lucky, because they can go out and they meet the others, you know, as equals. When they choose friends, it's just because of the person himself, not because he is Palestinian or he is Jewish, and it's really normal and sometimes if they shout at each other, or don't want to play with each other, it's because they had an argument, just a regular argument.

G: Yes, that's just a human trait. The Jewish-Palestinian conflict doesn't enter into it.

D: Quite right. This is something wonderful for me and my husband to see. It is so foreign to our own experience. We were so separate from the Jews. Both sides were so foreign to each other. In fact, when we first moved here it was very hard at the beginning because we weren't used to it. There were certain things I couldn't accept when my older son began his classes here. I have accepted it much more easily now with my younger son because I have also changed from the inside and I started to become much more open here.

At the beginning I was so suspicious and locked in because of the conflict. For example, when my older son came home from grade one and he brought his first reading book from the school library, it turned out to be in Hebrew, because Hebrew is easier to read and faster. You know in Hebrew each letter stands apart and it is easier to read and write in that language. Arabic is so much more complicated. The letter can change three times in a sentence. It depends if it is in the beginning, or the middle, or the end—much more complicated.

Anyway, when I saw him come home—so proud of himself that he could read this book in Hebrew—I felt really angry inside. All I could feel was that as a Palestinian he should be bringing home an Arabic book, not a Hebrew one first. And, of course, he did bring Arabic books home later on, but I didn't understand it at the time. I was so upset. All I could feel was that Hebrew was crowding out the Arabic as it does in the rest of the country, and which I had felt as a child.

Now, after some years here in the village, I am so different. I see the attempt to equalize the language situation as well as other things. I understand now that pedagogically it is natural for the kids to read Hebrew first because it is easier and of course this gives them self-confidence. For example, when my little one, my second child, came home with his Hebrew book this year from the library, I felt really good about it. I saw how proud he felt that he could read and I hugged him. This time I felt fine inside because I knew he would soon be able to read Arabic too and that he would be bilingual; knowing how to speak, read, and write in both languages with a feeling of worth. He would be able to enjoy both languages.

G: How wonderful. I think you're so right; the whole point is [to enjoy] the other language because you feel on the same level, not inferior.

D: Yes, I now believe that children can change their parents. Mine did. You see, when we first came here, it was based on an abstract, ideological feeling of wanting to improve our lot as Palestinians. We harbored a lot of anguish inside ourselves, which we kept hidden until we got here. In this place we began to feel safe enough to start to express our real feelings. At least I'm beginning to do that in meetings and, for example, in this interview. But it is because I see how real this place is and how much good it is doing for the children. So I feel better inside myself.

G: Well, thank you for feeling that you can say these things with me. The kids teach their parents, don't they?

D: Oh yes. They have convinced me.

Diana's views on the special qualities of the school:

G: That's so amazing and heartening. What is it about the school that is so successful?

D: Right from the beginning, we the teachers work with the kids at school. There is a lot of one-to-one time and the classes are all small, as I have mentioned. It is a really long-term process here, because they come here for five days a week each day of the school year. They arrive around eight o'clock and they leave around three in the afternoon and this is a long time, day after day. We have a lot of time together with them where we can really teach them about learning to live together peacefully, learning to respect each other, learning each other's language, each other's culture. And we work with the parents also, but I think that we need to develop that relationship even more.

G: That's a very big point.

D: You know, I believe that no matter what you will do with the kids, they go home and learn the real lessons from their parents. So you have to have the parents on your side. [We need] more meetings with parents, more gatherings for all the parents to meet each other. I think we need to explain more about what this school means to them.

G: And what is the reason why some parents will send their children to this school and some will not? What do you think makes the difference?

D: Well more and more parents are interested in the idea of a Jewish-Palestinian school. It's such a wonder here in this country. It's like a miracle almost. But you know it's also the fact that it's a really good school in terms of programs—the small size of classes attracts the parents; and now we have a language center and an art room and music lessons and the computer room. There's a real connection. And we're really close as teachers, and we develop a lot of curriculum materials together. We've built a reputation. This is what parents are looking for—really good education that is personal.

Diana's thoughts on learning Hebrew and Arabic:

G: It's interesting, and in terms of the language learning, the learning of Arabic, let's say by the Jewish kids, do you think that's very strong? Are they learning Arabic properly? Or is Hebrew still dominant?

D: The Hebrew language is still the real dominant language at this school, as it is in the village here, as it is in the whole country, and we are part of what's going on in the country, so as much as we are trying, the Hebrew language is still much more dominant than the Arabic language. And because of that we created the Language Center just a year ago. It took us two years just to study the idea and work on this til [it was] ready [and] they could come and learn there. You know, the Jewish kids as well as the Palestinian Arabs, if they are born here, will start right from the beginning—from the nursery, that means from three months old—to listen to their language, their mother language, as well as the second language, which is Arabic or Hebrew, and then they will start to speak it in a natural atmosphere. Then at the school they will start to read and write it, from the beginning.

But if you look around the village you will see that the Palestinian kids do speak Hebrew fluently, but the Jewish kids, although they may understand Arabic, do not speak it that much. Even though they live here and they were born here and hear the Arabic language daily, they still choose to speak Hebrew because that's what their parents do.

G: And of course it's easier.

D: Right, but you know it's also, I believe that it's not only the environment, it's something to do with the parents, it's something to do with the adults. They set the example and if they don't speak Arabic with each other, or with the Palestinians who come to visit them, then neither will their kids. I have a friend and when we get together we speak in Arabic often.

G: Is she Jewish or Palestinian?

D: She's Jewish, of course, and we speak Arabic and often she also speaks some Arabic with her daughter. She encourages the child to continue speaking in Arabic with her, because she feels very secure with her own (Hebrew) language and with everything, so why not do it, because she knows that the Arabic language needs more of a chance to be spoken in order to make it equal with Hebrew.

G: True enough. But maybe a lot of the Jewish parents don't know Arabic well enough to speak it fluently.

D: A lot of them don't know Arabic very well; but this is a big question, why don't they? If you want to be a journalist in Israel or a member of the Knesset [parliament] you must learn Arabic properly, as well as Hebrew. Some people take private lessons; it must be taken seriously.

G: It's interesting; this is a very difficult thing. There are certain similarities between the French and English in Canada because a lot of English Canadians don't speak French well. Again, it's the issue of dominant versus subordinate language. How do you change that attitude? We did have and we do have a program called French immersion which began in the 1970s, where anglophone children learn their school subjects in French in school—not just one class, but all their subjects are in French and that has made a very big difference. So you know language always mirrors what's going on in society, and I think that's what you're saying.

D: Absolutely. When I was on a tour in the United States, you know, speaking about our school, one woman asked why we still need the Arabic language. "Why don't you just do what we do here in the States? All of us speak English," she said . . . so narrow minded.

G: And what about the bilingual education programs in the United States? Did she know about them?

D: She said they should be canceled! And she was a young person, only about forty.

G: I find that very sad.

D: To me learning the other's language—when you are in the majority—is a mark of respect. I had to learn Hebrew, of course, and the content was full of issues of Jewishness and nothing to do with the Arabs. It was very hurtful. I hated learning Hebrew but I had to. I needed it for university and to get a good position. But I think we have to learn to like the language we are learning. This is happening here in Neve Shalom/Wahat Al-Salam. Here I have been able to start accepting the Hebrew language much more than I did before, of course, but this is something special here.

G: I really think you've hit it on the head. To like the language we are learning is crucial in terms of what it means for the society. What's important is that this should change in the entire school system.

D: Right. Some schools are trying to improve the instruction of Arabic. It is starting to change in some places. You know when the peace process began, they started to teach more Arabic, because up until this point it was the case that the [Jewish] students would learn English second and then Arabic third. Not high priority. It's only looked upon as a foreign language, not a second language, and that's what we're trying to change here. It needs to be compulsory.

   In this way the students will have to, and they will learn it. As it stands, it's not an equal language, but here [in the village] the way that we develop the language is to take it more seriously and we are theoretically and practically learning how to teach the Arabic language most effectively. But here we call it a second language because that is the status it deserves.

G: Yeah, I think it's a very important distinction because it's very different, learning a language as a second language as opposed to a foreign language. A number of people talked to me about this. And what about on the other side—in the Arab schools?

D: In the Arab schools, Hebrew is taken very seriously.

G: But they must learn it, as you say, with ambivalence because if they're learning that language without using Arab symbols from their own culture, it's a problem.

D: Yes, what's great here in this school is that the children learn Hebrew using Arab poetry, narratives, literature, and so on— something that belongs to their culture, but they learn it in the other language.

G: That's what counts, I think. It makes complete sense. I mean, if you want the student to like the other language, you should bring texts that belong to him or her, that [he or she is] familiar with, that [he or she can] appreciate.

D: Of course, we have to teach what the Ministry of Education expects because we have to prepare these students for the outside. But we look carefully at the materials and we omit some offensive ones and include a lot of materials that we prepared ourselves with the help of professors from the Tel Aviv and Hebrew Universities. We have regular staff meetings [in which] we discuss these issues and come together and organize the texts. The staff meets each week for a two-hour meeting, and once a month for some hours. So we decide and, of course, during the summer we have a holiday to work on ourselves and have some free time; but toward the end before school starts again, we come together to discuss what worked, what needs to be changed. It's all a new approach; there's no other school like it.

G: No, it's a pioneer situation. That's what's so incredible about it. So you negotiate with one another on what to include in the curriculum?

D: Yes, everyone has his own opinion and we deal with these things; and often, the language teachers will sit together and decide which books they are going to teach with, and they make up their own materials. Lots of negotiation, as you say. Also, there are arguments, which we handle. And there is so much interesting material that we have prepared especially for the language learning center, which we all helped to create ourselves, with the assistance of people at the Hebrew University.

G: That's wonderful.

"English as the foreign language for everybody":

D: At first we translated a lot of the materials from the English language courses but then we realized that teaching Arabic is different from teaching English because, as I said before, Arabic is a second language, not a foreign language like English. So we are beginning to deal with that difference.

G: Isn't that interesting!

D: You see, English is a foreign language for everybody; we're all on the same level. With Arabic, it's a very different story. There are different levels; and it means that you need to use more abstract ideas and keep it interesting.

G: It's more abstract, more complex.

D: We have to be that much more creative.

G: Yeah, it's a lot of work.

D: So we sit and figure out how to make language learning more interesting, challenging; creating new grammar exercises, new stories, new content so that the kids really will come there and they will enjoy it.

G: Yes, it looks like they do, because they see—I think what's interesting is—you're doing it together. I think that's already very different. You're doing it together and you're doing it as you go along; I mean, it's from real experience and real partnership.

Diana discusses the Language Center:

D: Our headmaster is in touch with Professor Olshtain at the Hebrew University and she and her associate, Judy, [are] helping us pedagogically. Our headmaster took a course with her and that's how the idea of the Language Center came into being.

So we started to work with her. She was very, very helpful and created this program for us. And her assistant comes and helps us implement the program with the kids. And she says she goes to other schools to help them but she never saw such a place as this—where everyone is eager to be creative and try something so new. But after a few months we told her that we need to teach Arabic as a second language, not a foreign language, and she is helping us create materials. It needs to be done in the right way psychologically so that the children can respect it. In the other schools across the country the Arabic language is still being taught as a foreign language, and that's not very helpful. The whole level of Arabic instruction has to be improved drastically.

G: Do you see the possibility that a school like this could become more of a role model outside?

D: Yes, and we have some people who really are in good contact with us. Lee Gordon from the Ministry of Education is considering creating a school like this in Jaffa or Ramle or Lod or Jerusalem. Our school now has been named an experimental school by the Ministry and gets some funding. It is becoming more accepted in the mainstream, which is really exciting, but we still have a long way to go to persuade many on both sides that it is OK for both Jews and Palestinians to go to school together. It will certainly take time. But it works here and I feel so good to be living and working here and knowing that my children are growing up in this atmosphere.

G: Thanks so much for sharing this time with me. I have learned a lot.

D: You're welcome. It was good to have a chance to talk about these things with you. Some things I have never spoken about before, especially some of my feelings.

What impressed me most about this interview was how Diana was able to connect the emotional upheaval of being a Palestinian feeling disenfranchised growing up in Israel with her new feelings of cautious optimism for her children at Neve Shalom/Wahat Al-Salam. Her story is valuable, and she carefully crafted it from the clarity of thought and richness of detail in the context of her professional experience.

Diana convincingly demonstrates how lived experience strongly influences our perceptions, our values, our decisions, and our choices within our professional enterprises. In that regard, perhaps I should have placed more emphasis in the interview on the ways in which her personal story interacts with the pedagogy that she uses in her everyday teaching. But time was short and I did not want to set any agendas. Diana offered me the parts of her story that she wanted to share and I am grateful for that. I found myself a fellow traveler on her journey of understanding in the face of difference, and I witnessed the power of hope within her. She embodies Kathryn Au's (1997, p. 79) claim that "empowerment is the confidence to act on one's own behalf." Her call is for developing a pedagogy that sees language and identity issues in the light of resistance and reinvention. The school of Neve Shalom Wahat Al-Salam responds to that call.

An Interview with Anwar Daoud

When I inteviewed Anwar Daoud in 1997, he was the headmaster of the school. He describes the pioneering efforts of the school in his own way. For him, changing the pedagogical landscape for the students is of utmost importance in order to ensure real equality. Educational issues are rarely straightforward because the personal and the pedagogical are so intertwined. It was ever thus. Maxine Greene warns us that "knowledge is value laden, and that teaching has moral as well as epistemological and social consequences" (in Pagano, 1998, p. 255). In 1933, William Sapir argued that language is a fundamental expression of collective social identity and a powerful symbol of group solidarity. Anwar is in search of language freedom for the teachers as well as for the students. He, too, focuses on the central issues of language and power in the school—which often result in intense staff meetings. They reflect the words of American poet Rikki Ducornet (1997): "There is no illumination without vertigo."

I see the teachers at Neve Shalom/Wahat Al-Salam on a metaphorical journey through cultural, historical, and personal borders (Derrida, 1979; Foucault, 1984; Giroux, 1991). Language is not solely a means of communication; it is also a way of constructing our cultural selves and creating a sense of belonging in the world within the context of the historical narratives of our particular group (Chambers, 1994; Fishman, 1991; Garcia, 1994; Lambert, 1982; Spolsky, 1989; Adams & Tulasiewicz, 1994). Indeed, the staff meetings of 1997, in which the issue of language and power came to the fore, became an exotic landscape where the "self" was revealed in unexpected ways—as a construction of experience and meanings which are always mediated through language, culture, and identity. I came to know Anwar through the quiet strength of his desire for true equality and affirmation of both Jewish and Arab identities in the school and in the village. There was a solidity and spirit in his words which never wavered from his goals as principal of this very special educational site. Opening new landscapes is a very tricky business: I was struck by Anwar's acute sense of responsibility, which underscored the whole of his interview. Excerpts from this interview follow.

Anwar's thoughts on some of the cultural values of the two groups:

> *Anwar (A):*   In this school, we as teachers and students want to be here, we have chosen to be here, and it is exciting but also very difficult because we want the children to accept one another and to find equality as well as to understand their differences. We need to be open to the parents' needs because they have made a conscious decision to send their children to this school which, because of what it stands for, is very controversial. It's not easy to talk about these issues; differences in family values, for example. In many cases, the Arab families are stricter and less permissive than the Jewish ones. It's complicated, especially for the Arab girls. It's a real challenge and the only way to handle it is with real dialogue, exchange of ideas.

> *Grace (G):*   How do the kids feel?

> *A:*   The kids show their anxiety sometimes because they are pioneers; they don't have role models. Nothing is absolute. And

certainly the teachers too feel this anxiety at being in new territory. The borders are not clear. Like when the kids bring in stuff for Actualia [current events] about family life, for instance. Some of the Jewish kids will bring in very modern pictures with women wearing bathing suits and it will offend some Palestinian parents. The cultural differences are great at times. And they need to be respected and talked out . . .

The asymmetry of Hebrew and Arabic—Anwar's point of view:

G: How long have you been here in the school as principal?

A: I have been here for twelve years and have learned so much in terms of education. So much has been done here that is completely new and it's a little scary for some, too. Lots of good curriculum materials have been developed. We discuss programs on an everyday basis. We are here because we want to construct a society [in which] we can feel like we belong and live together. But of course there are all sorts of issues that need to be negotiated. Recently, for example, the issue of language is coming up a lot. We talk about how language is power and many of us—especially the Palestinian teachers—feel that all the teachers should be bilingual. At the beginning [of the school's existence] we didn't stress that at all. Now this threatens the Jewish teachers because many of them are not so fluent in Arabic.

G: In what ways do they feel threatened?

A: Well, for example, we used to conduct the staff meetings in Hebrew only. But now we are saying that is copying what goes on in the rest of the country. And it means the Jews have to learn Arabic properly. It changes the balance of power, that's for sure. The fact that I, a Palestinian, am headmaster is such an important symbol. It's totally new—we are saying, let's be partners. Let's work together, that's our message. It immediately sets up a completely different model, and therefore new policies. We do need more teacher training. This is urgent. The teachers need to have even more dialogue and talk about their worries. This business of language equality has become more and more important. We have to face it.

G: How will you face such a sensitive issue?

A: I think we need some facilitation through the "School for Peace." It works for so many others in the country; I hope it will be useful for our teachers here. It's like finally the "crunch" has come, because of this language issue. I still think it means that there's much improvement, or else we [the Palestinians] would never have been able to raise the issue. But we didn't expect the opposition from some of the [Jewish] teachers.

G: I guess it's a question of having to learn a language fluently in adulthood. That's not easy. It doesn't sound like they're against the idea in theory. It's that it is so difficult to do in practice. It's much easier for their children than for themselves. And that is what was originally in their minds.

A: I guess that's true. But we have evolved here and we want to go further. And the next step is for the teachers (and other adults) to take Arabic seriously. As we have already talked about, language is identity. We had to learn Hebrew even if it wasn't our identity. So in this village at least, they should learn Arabic, especially to show that they respect the weaker language. I hope I don't sound too harsh. But we can set up language classes for the adults. We should give it a try. What a great role model that would be for the children, a very concrete example of coexistence. Real bilingualism, real binationalism. This is not an ordinary place and so we do things that are not ordinary. It's a big challenge.

G: Any other issues you want to talk about?

A: Another thing that bothers me a great deal is the attitude of the community, I mean the parents, in terms of language. Some of the Jewish parents need to be more serious about Arabic. Their children never see them using it. What kind of message is that? It still shows that Hebrew is dominant. Again, we're back to the idea of language and power. We really have to work on it. We need to bring in specialists from the university and discuss these issues in a very professional way.

A glimpse into Anwar's personal story:

G: You're so wonderfully committed. Where does your motivation come from?

A: Oh, that's a long story, but simply put, I was one of those Israeli Arabs that made it a point to excel in Hebrew. I studied at the Hebrew University in spite of the difficulties [of doing] so at that time [the 1970s]. I felt like an oddball, and many of my peers couldn't understand what I was doing. But I always have connected language with power. So I realized that if Hebrew is the language of power then I'd better learn it as well as I could, even though it sometimes repressed my own identity. And then there was the Intifada. It threw me into a tailspin. I was very upset. Where did I stand on the issues? Should I get totally involved? What about the violence?

Then I found out about Neve Shalom/Wahat Al-Salam. It was the answer to my prayers. Here I am proud to be a Palestinian and happy to live with Jewish neighbors and get to know them as human beings. It's just not like that in other areas of the country. Everything is so separate, although in some ways things are changing. Many people are really fed up with this conflict, maybe more than we realize. Maybe there is hope. I have to believe that, or else what is the point? Here in this village I feel like I am doing the right thing and that I am living the right way.

I conducted the interviews with Diana and with Anwar in June 1997 and remained in contact with them until my visit in November 1999. Since then, Diana became a codirector of the school in the fall of 1999, and Anwar became the mayor of the village in the spring of 2000.

Interestingly enough, in May 1999 the teachers at the school did get involved in a "School for Peace" encounter themselves in order to sort out the issue of their everyday working relationships, and especially their concerns about the asymmetry between Hebrew and Arabic, which had become a troubling issue for them. This dialogue has become an ongoing process. In the first years of the school, everyone was so focused on redressing the balance between Hebrew and Arabic for the children (see chapter 3) that they never thought about this inequity within their professional lives. I suppose it is a tribute to how far they have come that they are now able to acknowledge the problem and attempt to resolve it. It did create, however, quite a sense of psychological "vertigo" for the Jewish teachers. The interplay of desire and resistance was indeed dizzying. Again, dialogue triumphs and promises a more reciprocal relation in the face of this asymmetrical reality. Each participant continues to honor the other by contributing to and extending the discourse and thereby the process of coming to know.

The Neve Shalom/Wahat Al-Salam school, in spite of all its good intentions and accomplishments, is still a microcosm of the social world and offers interesting illustrations of the way the mainstream culture thinks about itself. What more can we expect? This is not a fantasyland and, therefore, there are bound to be problematic issues. Indeed, the unceasing attempts at opposing the conventional pedagogical asymmetries between the two peoples embodies the idea that "teaching and the moral universe are inextricably bound" (Keroes, 1999, p. 28). It would be unrealistic to expect the Jewish teachers to become fluent in Arabic overnight. They are, after all, products of the hegemonic society in which they grew up. They, however, have resisted the inequities of their original schooling with courage and goodwill against all odds, and that is what makes them special. Both groups need to be respectful of the complexities and ambiguities of this human enterprise. To my mind, what is crucial is to be progressing in good faith and with an open mind.

Language, again, becomes the site of human struggle. This is a moment when one needs to proceed with care and caution. According to the village newsletter (May 1999), "there was an awareness raised toward the inequalities between the two peoples and the complexity of the experiment they are undertaking at the school in the workshop session." (The SFP chose facilitators from outside the village for the purpose of professional distance.) This was an experiential encounter among the teachers but there was also a theoretical section devoted to issues of language and identity and an analysis of case studies. The encounter became a forum where the teachers could reflect on their work together and express matters that are seldom given expression in the course of everyday working relations. This is what a couple of the teachers said, as quoted from the village newsletter, May 1999:

> After this encounter I realized that I can speak all the time to the classes in Hebrew, whereas the Arab teachers are not able to speak all the time in Arabic. On an interpersonal level, the teachers learned that in a school like Neve Shalom/Wahat Al-Salam it is necessary to speak their hearts to their colleagues, even though this can feel very uncomfortable in a close working environment. (Hebrew-speaking teacher)

> "Exposing one's feelings doesn't endanger the teacher but opens ways of understanding and dialogue. The course drew the teachers nearer to one another and clarified many cloudy issues and points. (Arabic-speaking teacher)

The participants are searching for an equilibrium wherein conflicting desires for virtue and power can somehow live together in spite of the obvious tensions. I was told, through e-mail conversations and while I was in the village in November and December of 1999, that this session inspired a renewal of the quest for respective identity and language maintenance within a landscape of goodwill.

An Interview with Ilan Frisch

The following interview with Ilan Frisch was taken from the French-language village newsletter *La Lettre de la Colline* (April 1999). The interview was conducted by Anne Le Meignen, one of the original "dreamers" of the village. She pioneered this village alongside Father Bruno and has been in charge of the French newsletter from its beginning. She is very active in fundraising for the village, especially in French-speaking countries. Her dedication to the dream of what the village represents does not cloud her understanding of the magnitude of the Jewish-Palestinian conflict. She possesses an idealism that is etched with a hard-boiled realism—which I find stimulating as well as comforting. Being neither Jewish nor Arab (but very much an Israeli), she brings a special perspective to this story. She grew up in France but was attracted to Israel as a young adult and then met Father Bruno. The rest is history, as they say. Anne's activity and humility serves as a role model for all people interested in peace. She was very happy that I was including this interview with Ilan because of its crystal-clear portrayal of everyday situations in the village and in the wider society. Anne told me how much she identified with his thoughts.

Ilan, who came from a kibbutz, was also one of the original members of Neve Shalom/Wahat Al-Salam. His architectural and engineering skills have been instrumental in physically creating the village. His thoughts are both incisive and honest as he speaks to the issue of language and cultural differences. I translated the following excerpts of the interview into English.

Ilan's view of the sociohistorical background of the village:

Ilan (I):   When I came here I had an idea that had always been in my head even as I lived on a kibbutz: to make it a Jewish-Arab kibbutz. Well, I thought that that wasn't really feasible and then I found Neve Shalom/Wahat Al-Salam, and then I continued to think of a place where Jews and Arabs could live a collective life, not just a political idea; a life between the two that is not superficial like that sort of thing in politics with slogans and demonstrations. No, I was looking rather for a real life together where our personal everday lives with our wives and children would be included. Where we would make decisions together and bring up our kids together . . . far from just an abstract concept of Jewish-Arab relations.

At the beginning we were a very small number, only a few Jewish couples. And then the first Arab couple arrived. Little by little we discovered the good and difficult issues. But we could never have imagined the reality of today: a real village, with a collective life and established institutions in common. I have learned through the years how the ideal and the reality can be different. We live in some ways with very complicated situations and in other ways with very simple ones, more simple than I would have ever thought possible. For example, the friendship my wife and I have with [Abed and Aishe, a Palestinian couple who are also "pioneers" of the village]; it's so simple and natural. Something that would be considered impossible outside of this village. There is a chemistry between us.

Anne (A):   This chemistry, is it enough? Aren't there also some problems?

I: Sure. As citizens of Israel, we have something in common but our differences exist: our different languages, our different cultures, our different educational systems. It is impossible to erase those, nor should we deny that we are living in a paradoxical situation; it is possible to create an excellent personal relationship, and also to discover differences that can cause sharp problems. And we don't manage to surmount all of them. For example, there was the terrible tragedy of the son of one of the Jewish families in the village who was killed two years ago just as he was turning twenty-one years old and ending his army duty. He was in a helicopter maneuver accident. We, the people in the village, could never have foreseen that we would find ourselves in such a terrible situation. The issue of the Israeli army positioned in controversial areas like South Lebanon and the West Bank is a very tough one; but the Arab families stood side by side with us at the military funeral because of this horribly exceptional case. They knew Tom since he was a child and he was a son of one of their neighbors and friends. We could not have known in advance that we would one day find ourselves in such a situation.

A: Can one erase the differences, then?

I: It's a good question, but very difficult. Where would that lead us? Because here in Neve Shalom/Wahat Al-Salam, we have this double message which is paradoxical: We do not ignore our differences; on the contrary we discuss and highlight them. They start with our identity. And from that start comes all the conflicts, violence, war, and divisions.

Ilan's views on Jewish and Palestinian identities:

A: And what about your feelings about the establishment of the state of Israel, its history?

I: When I came to this village for the first time I was not aware that our "Day of Independence" was in fact a day of tragedy for the Arabs. Arafat is only now accepting the borders of 1947 after fifty years. All these issues are so complex.

A: And each side can't see them in the same way.

I: Absolutely not. In fact, we should not expect others to see it the same way. And we can't commit suicide, we the Israelis, because the situation is so difficult. We have a right to our being Israeli. We started with the premise that we cannot lose our identity. This village is built on that philosophy. The case of Tom, who was killed in the helicopter accident, created a very difficult situation for the Arab families in that there was a tension that emerged between their personal relationship with this family and their political and national identity which was at cross purposes with their honoring a Jewish soldier . . . and I understand their psychological conflict; it's real. They belong to the Arab community and therefore don't want to appear that they aren't as loyal as their peers [to the Palestinian cause]. And for us Jews, being in the army means taking part in combat. How does this affect our relations with our people and with our own identity?

We are bringing up our children here so that they understand things clearly and so that they will be able to make difficult choices. We talk about these issues together as well as individually; we're bringing up our children collectively. Lots of questions come up and even the feeling of fear. We must ask ourselves: Has the state of Israel done everything it could to improve the situation? After fifty years of existence, could we not be in a better situation of peace with our neighbors? How much should we continue to sacrifice our children [in terms of the Army service and casualties] almost on a daily basis to this conflict? Difficult questions.

A: Do you want to discuss any other issues?

The balance of power in the village according to Ilan:

I: The Arabs, who are a minority in Israel, complain often that the authority and power are in the hands of the Jews. At Neve Shalom/Wahat Al-Salam, today, most of the administrative positions of responsibility are in the hands of Palestinians: the present secretariat (and the two previous ones), the director of the "School for Peace" in the last two years, the elementary school, the kindergarten, the public relations office, and the treasury. Our structure is very egalitarian in numbers and direction. And therefore we must not be manipulated by this issue of "inferiority" or "subjugation" of the Arabs by the Jews in order to make us feel guilty, which indeed at the beginning motivated us to create Neve Shalom/Wahat Al-Salam in order to transform that reality. We, the Jews, need to maintain our freedom of expression and action.

A: Do you speak sincerely with the Arabs? Do they openly speak to you about their problems?

I: Certainly, with those who are good friends. And I tell them, "I'm not going to give you favors just because you are Arab. Don't come to me with your reckoning against the Jewish People. Those who do that—and there are some—do not believe in strength, in the real possibility of change, in those with whom they are in dialogue. If you say to yourself, "I find myself in front of someone who is my equal," he will not fall apart if I tell him what I think. He is mature like me, he has strength as I do—they [the Arabs] have experiences which I certainly did not have, and I tell them that. If I am made to feel that I have to "walk on eggshells" around them, then that is a heavy mistake. I have to deal with them as I do with everyone.

Some of Ilan's insights after twenty years:

A: What is your balance sheet here for the last twenty years?

I: In my opinion, it's very positive. We have become a vibrant society and, I believe, also successful. I would have liked for us to have grown more quickly. We are still too small; not exactly an organic or full-fledged community, as it were. A little too familial, with this pleasant approach of everyone knowing everyone else. In my opinion that's not good for Neve Shalom/Wahat Al-Salam. We must become a more nuanced society, bigger, with a range of more diverse encounters and experiences. When we [become] a community of 160 families, which is what we decided upon, the test will be much more interesting, more serious. I am not worried about the problems that might emerge due to a larger group of people in this community. I see in it, in fact, a greater possibility of realizing our goals. Now everything depends on financial aid that we get from the outside, and that's a problem. But we have to look ahead. And this year we have to invest in the foundations of the village. It is imperative that we grow.

A: How do you see the political significance of this village? Do you see one?

I: Neve Shalom/Wahat Al-Salam doesn't exist yet as an Israeli political entity; we are still too small, a sort of curiosity. But our existence is valuable because of our accomplishments to date: our educational work with the teenagers who come here from everywhere; our experimental elementary school; our public relations work with the outside—I receive a lot of Israeli groups who come to visit our village. It's interesting and very important. We explain to them that—yes—we exist, and we tell them what our goals are. A reality of peace in this country would make things so much easier and more pleasant. We would have a more optimistic feeling. What we lived with Rabin and Peres, this peace process which was on the verge, had given us energy, hope. If Israel today falls into endless wars and doesn't enter into dialogue with the Arab countries and with the Palestinians and therefore hope begins to wane, then Neve Shalom/Wahat Al-Salam could crumble and disappear.

A: In what way are there limitations to the challenges you face here in this village?

I: It's true. That's why I say that it doesn't only depend on us, but on what happens around us.

> *A:* It must also be mentioned that you obviously don't live here without problems. But can that be regarded as a positive thing?
>
> *I:* Absolutely. It's the sign that we are living in reality and that we are working together and bound to reality. We are not an island . . . we are not saints who live in heaven. No! We are involved in the complexities and difficulties of our two peoples. Certainly, the Palestinians lack a sense of security and are therefore frustrated. A real political peace is absolutely necessary.

To my mind, Ilan's interview, filled with profound insights, invites the possibility of creating a shared meaning with the reader. We can't help but recognize the troubling complexities of this project through Ilan's words, and we find ourselves confused and yet in awe. Ilan's authentic reflections are at the heart of coming to know what the struggle toward emancipation is all about. I see Ilan as the sort of chronicler which the great European philosopher Walter Benjamin (1940) describes in his writings: "a chronicler who recites events without distinguishing between major and minor ones in accordance with the following truth: nothing that has ever happened should be regarded as lost for history. . . . The tradition of the oppressed teaches us that the 'state of emergency' in which we live is not the exception but the rule. . . . In every era the attempt must be made anew to wrest tradition away from a conformism that is about to overpower it. . . . The past carries with it a temporal index by which it is referred to redemption. There is a secret agreement between past generations and the present one."

Ilan's ideas are congruent with Benjamin's writings when he speaks of social justice happening only when there is participation by all individuals, and that every point of view needs to be voiced, discussed, and negotiated in relational contexts and within a historical perspective. Facing the issues is the true essence of a healthy dynamic community.

Concluding Remarks

> *It is up to each of you to work out your own liberation.*
>
> —Siddhartha

The simplest way of telling a story is in the voice of the storyteller. I am fortunate to have had these participants open their hearts and minds to me in the telling of their personal and professional stories. These were honest and authentic encounters—spaces were created in which vulnerable feelings were shared in the safety of our conversations. The act of remembering, the act of narrating, and listening to retrospective reflection were all braided together into a melange of past experience of marginality and present quest for equality. It enhanced my own reflection on the issue of minority language learning and

Jewish-Palestinian relations in a new way. This self-understanding—which emerges out of the intersubjective experiences of relationships—becomes the impetus for deep inquiry and the construction of knowledge. In the dynamic mutuality of the relationship, I as the researcher tried to shape, as Sara Lawrence-Lightfoot (1997, p. 152) puts it, "the intellectual and emotional meanings that emerged," all the while being cognizant of my responsibility to "define the boundaries and protect the vulnerability and exposure of the actor." Most important, there was a sense of reciprocity in these conversations, which, I believe, showed commitment and legitimacy to what was being said.

What also strikes me about the conversations is the power of the teachers' educational dream: their imaginings and longings for a school and a society that offers something truly different, truly aesthetically and morally appealing. They are, to my mind, artists in their search for beauty and truth and social justice. Deborah Britzman (1995) describes artists as those "who still worry about this thing called pedagogy, about what it means to teach and to learn, and about the detours known as history. . . . We have artists unafraid to imagine differences within, to address those who may or may not understand, to fashion communities yet to become, and to engage life at its most incomplete. Unlike [the more usual] educators . . . they are interested in the mistakes, the accidents, the detours, and the unintelligibilities of identities. . . . They gesture to their own constructedness and frailties, troubling the space between representation and the real" (p. 105). This eloquent description of the "artist" is indeed congruent with the kind of educators who teach at Neve Shalom/Wahat Al-Salam. These teachers are not afraid to face their relationship to the "other," to their own experience, and hence to negotiate the interplay among identity, language, and cultural differences. They look within their own village school and within themselves for strategies of negotiation as well as seek conceptual guidance from outside professional and academic sources. All face the issues of desire and loss as they develop curriculum. It is a question of belonging and sense of ownership in order to retrieve that which has been expropriated emotionally. Thus they continue to push the limits in their dynamic interaction and to struggle for greater voice as they reach higher and higher and dig deeper and deeper in their efforts toward community building and social transformation.

Endnotes

1. This section "Tirzah and Ahmed: The SFP Facilitators" is based on material that appeared in *Theory into Practice*, 1997 vol. 36, no. 1. Due to the sensitive nature of the encounter group workshops, all names are pseudonyms.

Chapter Seven

The Dream of Peace

If one advances confidently in the direction of his [sic] *dreams and endeavors to live the life which he has imagined, he will meet with a success unexpected in common hours.*

—Henry David Thoreau

Hillary Rodham Clinton's Visit to the Village

On December 13th, 1998, Hillary Rodham Clinton, then First Lady of the United States, came to visit the village.[1] Unfortunately, I could not be in Israel to attend this exciting event but I heard and read all about it. This section describes that special day and documents what it meant for the village. Rayek Rizek, its secretary/mayor, came to visit me in June 1999. He showed me the videotape of the visit and of the speech Mrs. Clinton gave in the elementary school which captured the wonderful intensity of that morning. It was Mrs. Clinton's first official engagement of her three-day tour of Israel and of the Palestine Authority, and she was accompanied by Mrs. Sara Netanyahu, wife of the then Prime Minister of Israel.

Welcomed by Rayek and by a group of children holding the drawings of peace they had produced for this special event, the First Lady and Mrs. Netanyahu were escorted to the White Dove restaurant located next to the village. Here a photographic exhibition of the village activities were on display. Representatives and delegates of the village were there to speak with Mrs. Clinton. Then she walked through the village to the kindergarten where she was received by three little children—Jewish, Christian, and Moslem.

It was the eve of the Jewish Festival of Lights, Hannukah, as well as the holy Muslim month of Ramadan and close to Christmas, the holiday that celebrates the birth of Jesus (Yeshua). I will not forget the picture of Mrs. Clinton standing at a table with the three children all dressed up for the occasion: a little boy in a suit standing in front of a lantern for Ramadan; a little girl in a dress with a lace collar standing in front of a small Christmas tree; and another young girl whose dress was adorned with ribbons in front of a little Hannukah menorah (an

181

Figure 7–1   Ramadan, Christmas, and Hannukah are represented by the lantern, tree, and menorah, respectively, in the kindergarten during Hillary Rodham Clinton's visit in December, 1998. Mrs. Sara Netanyahu is behind Mrs. Clinton. Aishe Najjar, the kindergarten teacher, looks on. (Courtesy of NS/WAS.)

eight-branched candelabra). Mrs. Clinton, holding a candle in her hand, admired the three different religious objects of the season which had been placed side by side in harmony on the table. It was a beautiful symbol of peace. (See Figure 7–1.)

The elementary students (more than 200 of them!) were waiting for her on the school steps and singing "A Time for Peace." Emotions ran high, especially for those villagers who could remember when this place of trees, fruit, flowers, and children was only a barren hill with rocks and brambles, a mere two decades earlier. Then Mrs. Clinton gave her speech. It was clearly from the heart and very personal. She spoke about how the Ayalon Valley below is a particularly appropriate location for the village:

> . . . I looked out across the Ayalon Valley, and I know how often that valley has seen war and conflict going back thousands of years. And it

seems particularly fitting that your village would sit here above that valley, looking down, being reminded of the cost that violence and conflict takes on all of us, but particularly on children.

She went on to speak about the wisdom of Father Bruno in his understanding of the importance of Jews and Arabs living together and sharing their experiences daily. She explained how as a young girl she grew up in an exclusively White neighborhood, monocultural, monolingual. Only as an adolescent did she begin to meet Blacks and Latinos and to sit down, talk with them, and realize they had much in common with her:

As a young girl growing up in the United States, I lived in a community that was all White. I knew no Black Americans. And it was because of another person of faith that I began as a teenager to meet Black Americans, and Americans who came from Spanish-speaking countries. And for the first time to sit and talk with them, and to understand that we had so much in common, that I had never understood before. . . ."

Mrs. Clinton said that when she was with the three little children in the kindergarten and in the midst of the symbols of the three monotheistic religions of the world what she remembered was that steadfast feeling she had as a young girl:

[I believe] that religion should not be an instigator of war but a bridge to peace. The children should learn to respect their own traditions, and also to understand the traditions of others. It is particularly appropriate that we would gather here, today, at the beginning of Hannukah—a time of rededication for the Jewish people—and a reminder of how important it is to rededicate ourselves to peace.

Despite the setbacks that come any time that any great challenges are being pursued, the strong belief that peace will prevail must once again be reinforced. People who choose to live free from violence, blessed with security and peace, must prevail. And the way to prevail is not only through our leaders sitting down and negotiating—a process that cannot be imposed from the outside, but can be nurtured and supported—but also from the daily lives and interactions of people like yourselves . . . peace actually begins in our homes, in communities like this, and in our hearts . . . well, I hope that we will move toward a time when it [pointing to a picture of a Jewish child and an Arab child holding hands] is not newsworthy, when it is more as it is here [in Neve Shalom/Wahat Al-Salam] where children from three different faiths, from different backgrounds, from different experiences, are living with one another in such a normal way that they are not making news at all, but living their lives. And, of course, in order to do that, we have to abolish the stereotypes that keep people apart. And this is not just an issue for this region of the world, it is an issue throughout the world. . . .

I would like to imagine a time when, as we heard the children singing in the song called "A Time of Peace," that that will be a reality here and around the world. In Arabic and Hebrew they sang, "between the lightning a rainbow will appear not just in the sky, but in our hearts and minds," and, God willing, we will create peace and security, and justice and freedom, and we will provide all children with the experience that you are giving them here: to be looked at and judged as an individual, to learn to build trust with one another.

There was faith in the language and in the image of Mrs. Clinton speaking so simply in this little village. There she stood, a frontier spirit, traveling to the "border" to speak and to help create a space for contemplation. There seemed to be a dreamlike quality that enveloped the entire event—full of excitement and hope. In that perfect moment, the dream was indeed realized. I am grateful for Hillary Clinton's decision to visit this village. In so doing, she became a true role model and a moral leader projecting the courage to *not* give up on the possibility of peace in the world, and especially to stand up against the emptiness of despair. There was no pomp and ceremony to her visit; it was just an ordinary gathering and yet it was extraordinary at the same time. I can only think of the metaphor of light banishing the shadows in the simplicity of her act. She was just "there," making the children feel special. She thanked the villagers for doing God's work daily; but I think that by deciding to come and to shine the spotlight on the village, she was doing God's work as well.

I watched Mrs. Clinton on the video with genuine pleasure, knowing how much she had reinforced the villagers through her appearance and with her words. Mrs. Clinton said, quoting President John F. Kennedy: ". . . on this earth, God's work is our own, and certainly the work of building peace, and building trust is among the most important work we have to do." She ended the speech by thanking the community "for doing God's work—the everyday work of peace. Thank you very much."

I told Rayek how nourished I felt by Mrs. Clinton's words; he said that is exactly how they all had felt on that day and for many days and weeks afterwards. Hers was a gesture of support, admiration, and gratitude. It was as though she was discussing social redemption and communal activity as a form of love in the Freirian sense. Perhaps her own personal and professional state of liminality[2] intersected with that of the villagers; that is, being on the threshold of transformation and redefinition. Her oral text provided context and patterns through which everyone connected to the village could realize and transmit their own experience. Her reassuring words brought public justification, validation, and power. To use Julia Kristeva's words from another context, "It was a living speech shared by the community."[3] To feel a sense of belonging to a community and to something good and hopeful, something much larger than ourselves—a liminal space that enables other possibilities, other options, other choices to emerge—this is what Hillary Clinton captured in her speech about the village.

Dreaming of Peace: A Pedagogical Adventure

Many people see the Tower of Babel as a disaster that unleashed confusion onto humanity, but I see it as a personal salvation. We all have our own perceptions of reality and our own needs. We all have to find meaning in our unique life experiences. That is the challenge placed before us. The dream of transcendence and transformation in the interstices of my multicultural longings have literally kept me alive. Therefore, it is not surprising that I was drawn to this village of Jewish-Palestinian reconciliation as a site of research as soon as I had heard about it. Metaphorically speaking, it offered solid ground beneath my feet.

As a child of survivors in the post-Holocaust era, I have always searched for a sense of personal belonging within the protective layers of my professional life—in school when I was very young, and in the university when I was older. I discovered at a very early age that languages and cultures could offer me an escape from the bleak nightmares that dominated my family's existence. As mentioned in my personal narrative in chapter 3, learning languages and writing about the cultures they represented became a foster home: a place where I could negotiate communities that were full of life and energy and continuity. The stories that I wrote in my childhood, describing the lives of others, nourished me through their dynamic relationship to the world. I felt safe in my writings because they opened up an escape route from the six million ghosts that haunted my everyday conscious and unconcious moments. I am comforted by the words of Hélène Cixous (1996), who states that she began writing in order to overcome her personal experience of loss: "I believe that one can only begin to advance along the path of discovery . . . from mourning and in the reparation of mourning . . . One writes from death toward death in life" (in Sellers, 1996, pp. xii, xiii).

Understanding the experience of the Jews and Palestinians at Neve Shalom/ Wahat Al-Salam in their quest for peaceful coexistence within the social hegemony of the state of Israel necessarily involved positioning myself in their world, albeit as an outsider—a non-Israeli Diaspora Jew—but nevertheless concretely placed as a bona fide educational researcher. Listening to and talking with these participants was one necessary part of my research work. Furthermore, reflecting on their moral project of intercultural and interpersonal understanding, through the writing of this book, has forced me to recognize that my own part in the dialogue was very much an essential aspect of the whole enterprise. This reflexive research thus represents for me a "critical return, a personal quest," as Grimshaw (1992, p. 62) puts it, and an attempt at settling a psychological account with my own cultural inheritance through this investigation into the routes toward peace in this Jewish-Palestinian community. In addition, the social landscape of this little village contrasts with the textures of the North American "big city" atmosphere in which I grew up. Therefore, the duration of my ethnographic "gaze" and of the everyday activities thus depicted emphasizes the act of looking at the "other" and, through them, at myself. Throughout this book I have emphasized how my focus on re-flexivity in ethnographic research is congruent with many contemporary qual-itative researchers. Indeed, Robert Coles (1997, pp. 4–5), in his discussion of the moral underpinnings of social inquiry, points out that "the intense self-scrutiny is, one hopes, an aspect of all writing, all research" and furthermore "the search for objectivity is waylaid by a stubborn subjectivity."

It was therefore, I believe, valuable and necessary to share with the partici-pants my own reflective narrative of a child growing up in a multicultural and multilingual home in Montreal, psychologically scarred and tormented by the events of the Holocaust. This was a way to open a textual space for under-standing and honoring the struggle toward conflict resolution and peacemak-ing in education at Neve Shalom/Wahat Al-Salam. Perhaps most important, this community endeavor provided an opportunity to celebrate life and the possibility of renewal that life offers. Interestingly, the multilayered realities of this village became entangled with my own inner personal desires and fantasies. These had always manifested themselves in my professional work as a teacher/educator, and as a sociolinguist and ethnographer focusing on sites of diversity, conflict resolution, multicultural/multilingual education, and minor-ity language issues. I didn't choose this research topic; it chose me. In the French tradition of *histoires de vies* (Bayle-Lani, 1997; Josso, 1991; Lainé, 1998; Leray, 1997), this book can legitimately be considered an individual ex-perience, a personal inquiry into the collective consciousness of these villagers, in order to bring to the page the nuanced meaning inherent in all their individ-ual personal and professional decisions and actions.

Personal Place in the Research

I situate my own research within the framework of this border discourse—at the intersection of the local and the global against the historical backdrop of a long-standing complicated and deadly cultural rivalry. I envisaged, from the beginning, an interactive and holistic approach which would reflect the relation-ship between the community and the school, as well as between individual participants and myself as researcher. By means of participant observation and interviewing techniques, I explored the bicultural, binational, bilingual initia-tive of both the elementary school and the "School for Peace" conflict resolu-tion program within the microcontext of this village society. I tried to get at the very nature of language, culture, and identity in this unique place of reconcili-ation, and to witness a new educational universe being intricately constructed. It was the sense of discovery in this fieldwork, moved primarily by the devo-tion of the participants to peaceful coexistence, that enticed me to "dig deeper" in search of a faithful documenting of this extraordinary binational space for action and transformation. The shared imagining of "peace on Earth" among myself and my participants is the profound "mover and shaker" of this research project.

Perhaps we are hooked on a fantasy of utopia, but at least it provides a more hopeful view of what the world has the potential to be, and permits us to come together and engage in the "impassioned and significant dialogue" about which Maxine Greene speaks (1988, p. 4). Indeed, I witnessed the dialectical relationship between imagination and social responsibility in this village. I realize now that it is in our disconcerting incompleteness, in our melancholic longings, in our painful woundedness that we are summoned to, in Greene's words, "the tasks of knowledge and action." "Living on the margins may be dangerous," says William Pinar, "but at least you can breathe there." We must strive pedagogically for what Franz Fanon calls the "invention of new souls." The cynics will shrug their shoulders; the pragmatists will shake their heads; and the evildoers will raise their fists and call it an illicit story line. This book is filled with "messy texts" of a dream landscape—open ended, uncertain, incomplete, anxious and yet hopeful, ambitious, and dynamic because the people involved with Neve Shalom/Wahat Al-Salam may be on the threshold of societal transformation. They are my heroes.

There are those in academe who are in the midst of poststructuralist debates about what is real and what is representational in educational research. I believe, as a peace worker, that the authentic debates are those in which theory and practice are sculpted into an educational discourse devoted toward the striving for conflict resolution, moral integrity, and a true respect for diversity; a respect for *all* humanity in the name of those who have suffered and those who continue to suffer at the hands of oppression all over the world. Neve Shalom/Wahat Al-Salam is one example of those courageous few who rise above the fray and say, "We must come together to teach and learn about how to find an end to violence, poverty, oppression, and war, no matter what color of the rainbow we happen to be, and no matter where we are coming from." The ultimate goal of this research work is to bear witness to the power of what these villagers are trying to accomplish in this place. Ruth Behar's (1996, p. 16) words still echo: "When you write vulnerably, others respond vulnerably." The writing of this book (and the opportunity which it offers me in terms of sharing my professional journey) is situated in the social, pedagogical, political, and personal longing for a postmodern notion of moral compassion and social justice in which relationships between national identity and cultural difference can be critically negotiated. But there is too much at stake for mere reflection; we must *act* on our historical inheritance and we need to connect it to a future that re-invents the complex and paradoxical notions of national belonging within the contexts of coexistence. All I have tried to accomplish in this book is to offer a participant-observer's microsense of the realms of discourse and modes of thought that make this unique Jewish-Arab cooperative village what a grade–six child called it: an "oasis of peace in a desert of war." I leave the "macro, prophetic" view, as George Marcus (1998, p. 232) puts it, for the gurus—or perhaps for another time. At the core of this reflexive ethnography lies a search for a safe place in the world—a site of refuge, reconciliation, and hope for humanity in spite of the possibility that this search may be never ending. I was fueled by the desire to claim a professional "home" by writing about this village dedicated to peace. I shall always be dominated by my sense of being a border-dweller, someone forever in search of "home."

The people at Neve Shalom/Wahat Al-Salam taught me to have faith in something that I have always believed in: that education has the power to create a collective "home"—a vision of the future nurtured by the reflective narratives and stories of all the players involved—teachers, students, parents, policymakers, researchers, and others too—so that they might clarify and interconnect their dreams for transformative pedagogies of an inclusive social consciousness. The hope is to create a communicative space in which dislocation and marginality, suspicion and fear can be transcended through open dialogue. This book is dedicated to the dream and to the vision, as well as to the stories of all of those involved with Neve Shalom/Wahat Al-Salam who have created a remarkable space of in-betweenness where they authentically explore the cultures of displacement and diaspora, issues of asymmetrical power relations, and above all, their shared quest for peace.

Endnotes

1. Hillary Rodham Clinton was elected to the United States Senate (D–New York) in November, 2000.
2. It is the condition of liminality of which Carolyn Heilbrun (1999, p. 1) speaks: "the word 'limen' means 'threshold,' and to be in a state of liminality is to be poised upon uncertain ground, to be leaving one condition or country or self and entering upon another."
3. These words were part of a lecture Julia Kristeva gave at the University of Toronto in October, 1999.

Bibliography

Abella, I., & Troper, H. (1986). *None is too many: Canada and the Jews of Europe 1933–1948.* Toronto, Ontario: Lester & Orpen Dennys, Publishers.

Abu-Rabia, S., & Feuerverger, G. (1996). Towards understanding the second language learning of Arab students in Israel and Canada. *Canadian Modern Language Review, 52* (3), 359–385.

Acker, S., & Feuerveger, G. (1996). Doing good and feeling bad: The work of women university teachers. *Cambridge Journal of Education, 26* (3), 401–22.

Ada, A. F. (1988). The Pajaro Valley experience: Working with Spanish-speaking parents to develop children's reading and writing skills in the home through the use of children's literature. In T. Skutnabb-Kangas & J. Cummins (Eds.) *Minority education: From shame to struggle,* 223–228. Clevedon, Avon, England: Multilingual Matters.

Adams, A., & Tulasewicz, W. (1994). Language awareness in an intercultural curriculum for schools. *Modern Languages: Entente Internationale. Education, 3,* xii. Cambridge University Press.

Adorno, T. W., Frenkel-Brunwik, E., Levinson, D. J., & Sanford, R. M. (1950). *The authoritarian personality.* New York: Harper Books.

Ajami, F. (1998). *The dream palace of the Arabs: A generation's odyssey.* New York: Pantheon Books.

Al-Haj, M. (1995). *Education empowerment and control in the case of Arabs in Israel.* Albany: SUNY Press.

Amir, Y. (1976). The role of intergroup contact and change of prejudice and ethnic relations. In P. H. Katz (Ed.), *Toward the elimination of racism,* 245–308. New York: Pergamon Press.

Anzaldua, G. (1987). *Borderlands/La frontera: The new mestiza.* San Francisco: San Francisco/Aunt Lute.

Aronowitz, S., & Giroux, H. (1991). *Postmodern education: Politics, culture, and social criticism.* Minneapolis: University of Minnesota Press.

Ayers, W. (1993). *To teach: The journey of a teacher.* New York: Teachers College Press.

Bakhtin, M. (1981). *The dialogic imagination.* Austin: University of Texas Press.

Bakhtin, M. (1986). *Speech genres and other late essays.* (V. McGee, Trans.). Austin: University of Texas Press.

Banks, J. (1989). *Teacher education and ethnic minorities: Conceptualizing the problem.* Paper presented at the annual conference of the American Educational Research Association, San Francisco.

Bar, H. & Bargal, D. (1988). *The "School for Peace" at Neve Shalom/Wahat Al-Salam: Encounters between Jewish and Palestinian youth.* Tel Aviv: The Israel Institute for Applied Social Research.

Bar-On, D. (1991). Trying to understand what one is afraid to learn about. In D. A. Schön (Ed.), *The reflective turn: Case studies in and on educational practice,* 321–341. New York: Teachers College Press.

Bar-On, D. (1993). First encounter between children of survivors and children of the perpetrators of the Holocaust. *Journal of Humanistic Psychology, 33* (4), 6–14.

Bar Tal, D. (1995). Changes in social beliefs in Israel: From conflict to peace. In *Leaves of peace.* Unpublished document, Department of Curriculum, Ministry of Education, Jerusalem.

Barkan, E., & Shelton, M. D. (Eds.). (1998). *Borders, exiles, diasporas.* Stanford, CA: Stanford University Press.

Bateson, M. C. (1989). *Composing a life.* New York: The Atlantic Monthly Press.

Beckett, Samuel. (1961). *Comment c'est.* Paris: Les Editions de Minuit.

Belenky, M. F., McVicker Clinchy, B., Goldberger, N. R., & Tarule, J. M. (1986). *Women's ways of knowing: The development of self, voice, and mind.* New York: Basic Books.

Benevenisti, M. (1995). *Intimate enemies: Jews and Arabs in a shared land.* Berkeley: University of California Press.

Benjamin, W. (1969). Theses on the Philosophy of History (B. Zohn, Trans.) In Hannah Arendt (Ed.), *Illuminations,* New York: Schocken Press.

Ben Jelloun, T. (1989). *The sand child.* New York: Ballantine Books.

Bentwich, J. (1965). *Education in Israel.* Philadelphia, PA: Jewish Publication Society of America.

Berryman, J. (1988). Ontario's heritage languages program: Advantages and disadvantages of three models of organization. *Multiculturalism/Multiculturalisme, 11* (3), 18–21.

Bettman, E. H., & Moore, P. (1994). Conflict resolution programs and social justice. *Education and Urban Society, 27,* 11–21.

Bloom, L. R. (1998). *Under the sign of hope: Feminist methodology and narrative interpretation.* Albany: SUNY Press.

Britzman, D. (1998). On doing something more. In W. Ayers & J. Miller (Eds.), *Maxine Greene: A light in the dark times,* 97–107. Columbia University: Teachers College Press.

Bhaskar, R. (1986). *Scientific realism and human emancipation.* London: Verso.

Bhaskar, R. (1989). *Reclaiming reality: A critical introduction to contemporary philosophy.* London: Verso.

Blasi, A. (1980). Bridging moral cognition and moral action: A critical review of the literature. *Psychological Bulletin 88* (1), 1–45.

Bourdieu, P. (1996, April 6). *Democracy, society, and education.* Lecture given at the University of California at Berkeley, Wheeler Auditorium.

Briggs, J. L. (1970). *Never in anger: Portrait of an Eskimo family.* Cambridge, MA: Harvard University Press.

Buber, M. (1958). *I and thou.* New York: C. Scribner's Sons.

Buber, M. (1965). *The knowledge of man.* New York: Harper & Row.

Byram, M. S. (1993). Foreign language teaching and multicultural education. In A. S. King & M. J. Reiss (Eds.), *The multicultural dimension of the national curriculum,* 73–186. London: The Falmer Press.

Carr, D. (1986). *Time, narrative and history.* Bloomington: Indiana University Press.

Carse, J. (1986). *Finite and infinite games: A vision of life as play and possibility.* New York: Ballantine Books.

Carter, K. (1993). The place of story in the study of teaching and teacher education. *Educational Researcher, 22* (1), 5–12.

Cazden, C. (1989). Richmond Road: A multilingual/multicultural primary school in Auckland, New Zealand. *Language and Education, 3,* 143–166.

Chambers, I. (1994). *Migrancy, culture, identity.* New York: Routledge Press.

Church, K. (1995). *Forbidden narratives: Critical autobiography as social science.* Amsterdam: Gordon and Breach.

Clandinin, D. J. (1988). Metaphor and folk model as dimensions of teachers' personal practical knowledge. Unpublished paper: University of Calgary.

Clandinin, D. J., & Connelly, F. M. (1994). Personal experience methods. In N. K. Denzen & Y. S. Lincoln (Eds.), *Handbook of qualitative research,* 413–427. Thousand Oaks, CA: Sage Publications.

Clandinin, D. J., & Connelly, F. M. (1995). *Teachers' professional knowledge landscapes.* New York: Teachers College Press, Columbia University.

Clandinin, D. J., & Connelly, F. M. (2000). *Narrative inquiry: Experience and story in qualitative research.* San Francisco: Jossey-Bass.

Clark, C. (1990). What you can learn from applesauce: A case of qualitative inquiry in use. In E. Eisner & A. Peshkin (Eds.), *Qualitative inquiry in education: The continuing debate.* New York: Teachers College Press.

Clark, K., & Holquist, M. (1984). *Mikhail Bakhtin.* Cambridge: Harvard University Press.

Clifford, J., & Marcus, G. (Eds.) (1986). *Writing culture: The poetics and politics of ethnography.* Berkeley: University of California Press.

Cole, A., & Knowles, G. (2000). *Researching teaching: Exploring teacher development through reflexive inquiry.* Boston, Toronto: Allyn and Bacon.

Coles, R. (1989). *The call of stories: Teaching and the moral imagination.* Boston: Houghton Mifflin Co.

Coles, R. (1997). *Doing documentary work.* New York: Oxford University Press.

Connelly, F. M., & Clandinin, D. J. (1988). *Teachers as curriculum planners: Narratives of experience.* New York: Teachers College Press, Columbia University.

Connelly, F. M., & Clandinin, D. J. (1990). Stories of experience and narrative inquiry. *Educational Researcher, 19* (5 June/July), 2–14.

Corson, D. (1990). *Language policy across the curriculum.* Clevedon, Avon, England: Multilingual Matters.

Corson, D. (1993). *Language, minority education, and gender: Linking social justice and power.* Toronto: OISE Press.

Corson, D. (1999). *Language policy in schools: A resource for teachers and administrators.* Mahwah, New Jersey: Lawrence Erlbaum Associates.

Crites, S. (1971). The narrative quality of experience. *Journal of the American Academy of Religion, 39* (3), 292–311.

Cuffaro, H. (1995). *Experimenting with the world: John Dewey and the early childhood classroom.* New York: Teachers College Press.

Cummins, J. (1988). From multicultural to antiracist education: An analysis of programmes and policies in Ontario. In T. Skutnabb-Kangas and J. Cummins (Eds.), *Minority education: From shame to struggle.* Clevedon, Avon, England: Multilingual Matters.

Cummins, J. (1989). *Empowering minority students.* Sacramento: California Association for Bilingual Education.

Cummins, J. (1994). From coercive to collaborative relations of power in the teaching of literacy. In B. M. Ferdman, R. M. Weber, & A. G. Ramirez (Eds.), *Literacy across languages and cultures,* 295–331. Albany: SUNY Press.

Cummins, J., & Danesi, M. (1990). *Heritage languages: The development and denial of Canada's linguistic resources.* Toronto: Our Schools/Ourselves Educational Foundation.

Darwich, M. (1997). *La Palestine comme métaphore.* Arles, France: Sindbad, Actes Sud.

Davies, C. A. (1999). *Reflexive ethnography: A guide to researching selves and others.* London, New York: Routledge.

de Lauretis, T. (Ed.). (1986). *Feminist studies/critical studies.* Bloomington: Indiana Press.

Delpit, L. (1992). The politics of teaching literate discourse. *Theory into practice, 31,* 285–295.

Denzin, N. (1988). *The research act* (Rev. ed.). New York: McGraw-Hill.

Derrida, J. (1979). Living on border lines. In H. Bloom, et al. (Eds.), *Deconstruction and criticism.* London: Routledge & Kegan Paul.

Dewey, J. (1938). *Experience and education.* New York: Collier Books.

Dewey, J. (1909/1975). *Moral principles in education.* Carbondale, IL: Southern Illinois University Press, Arcturus Books.

Dilthey, W. (1894/1977). The understanding of other persons and their expressions of life. In W. Dilthey, *Descriptive psychology and hisorical understanding* (R. Zaner & K. Heiges, Trans.). The Hague, Netherlands: Martinus Nijhoff.

Dolphin, L., & Dolphin, B. (1993). *Neve Shalom/Wahat Al-Salam: Oasis of Peace.* New York: Scholastic, Inc.

Donmall, B. S. (1985). Some implications of language awareness work for teacher training. In B. C. Donmall (Ed.), *Language awareness* (4th ed.), 1–13.

National Congress on Languages in Education, assembly (4th ed.), York, England.

Ducornet, R. (1997). *The word "desire."* New York: Henry Holt.

Durkheim, E. (1973). *Moral education.* New York: Free Press.

Durrell, Lawrence (1960). *Reflections on a marine Venus: A companion to the landscape of Rhodes.* London: Faber and Faber.

Eisenstadt, S. N. (1969). The absorption of immigrants, the amalgamation of exiles and the problems of transformation of Israeli society. In O. Kohen (Ed.), *The integration of immigrants in Israel from different countries of origin,* 6–15. Jerusalem: Magnes Press.

Eisenstadt, S. N. (1985). The transformation of Israeli society: An essay in interpretation. Boulder, CO: Westview Press.

Eisner, E. (1991). *The enlightened eye: Qualitative inquiry and the enhancement of educational practice.* New York: Maxwell MacMillan International Publishing Group.

Eisner, E., & Peshkin A. (1990). *Qualitative inquiry in education: The continuing debate.* New York: Teachers College Press.

Elazar, D. J. (1985). Israel's compound policy. In E. Krausz (Ed.), *Politics and society in Israel.* New Brunswick, NJ: Transaction Books.

Epstein, H. (1979). *Children of the Holocaust: Conversations with sons and daughters of survivors.* New York: Putnam's.

Fairclough, N. (1993). *Discourse and social exchange.* Cambridge: Polity Press.

Fanon, F. (1967/1952). *Black skin, white masks.* (C. L. Markmann, Trans.). New York: Grove Press.

Felman, S., & Laub, D. (1992). *Testimony: Crises of witnessing in literature, psychoanalysis, and history.* New York: Routledge.

Fellman, J. (1973). *The revival of a classical tongue: Eliezer Ben-Yehudah and the modern hebrew language.* The Hague, Netherlands: Mouton.

Feuerverger, G. (1989). Ethnolinguistic vitality of Italo-Candian students in integrated and non-integrated heritage language programs in Toronto. *The Canadian Modern Language Review, 46,* 50–72.

Feuerverger, G. (1991). University students' perceptions of heritage language learning and ethnic identity maintenance in multicultural Toronto. *Canadian Modern Language Review, 47* (4), 660–677.

Feuerverger, G. (1994). A multicultural literacy intervention for minority language students. *Language and Education, 8* (3), 123–146.

Feuerverger, G. (1995). Oasis of peace: A community of moral education in Israel. *Journal of Moral Education, 24* (2), 113–141.

Feuerverger, G. (1996). Peacemaking through emancipatory discourse: Language awareness in a Jewish-Arab school in Israel. *Curriculum and Teaching, 11* (2), 53–61.

Feuerverger, G. (1997). An educational program for peace: Jewish-Arab conflict resolution in Israel. *Theory into Practice, 36* (1), 17–25.

Feuerverger, G. (in press) My Yiddish voice. In M. Morris and J. Weaver (Eds.), *Difficult memories: Talk in a (post) Holocaust era.* New York: Peter Lang.

Fine, M. (1993). You can't just say that the only ones who can speak are those who agree with your position: Political discourse in the classroom. *Harvard Educational Review, 63,* 412–433.

Fishman, J. (1991). *Reversing language shift: The influence of language, culture, and thought.* New York: Random House.

Freire, P. (1970). *Pedagogy of the oppressed.* New York: Seabury Press.

Friedlander, S. (1979). *When memory comes.* New York: Farrar, Strauss, Giroux.

Friedman, A. (1992). Legitimation of national identity and the change in power relationships in workshops dealing with the Israeli/Palestinian Conflict. Unpublished paper, Neve Shalom/Wahat Al-Salam.

Friedman, T. (1989). *From Beirut to Jerusalem.* New York: Doubleday.

Garcia, E. E. (1994). Language, culture, and curriculum. In L. Darling-Hammond (Ed.), *Review of research in education,* 51–98. New York: Teachers College Press.

Garcia, E. E. (1999). *Student cultural diversity: Understanding and meeting the challenge.* Boston: Houghton Mifflin.

Geertz, C. (1973). *The interpretation of cultures.* New York: Basic Books.

Geertz, C. (1988). *Works and lives: The anthropologist as author.* Stanford, CA: Stanford University Press.

Geertz, C. (1995). *After the fact: Two countries, four decades, one anthropologist.* Cambridge, MA: Harvard University Press.

Geretz, N. (1995). *Captives of a dream: National myths in Israeli culture*. Tel Aviv: Am Oved.

Gilligan, C. (1982). *In a different voice: Psychological theory and women's development*. Cambridge, MA: Harvard University Press.

Gilligan, C. (1988). *Oedipus and Psyche: Two stories about love*. Worcester, MA: Clark University.

Gilligan, C, Ward, J., & Taylor, J. (Eds.). (1988). *Mapping the moral domain: A contribution of women's thinking to psychological theory and education*. Cambridge, MA: Harvard University Press.

Gilligan, C., Brown, L., & Rogers, A. (1990). Psyche embedded: A place for body, relationships, and culture in personality theory. In A. Rabin (Ed.), *Studying persons and lives*. New York: Springer Verlag.

Giroux, H. (1988). *Schooling and the struggle for public life*. Minneapolis: University of Minnesota Press.

Giroux, H. A. (1991). Democracy and the discourse of cultural difference: Towards a politics of border pedagogy. *British Journal of Sociology of Education, 12* (4), 501–519.

Giroux, H. A. (1994). Insurgent multiculturalism and the promise of pedagogy. In D. T. Goldberg (Ed.), *Multiculturalism: A critical reader*. Cambridge, MA: Blackwell.

Glesne, C., & Peshkin, A. (1992). *Becoming qualitative researchers: An introduction*. New York: Longman.

Goodman, K., Brooks-Smith, E., Meredith, R. & Goodman, Y. M. (1987). *Language and thinking in school: A whole-language curriculum*. New York: Richard C. Owen.

Goodson, I. (1991). Teachers' lives and educational research: Biography, identity and schooling. In Goodson, I. & Walker, R. (Eds.), *Episodes in educational research*, 137–149. London: Falmer Press.

Gumpel, Y. (1996). The endless turmoil of social violence. In P. Lemish (Ed.), *Education in deeply conflicted societies*. New York: The International Center for Peace in the Middle East.

Gumperz, J. (1977). Sociocultural knowledge in conversational inference. In M. Saville-Troike (Ed.), *Twenty-eighth annual roundtable monograph series in language and linguistics*. Washington: Georgetown University Press.

Hammersley, M., & Atkinson, P. (1995). *Ethnography* (2nd ed.). London: Routledge.

Hartshorne, H., & May, M. A. (1928–1930). *Studies in the nature of character.* (Vols. 1–3). New York: Macmillan.

Hawkins, E. (1984). *Awareness of language.* Cambridge, MA: Cambridge University Press.

Heath, S. B. (1983). *Ways with words: Language, life, and work in communities and classrooms.* Cambridge, MA: Cambridge University Press.

Heilbrun, C. (1988). *Writing a woman's life.* New York: W. W. Norton.

Heilbrun, C. (1999). *Women's lives: The view from the threshold.* Toronto, Ontario: University of Toronto Press.

hooks, b. (1990). *Yearning: Race, gender, and cultural politics.* Toronto, Ontario: Between the Lines.

hooks, b. (1994). *Teaching to transgress: Education as the practice to freedom.* New York: Routledge.

Hopkins, D. (1987). *Enhancing validity in action research.* (Research paper #16), British Library.

Hopkins, D., Bollington, R., & Hewett, D. (1989). Growing up with qualitative research and evaluation. *Evaluation and Research in Education, 3,* 61–80.

Hornberger, N. (1990). Creating succesful contexts for bilingual literacy. *Teachers College Record, 92* (2), 212–229.

Huberman, A. M., and Miles, M. B. (1984). *Innovation up close.* New York: Plenum.

Hunt, D. (1991). *Beginning with ourselves.* Toronto, Ontario: Ontario Institute for Studies in Education (OISE).

Hussar, B. (1983/1989). *When the cloud lifted.* (A. Megroz, Trans.). Dublin: Veritas Press.

Hymes, D. (Ed.) (1969). *Reinventing anthropology.* New York: Random House.

Iram, Y., & Schmida, M. (1998). *The education system of Israel.* Westport, Connecticut: Greenwood Press.

Jabès, E. (1980). *From the desert to the book* (P. Joris, Trans.). Barrytown, NY: Station Hill.

Jackson, S. (1995). Autobiography: Pivot points for engaging lives in multicultural contexts. In J. M. Larkin & C. E. Sleeter, *Developing multicultural teacher education curricula,* 31–44. New York: SUNY Press.

Jalongo, M. R., & Isenberg, J. P. (1995). *Teachers' stories: From personal narrative to professional insight.* San Francisco: Jossey-Bass.

Janesick, V. J. (1979). Ethnographic inquiry: Understanding culture and experience. In Short, E. (Ed.), *Forms of curriculum inquiry,* 101–119. Albany: SUNY Press.

Janks, H. (1991). A critical approach to the teaching of language. *Educational Review, 43*(2), 191–199.

Jay, G. (1991). The end of "American" literature: Toward a multicultural practice. *College English, 53* (3), 264–281.

Josso, C. (1991). *Cheminer Vers Soi.* Lausanne, Suisse: Editions L'Age d'Homme.

Kaser, S., & Short, K. (1998). Exploring culture through children's connections. *Language Arts, 75* (3), March (pp. 185–92).

Katz, I., & Cahanov, M. (1990). A review of dilemmas in facilitating encounter groups between Jews and Arabs in Israel. *Megamot, 33* (1).

Keiny, S. (1999). Response to "Human rights in history and civic textbooks: The case of Israel." *Curriculum Inquiry, 29* (4), 513–522.

Krashen, S., & Biber, D. (1988). *On course: Bilingual education's success in California.* Sacramento, CA: California Association of Bilingual Education.

Kridel, C. (1998a). Landscapes, biography, and the preservation of the present. In W. Ayers & J. Miller (Eds.), *Maxine Greene: A light in the dark times.* New York: Columbia University, Teachers College Press.

Kridel, C. (Ed.) (1998b). *Writing educational biography: Explorations in qualitative research.* New York: Garland.

Kristeva, J. (1980). *Desire in language: A semiotic approach to literature and art* (L. S. Roudiez, Trans.). New York: Columbia University Press.

Kristeva, J. (1991). *Strangers to ourselves* (L. S. Roudiez, Trans.). New York: Columbia University Press.

Kohlberg, L. (1966). Moral education in the schools: A developmental view. *The School Review, 74,* 1–30.

Kohlberg, L. (1971). Cognitive-developmental theory and the practice of collective moral education. In M. Wolins & M. Gottesman (Eds.), *Group care: An Israeli approach.* New York: Gordon and Breach.

Kohlberg, L. (1981). *Essays on moral development. Vol. 1: The philosophy of moral development.* San Francisco, CA: Harper & Row.

Kohlberg, L. (1985). The Just Community approach to moral education in theory and practice. In M. Berkowitz & F. Oser (Eds.), *Moral education: Theory and application,* 27–87. Hillsdale, NJ: Lawrence Erlbaum.

Kozol, J. (1991). *Savage inequalities: Children in America's schools.* New York: Crown.

Kozol. J. (1996). *Amazing grace.* New York: Penguin.

Lainé, A. (1998). *Faire de sa vie une histoire: Théories et pratiques de l'histoire de vie en formation.* Paris: Desclée de Brouwer.

La Lettre de la Colline. (2000). French version. Anne LeMeignen (Ed.).

Lambert, W. E. (1982). Language as a factor in personal identity and intergroup relations. Unpublished document, McGill University, Montreal.

Lani-Bayle, M. (1997). *L'Histoire de Vie Généalogique: D'Oedipe à Hermès.* Paris et Montréal: L'Harmattan.

Lawrence-Lightfoot. S., & Hoffman Davis, J. (1997). *The art and science of portraiture.* San Francisco: Jossey-Bass.

Lemish, P. (1996). Knowledge/power dimensions of educating in conflicted societies. In V. Morgan & J. Darby (Eds.), *Conflict and change,* 224–235. Tokyo: United University Press.

Leray, C. (1995). "Recherche sur les histoires de vie en formation," *Revue Française de Pédagogie, 112,* pp. 77–84.

Levi, Primo. (1988). *The drowned and the saved* (R. Rosenthal, Trans.). New York: Vintage Books.

Lewin, K. (1958). Group decision and social change. In E. Maccoby (Ed.), *Reading in social psychology,* 197–211. New York: Holt Rhinehart.

Lo Bianco, J. (1989). Revitalizing multicultural education in Australia. *Multiculturalism, 12,* 30–39.

Marcus, G. E. (1998). *Ethnography through thick and thin.* Princeton, NJ: Princeton University Press.

Mari, S. (1985). *The Arab education in Israel.* New York: Syracuse University Press.

Maroshek-Klarman, U. (1993). Education for democracy: Replacing conflict with dilemma. Paper presented at the International Conference on Education for Democracy in a Multicultural Society, Jerusalem, Israel.

Mascia-Lees, F. E., Sharpe, P., & Cohen, C. B. (1989). The postmodern turn in anthropology: Cautions from a feminist perspective. *Signs, 15* (1), 7–33.

Masemann, V., & Iram, Y. (1987). The right to education for multicultural development: Canada and Israel. In N. Bernstein-Tarrow (Ed.), *Human rights and education*. Oxford: Pergamon Press.

Michaels, S. (1981). Sharing time: Children's narrative styles and differential access to literacy. *Language in Society, 10*, 423–442.

Mishler, E. (1986). *Research interviewing: Context and narrative*. Cambridge, MA: Harvard University Press.

Morrison, T. (1987). *Beloved*. New York: Alfred K. Knopf.

Morin, E. (1989). *Vidal et les Siens*. Paris: Editions du Seuil.

Mosher, R. (Ed.). (1980). *Moral education: A first generation of research and development*. New York: Praeger.

Newsletter. *Neve Shalom/Wahat Al-Salam* (2000). English version. Aron, C. & Shippin, H. (Eds.).

Nieto, S. (1992). *Affirming diversity: The sociopolitical context of multicultural education*. White Plains, NY: Longman.

Noddings, N. (1984). *Caring: A feminine approach to ethics and moral education*. Berkeley, CA: University of California Press.

Noddings, N. (1991). Stories in dialogue: Caring and interpersonal reasoning. In C. Witherell & N. Noddings (Eds.), *Stories lives tell: Narrative and dialogue in education*, 157–170. New York: Teachers College Press.

Ogbu, J. (1974). *The next generation: An ethnography of education in an urban neighborhood*. New York: Academic Press.

Ogbu, J. (1978). *Minority education and caste*. New York: Academic Press.

Olesen, V. (1992). Extraordinary events and mundane ailments: The contextual dialectics of the embodied self. In C. Ellis & F. Flaherty (Eds.), *Investigating subjectivity: Research on lived experience*. Newbury Park, CA: Sage.

Pagano, J. (1998).The end of innocence. In Ayers, W. & Miller, J. (Eds.), *A light in dark times: Maxine Greene and the unfinished conversation*, 254–261. New York: Teachers College Press.

Pajak, E. (1986). Psychoanalysis, teaching, and supervision. *Journal of Curriculum and Supervision, 1* (2), 122–131.

Paré, A. (1994). L'enseignant est une personne: Analyse evolutive d'une pratique pedagogique. *Revue de Psychologie de la Motivation, 18,* 133–147.

Patterson, D. (1998). *Sun turned to darkness: Memory and recovery in the Holocaust memoir*. New York: SUNY Press.

Peshkin, A. (1988). Virtuous subjectivity: In the participant-observer's I's. In D. Berg & K. Smith (Eds.), *The self in social inquiry,* 267–282. Newbury Park, CA: Sage Publications.

Pinar, W. F. (1988). Autobiography and the architecture of self. *Journal of Curriculum Theorizing, 8* (1), 7–35.

Pinar, W. F. (1998). *Curriculum: Toward new identities.* New York: Garland.

Pivovarov, V. (1994). *Towards a culture of peace: International practical guide to the implementation of the recommendations concerning education for international understanding, cooperation, and peace education relating to human rights and fundamental freedoms.* Paris: UNESCO.

Polkinghorne, D. E. (1988). *Narrative knowing and the human sciences.* Albany, NY: State University of New York (SUNY) Press.

Potok, R. N. (1988). Borders, exiles, minor literatures: The case of Palestinian-Israeli writing. In E. Barkan & M. D. Shelton (Eds.), *Borders, exiles, diasporas,* 291–310. Stanford, CA: Stanford University Press.

Powdermaker, H. (1966). *Stranger and friend: The way of an anthropologist.* New York: W. W. Norton.

Power, F. C. (1988). The Just Community approach to moral education. *Journal of Moral Education, 17* (3), 195–208.

Power, F. C., Higgins, A., & Kohlberg, L. (1989). *Lawrence Kohlberg's approach to moral education.* New York: Columbia University Press.

Ray, D. (1990). Languages and political purpose: The Canadian case. *Canadian and International Education, 19* (1), 4–15.

Resnik, J. (1999). Particularistic vs. universalistic content in the Israeli education system. *Curriculum Inquiry, 29* (4), 485–512.

Rich, A. (1979). *On lies, secrets, and silence.* New York: Norton.

Rich, A. (1986). *Blood, bread, and poetry: Selected prose 1975–1985.* New York: Norton.

Richardson, V. (1994). Conducting research on practice. *Educational Researcher, 23* (5), 5–10.

Rodham Clinton, H. (1996). *It takes a village and other lessons children teach us.* New York: Touchstone, Simon & Shuster.

Roethke, T. (1966). *Collected poems.* New York: Doubleday Books.

Rosenberg, E. R. (1991). Living together side by side: Palestinians and Jews in Neve Shalom/Wahat Al-Salam. Unpublished, Master of Arts Paper in Social Sciences, University of Chicago.

Said, E. (1990). Reflections on exile. In R. Ferguson, M. Gever, T. Minh-Ha, & C. West (Eds.), *Out there: Marginalization and contemporary cultures*, 159–172. Boston: MIT Press.

Said, E. (1996*)*. *Representations of the intellectual: The 1993 Reith lectures.* New York: Vintage.

Samuda, R. (1986). The Canadian brand of multiculturalism: Social and educational implications. In S. Modgil, G. K., Verma, K. Mallick & C. Modgil (Eds.), *Multicultural education*, 101–109. London, Philadelphia: The Falmer Press.

Sarbin, T. R. (Ed.). (1986). *Narrative psychology: The storied nature of human conduct.* New York: Praeger.

Schofield, J. W. (1982). *Black and white in school: Trust, tension, or tolerance?* New York: Praeger.

Scholes, R., & Kellogg, R. (1966). *The nature of narrative.* New York: Oxford University Press.

Schön, Donald. (1987). *Educating the reflective practitioner.* San Francisco: Jossey-Bass.

Schön, D. (Ed.). (1991). *The reflective turn: Case studies in and on educational practice.* New York: Teachers College Press.

Schweitzer, Freidrich. (1989). Forgetting about Auschwitz? Remembrance as a difficult task of moral education. *Journal of Moral Education, 18* (3), 163.

Sellers, S. (1996). *Helene Cixous: Authorship, autobiography, and love.* Cambridge, MA: Blackwell.

Selman, R. (1980). *The growth of interpersonal understanding.* New York: Academic Press.

Shabatay, V. (1991). The stranger's story: Who calls and who answers? In C. Witherell & N. Noddings (Eds.), *Stories lives tell: Narrative and dialogue in education*, 136–152. New York: Teachers College Press.

Shipler, D. K. (1986). *Arab and Jew: Wounded spirits in a promised land.* New York: Times Books.

Shohamy, E. (1993, June). A monolingual language policy in a diverse cultural society: The case of Israel. Paper presented at the International Conference on Education for Democracy in a Multicultural Society, Jerusalem.

Shohamy, E., & Spolsky, B. (2000). *New perspectives and issues in educational language policy: A festschrift for Bernard Dov Spolsky.* Philadelphia: J. Benjamins.

Shohat, D. (1993, June). Democracy and education in Israeli schools. Paper presented at the International Conference on Education for Democracy in a Multicultural Society, Jerusalem.

Simon, K. (1997). A journey toward peace, equality and co-existence: A case study of education programs at Neve Shalom/Wahat Al-Salam. Unpublished masters thesis, Dept. of Curriculum and Instruction, Univ. of Minnesota.

Simon, R. I. (1992). *Teaching against the grain.* New York: Bergin & Garvey Press.

Sockett, Hugh (1993). *The moral base for teacher professionalism.* New York: Teachers College Press.

Sonnenschein, N., & Halaby, R. (1991). The project for Israeli-Palestinian conflict management training. Unpublished document, Neve Shalom/Wahat Al-Salam, Israel.

Spolsky, B. (1989). *Conditions for second language learning.* New York: Oxford University Press.

Smooha, S. (1978). *Israel: Pluralism and conflict.* New York: Routledge and Kegan Paul.

Smooha, S., & Peretz, D. (1982). The Arabs in Israel. *Journal of Conflict Resolution, 26* (3), 451–484.

Stephan, W. G. (1987). The contact hypothesis in intergroup relations. In C. Hendrick (Ed.), *Group process and intergroup relations,* 7–40. Beverly Hills: Sage Publications.

Strathern, M. (1987). An awkward relationship: The case of feminism and anthropology. *Signs, 12* (2), 276–92.

Swirski, S. (1999). *Politics and education in Israel.* New York: Routledge.

Tabachnick, B. R., & Zeichner, K. M. (1993). Preparing teachers for cultural diversity. In P. Gilroy & M. Smith. *International analyses of teacher education (JET Papers One),* 113–124. London: Carfax Publishing.

Tajfel, H., & Turner, J. C. (1985). The social identity theory of intergroup behavior. In S. Worchel & W. G. Austin (Eds.), *Psychology of intergroup relations.* Chicago: Nelson Hall.

Tappan, M. (1991). Narrative, language, and moral experience. *Journal of Moral Education, 20* (3), 243–256.

Tappan, M., & Brown, L. (1989). Stories told and lessons learned: Toward a narrative approach to moral development and moral education. *Harvard Educational Review, 59,* 182–205.

Trueba, H. T. (1989). *Raising silent voices: Educating the linguistic minorities for the twenty-first century.* Cambridge, MA: Newbury House.

Van Manen, M. (1990). *Researching lived experience: Human science for an action sensitive pedagogy.* London: University of Western Ontario.

Vygotsky, L. S. (1962). *Thought and language* (A. Kozulin, Trans.). Cambridge, MA: MIT Press.

Walsh, C. E. (1987). Language, meaning, and voice: Puerto Rican students' struggle for a speaking consciousness. *Language Arts, 64,* 196–206.

Weingrod, A. (1996). How Israeli culture was constructed: Memory, history and the Israeli past. *Israel Studies 2* (1), 228–237.

Witherell, C. (1991). Narrative and the moral realm: Tales of caring and justice. *Journal of Moral Education, 20* (3).

Witherell, C., & Noddings, N. (Eds.). *Stories lives tell: Narrative and dialogue in education.* New York: Teachers College Press.

Wolcott, H. F. (1988). Ethnographic research in education. In R. M. Jager (Ed.), *Complementary methods for research in education,* 187–206. Washington, DC: American Educational Research Association.

Wolcott, H. F. (1994). *Transforming qualitative data: Description, analysis, and interpretation.* Thousand Oaks, CA: Sage.

Wolf, M. (1992). *A thrice-told tale: Feminism, postmodernism, and ethnographic responsibility.* Stanford, CA: Stanford University Press.

Wong-Fillmore, L. (1991). When learning a second language means losing the first. *Early Childhood Research Quarterly, 6,* 323–346.

Yin, R. K. (1984). *Case study research.* London: Sage.

Zak, M. (1992). Walking the tightrope. Unpublished document, Neve Shalom/Wahat Al-Salam, Israel.

Index

205